Killing the Messenger
Journalists at Risk in Modern Warfare

Herbert N. Foerstel

Foreword by Danny Schechter

PRAEGER

Westport, Connecticut
London

Library of Congress Cataloging-in-Publication Data

Foerstel, Herbert N.

   Killing the messenger : journalists at risk in modern warfare / Herbert N. Foerstel ;
foreword by Danny Schechter.

      p. cm.

   Includes bibliographical references and index.

   ISBN 0-275-98786-8

1. War—Press coverage. 2. War correspondents—United States—Biography. I. Title.

PN4784.W37F62   2006

070.4'333—dc22   2005034112

British Library Cataloguing in Publication Data is available.

Library of Congress Catalog Card Number: 2005034112
ISBN: 0-275-98786-8

First published in 2006

Praeger Publishers, 88 Post Road West, Westport, CT 06881
An imprint of Greenwood Publishing Group, Inc.
www.praeger.com

Printed in the United States of America

(∞)™

The paper used in this book complies with the
Permanent Paper Standard issued by the National
Information Standards Organization (Z39.48-1984).

10   9   8   7   6   5   4   3   2   1

Contents

Foreword

Groucho Marx famously once said that he would never join a club that would have him as a member. Herb Foerstel, author of *Killing the Messenger*, might agree, but he would feel comfortable joining London's Frontline Club, located, appropriately enough, across the street from a hospital and down the block from a train station with the quickest connection in town to the airport. There, in a small building, is a club dedicated to and used by foreign correspondents, the heroes (and cads) that Foerstel's new book discusses in great detail and with a well-informed and nuanced argument. In the club's main room there are the photos of media martyrs, the men and women who lost their lives in the service of reportage abroad. There are artifacts and memorabilia, including license plates from Sarajevo, T-shirts with bullet holes, and posters singing the praises of the stories they covered: Pinochet, Arafat, Khomeini, and Mandela. This is a museum of the present, chronicling the ongoing challenge of keeping the world informed about itself.

Foerstel is concerned about this challenge, not just as a writer immersed in press issues, but also as a citizen concerned with peace and justice in a world of too many wars. In treating the lives and issues associated with this dangerous enterprise, he brings a set of values and passions that, alas, are often missing in the work he investigates. He is keenly aware that something dramatic is happening to the nature of war and its coverage. Reporters are no longer passive observers, if they ever were, but are often engaged participants. Sometimes their media wars become part of the larger conflicts they observe, often inflaming them. And most certainly, they are more at risk than ever, targeted by military forces and terrorists alike. "Has war reporting changed," he asks, "making journalism a second front in the war against terrorism? How has the scope and objectivity of war reporting been compromised by the dangers on the beat?" These are good questions, and this tightly written treatise offers helpful answers. It also offers what is often missing in much of the news coverage he writes about—context and background. These are the dimensions that help us make meaning out of what we read and see and that elevate real journalism from the "bang-bang" reporting of incidents and occasional atrocities.

There are other dimensions that are sometimes less visible. An individual reporter can do a great job braving bullets and bullshit on every front and still have to fight his or her own news organization to run or air the story without it first being gutted in the edit room or sanitized by editors and news executives. Sometimes that "front" is more frustrating and perilous in terms of career survival than just doing the job. News cultures sometimes demand self-censorship of a type that can be morally compromising and professionally suicidal. The dangers faced by today's correspondents extend beyond the battlefield to the news world, where media messengers are being killed by corporate indifference, as well as reader disinterest that is fed by years of downplaying stories from around the world. As overseas bureaus are cut and important stories left uncovered, the result is chronicled in memoirs by the likes of CBS's now-retired chief foreign correspondent Thomas Fenton, who decries such coverage cutbacks. His book is appropriately titled *Bad News*. Bad news can be found in *Killing the Messenger* as well, but there is also an appreciation of the courage of media legends who went to war so the rest of us could know what it was like. I marveled in the stories of those who came before, including Martha Gellhorn, Ernie Pyle, Walter Cronkite, and Andy Rooney. Pyle became a victim of war, and Gellhorn became a conscience; Cronkite became a newscaster, and Rooney became a curmudgeonly critic, even though in the fall of 2005 he provided television viewers with the boldest frontal assault on the Iraq War that I have seen in my media watching.

I found some of Foerstel's rigorous research startling. Gellhorn, the grand dame of war reporting, apparently wanted to return to the front during the Gulf War—at age 82! Pyle, beloved by all the GIs in World War II's European theater, grew to hate war, yet he felt duty-bound to cover the Pacific front, where a sniper's bullet killed him just months before the Japanese surrender. We learn that Cronkite fired weapons on an air raid over Germany, an action that would be considered a "no-no" for reporters today who are taught to let *them* do the fighting while *we* do the reporting. And Andy Rooney was awarded the bronze star for valor—something journalists don't like to talk about.

Foerstel reveals the heroic lives of people who inspired me and the people I've met, such as Edward R. Murrow and Peter Arnett. Murrow's distinguished career was virtually extinguished by the lack of support in the executive suites (aided and abetted later on by his on-air chain smoking). But in the days of his eloquent "This is London" reports, he often took risks against the direct orders of his network overlords. Arnett, who was responsible for passing on one of the great quotes of the Vietnam era—the lieutenant who said, "We destroyed the village in order to save it."—was targeted by right-wing media groups during his Iraq coverage and was forced to the sidelines, as documented in my film *WMD: Weapons of Mass Deception.*

So there is also a corporate battlefield that great correspondents have to navigate. But despite all the pressures, the correspondent still has the opportunity to do the kind of reporting that, to borrow a famous phrase, "alters and illuminates" our times. Herb Foerstel has spent his time well in documenting the story of a profession under fire, and yet a profession whose sense of mission he wants us to respect. The reason, I think, goes to his sense of how important it is to understand what's happening in this volatile world of ours, a world in which interdependence is key and tolerance is essential. He wants to create an empathetic connection between the reader and those suffering in devastating conflicts. He quotes Gellhorn as saying, "War is always worse than I know how to say." In addition, he wants us to know the challenges that correspondents face.

In that respect, all of the issues of war coverage are carefully laid out and backed up by a wide range of sources. He deals with the dangerous nature of the work and the psychology of the men and women who take it on. He shows how war has changed and what that has meant for those who travel with the troops or try to report unilaterally. He does not duck the difficult question of "To Embed or Not Embed?"; he introduces us to war correspondents who were kidnapped, tortured, and, in the case of Daniel Pearl, killed, and then he explores possible motivations for such brutality. One such motivation being that reporters are increasingly perceived by the other side—there is always the "other side" in wars—as being combatants doing the bidding of their governments through one-sided stories. And finally, he tackles the "What Is to Be Done?" question, including how to better protect correspondents by encouraging personal caution or requiring formal safety training.

A number of books have touched these subjects, but *Killing the Messenger* strikes me as more thorough because it raises questions that go outside the vocational approach that characterizes many journalistic tomes. If you have only one new book to read on the subject of war correspondents, make this the one. At the same time, the Internet age poses new challenges, including the need to build collaboration between Western news organizations and indigenous journalists. Foerstel points out that local Iraqi reporters, stringers, and fixers, working for Western news organizations, have become the most vulnerable war correspondents, sustaining the overwhelming majority of press casualties during the past two years. Can war reporting itself evolve into a form of peace journalism as advocated by our colleagues at Reportingtheworld.org?

War reporting has become tougher than ever, with correspondents threatened from all sides, including both the U.S. military and insurgents. Veteran journalist Robert Fisk says the situation in Iraq is now so dangerous that he doesn't know whether he can go on reporting from the country. Britain's *Press Gazette* reports, "Fisk, who has previously accused colleagues of practicing 'hotel journalism' in Iraq, said that 'mouse journalism' is now the best he can do in the country." We all have a stake in being informed and getting the truth. That's why we need a public campaign to support at-risk journalists and we need to demand that media outlets carry their reportage more prominently. We also need to advocate for: (1) *Inside-Out Reporting.* Today's journalists are still locked into an old paradigm of "outside-in" journalism when what is needed is "inside-out" coverage. We need to hear more from the victims of war and the indigenous journalists. (2) *Reports That Question Official Claims.* We need more aggressive coverage, like the recent *Washington Post* story that revealed high civilian casualties in air raids that the military said were only targeting Iraqi insurgents. The person who sent me the link commented, "The U.S. media may be more willing to expose U.S. atrocities in Iraq as Bush's war popularity sinks into the mire." (3) *Independent Assessments of Political Developments.* When U.S. elections seem shamelessly rigged, why would we think that U.S. stage-managed voting in Iraq is clean? Example: Most of the U.S. media claimed that the new Iraq constitution won by a landslide. Historian Gareth Porter did some digging over the phone from Washington and contradicted that narrative. "The final official figures for the province, obtained by IPS from a U.S. official in Mosul, actually have the constitution being rejected by a fairly wide margin, but less than the two-thirds majority required to defeat it outright," he writes. "Both the initial figures and the new vote totals raise serious questions about the credibility of the reported results in Nineveh. A leading Sunni political figure has already charged that the Nineveh vote totals have been altered." (4) *Unembedded Photography.* There are images of the war that media outlets possess but that they are not showing. The newspaper, *Liberation in Paris,* did an entire spread of graphic photos depicting what the war really looks like that could easily be run in the United States. A powerful new book, *Unembedded,* from Chelsea Green Publishers, offers gripping photography from the war by four outstanding independent photojournalists. We need to press every newspaper and magazine in America to run spreads by them and others like them. (5) *Footage, Footage, Footage.* It's there. Why can't we see it? At a recent protest in front of CNN headquarters in Atlanta, I was told by network staffers that they receive dramatic footage from the Iraq and Afghanistan conflicts every day that they do not air. Why? It's time to end such corporate censorship and self-censorship. A CNN producer told the protesters, who carried signs demanding "Show Us the War," that he hoped they would return every day, because their pressure could move the PR-sensitive media executives to respond to the public demands for openness.

My own experiences of writing about the war coverage and of making the film *WMD: Weapons of Mass Deception* have persuaded me that there is a large demand out there for the truth. One book can't cover everything, but *Killing the Messenger* does a lot, offering disturbing facts you didn't know along with provocative challenges to a media industry that needs to begin re-creating itself.

Danny Schechter[1]

Introduction

The power of the press to directly affect war and peace was most prominently displayed in 1898 when newspaper magnate William Randolph Hearst made it his personal business to foment war in Cuba. Having sent illustrator William Remington to Cuba to document the reported insurrection there, Hearst was outraged when Remington cabled him that there was no war to cover. Hearst allegedly replied, "Please remain. You furnish the pictures, I'll furnish the war." Within days, Hearst's *New York Journal* was banging the war drum with headlines like, "War? Sure!"[1] The Spanish American War followed soon thereafter.

Such was the influence of wealthy media barons like Hearst. But the first evidence of the power of individual journalists to build a national war effort came during World War II when a talented band of celebrity journalists whetted the public's appetite for tales of war. With their celebrity status came a new vulnerability. The public demanded eye-witness accounts of battle from these new press icons, and the competition among them for the big story often put them on the front lines.

Reporting news from the front lines of battle has always been dangerous business. In past wars, when soldiers and war correspondents shared a foxhole, bullets and bombs made no distinction between them. World War II reporters such as Ernie Pyle and Edward R. Murrow placed themselves in harm's way to bring stories of courage and sacrifice to the home front. Pyle put a human face on heroism. Murrow virtually invented broadcast journalism with his live coverage of the German blitz on London. Walter Cronkite and a host of other celebrated correspondents followed in their footsteps. But the dangers they faced were, more often than not, accidental.

In today's modern urban warfare there are no front lines, and journalists are no longer "collateral casualties." They have become primary targets. The modern war correspondent is in the cross hairs, and the international press corps is understandably concerned at the rising toll of kidnapped and murdered journalists covering military conflicts around the world. Why have terrorists, insurgents, and even Western armies made "unfriendly" journalists fair game? Has war reporting changed, making journalism a second front in the war against terrorism? How has the scope and objectivity of war reporting been compromised by the dangers on the beat? What actions can governments and press organizations take to protect war correspondents?

In their book *War and the Media*, Daya Thussu and Des Freedman describe the three roles of mainstream media in reporting on military conflict: critical observer, publicist, and, most recently, battleground, "the surface upon which war is imagined or executed."[2] As modern war correspondents enter this surface they become players in the conflicts they cover, essentially unarmed combatants, and thus doubly vulnerable.

One might reasonably ask why reporters continue to flock to battle zones around the world. The glamour of the profession is, of course, notorious, and those who endure its horrors form an elite club whose members rejoice in the fellowship of danger. But magazine editor Bill Buford has a less romantic view of war correspondents. He calls war journalism "voyeuristic travel writing," and says of the reporters who do such writing, "War correspondents are some of the sickest people you'll ever meet. I've been lucky enough to publish quite a few of them. . . . War correspondents do everything that we don't do. If there's a fight, they try to get close to it. . . . You know, there is nothing more exciting than violence."[3]

Jerry Levin, former CNN correspondent who was kidnapped and held for a year in Lebanon, recently described the circumstances under which he was given the fateful assignment in Beirut. "In December 1983, while I was running the Chicago bureau, Burt Reinhart called me in and said, 'Jerry, you don't have to say yes.' I said, 'To what, Burt?' He said, 'We're having some problems in the Beirut bureau and we'd really like you to go over and run it.' I said, 'Okay, Burt,' but he continued, 'Remember Jerry, you don't have to do this, because this is a very dangerous zone, so it's your decision. . . .' I said, 'Burt, . . .' but he kept going on about how I didn't need to do this. I kept saying, 'Burt, are you listening? My bags are packed.' Finally, he chuckled. My point is, I wanted to be a foreign correspondent, and you pays your money and you takes your chances."[4]

Such is the attitude of most war correspondents. *Killing the Messenger* describes the dangers of war reporting in the words of the reporters themselves. Chapter 1 provides a retrospective look at the dangers of reporting on conventional wars from the American Civil War up to the first Gulf War (Operation Desert Storm). These were the wars that relied on the most advanced military technology of the day. The enemy was engaged on a battlefield of one sort or another, whether it was a forest in Verdun, a beach at Anzio, or a rice paddy in Vietnam. Wherever the airmen or soldiers went, the reporters went with them, facing the same dangers. In this chapter, war correspondents such as Ernie Pyle, Edward R. Murrow, Walter Cronkite, Peter Arnett, and others tell the story of war and why they risked their lives to cover it.

Chapter 2 introduces us to the new face of war and the unprecedented risks faced by war correspondents. These are the wars of quick, relatively painless conquest followed by protracted, bloody occupation, the urban wars with no front lines, no uniformed enemy, and with little distinction made between combatant and civilian. In particular, these wars regard journalists as legitimate military targets. In this chapter, we hear from dozens of journalists who describe the growing risk of murder and kidnapping in places such as Lebanon, Afghanistan, and Iraq. The Middle Eastern spokesperson for the Committee to Protect Journalists tells of the agonizing choices made by news organizations and individual reporters who try to cover these unpredictable war zones.

Chapter 3 presents the personal stories of five war correspondents who were abducted, tortured, and, in one case, murdered as they tried to report on the modern face of war. Philip Caputo, Jerry Levin, Terry Anderson, Daniel Pearl, and Scott Taylor are the new breed of war correspondent, bold journalists who have become part of the story they set out to cover. Their chilling ordeals are the best illustration of the climate of terror in which today's journalists work.

Chapter 4 seeks to explain why journalists have become targets of combatants on both sides of conflicts in the Middle East. The carefully planned attacks on war correspondents suggest something more complex than wanton brutality. Have Western reporters become military propagandists, shedding the neutrality that protected them in the past? Are some journalists working for the CIA, as the insurgents repeatedly charge? Are U.S. and Coalition troops justified in regarding Arab journalists as supporters of terrorism? These and other questions are debated by a cross section of journalists, including some who have suffered abduction and torture at the hands of insurgents.

Chapter 5 offers suggestions from journalists, editors, and press organizations on how to minimize the danger of reporting on modern warfare. None of these voices offer hope of a return to the relatively secure days of Ernie Pyle and Walter Cronkite. Instead, their words of caution imply an era of retrenchment and isolation in modern war reporting, including an increasing reliance on local stringers and fixers to do the actual reporting while the western correspondents await their copy in militarized "Green Zones" or fortified hotels. Is this to be the fate of modern war reporting?

Chapter 1

The Dangers of Reporting Conventional War

Background

Great war correspondents have always been products of media technology. During America's Civil War, photographer Mathew Brady gained worldwide fame for his dramatic photos of war. Brady saw action himself, continuing to photograph even after his wagon came under fire at Bull Run. The *New York Times* said that Brady brought "home to us the terrible reality and earnestness of war."[1] But Brady was not really a journalist. He owned fashionable portrait studios in New York and Washington and often sent employees out to photograph the war in his name. As a result, many of the Civil War photographs attributed to him were not his work.

It was the telegraph that actually revolutionized reporting during the Civil War, making it possible for reporters to send news from the front lines in the morning and have an account in the newspapers by the following afternoon. Using this new technology, Charles Anderson Page emerged as the preeminent war correspondent of the day. Covering the war for Horace Greeley's *New York Tribune*, Page provided his readers with a stark description of the horrors of battle. In his very first report, he described a horse racing past him with nothing but a disembodied leg in the stirrup. He wrote, "During the stampede, for a moment the attention of hundreds was attracted to a horse galloping around carrying a man's leg in the stirrup—the left leg, booted and spurred."

Upon reading Page's story, the managing editor of the *Tribune* said, "Page shows a nice eye for the grotesque."[2]

Despite the prominent work of Brady and Page during the American Civil War, the first celebrity correspondent was created during the Spanish-American War when Richard Harding Davis became a household name. Davis was a short story writer, not a reporter, and his stories from the front lines were orchestrated by newspaper magnate William Randolph Hearst, whose propaganda mill is widely acknowledged to have precipitated the war. Davis hitched his star to a charismatic lieutenant colonel named Theodore Roosevelt, and by the end of the Spanish-American War both Davis and Roosevelt were celebrities. A typical Davis report from the front was: "Roosevelt, mounted high on horse back, . . . made you feel that you would like to cheer."[3]

By the time World War I began, Davis had lost much of his luster, and because none of the countries involved in the war would allow reporters near the front, no war correspondent would achieve prominence until twenty years later, when war clouds once again gathered over Europe. World War II and its precursor, the Spanish Civil War, formed the European stage on which countless war correspondents would achieve greatness. The introduction of "real-time" broadcast journalism added luster to what, in any age, would have been a compelling story of high drama: the fight to stop fascism. Later chapters in this book will examine the unique dangers of reporting on wars without front lines, but first we acknowledge the courage and skills of some of the great correspondents in America's traditional wars.

Martha Gellhorn

Female war correspondents have always been a small but celebrated minority in the press corps. They have often been discriminated against, frequently denied access to the front, but those women who were allowed to cover the war have proved themselves to be the equal of any of their male colleagues. Martha Gellhorn may be the most prominent of such women. Both her professional life and private life were matters of public fascination. Her mother's friendship with Eleanor Roosevelt made Martha a frequent visitor to the White House.

In 1937, Gellhorn went to Madrid to report on the Spanish Civil War between the Republicans and the Fascists, and while covering that war she met and married Ernest Hemingway. The United States government offered no assistance to the Republican forces fighting the Fascists in Spain, but a significant number of idealistic Americans went to Spain to join the fight. They were accompanied by a handful of writers and journalists, including John Dos Passos, Lillian Hellman, Ernest Hemingway, and Gellhorn, then a little-known reporter. From 1937 through 1938, Gellhorn made a name for herself by reporting on the brutal civil war, and although Ernest Hemingway may have been the best-known war correspondent covering that war, Gellhorn was there before Hemingway and was the more respected journalist. Indeed, Ward Just, another celebrated war correspondent and author, calls Gellhorn "the greatest war correspondent of the 20th century."[4]

"My idea was just to go and join the people and do whatever I can do." Gellhorn later recalled. "From the minute one was in Madrid one was at war. The artillery was so near that you could hear the shell leave the gun. . . . If fascism was not defeated there, then the second World War was inevitable, and we were totally and absolutely convinced that they had to be beaten there."[5]

Under a July 1937 dateline from Madrid she wrote, "At first the shells went over: you could hear the thud as they left the Fascists' guns, a sort of groaning cough; then you heard them fluttering toward you. As they came closer the sound went faster and straighter and sharper and then, very fast, you heard the great booming noise when they hit. . . . There wasn't anything to do, or anywhere to go: you could only wait."[6]

Gellhorn said it seemed a little crazy to be living in a hotel with an ordinary lobby, chairs in the lounge, signs on the doors telling you how to get your clothes pressed, and "meantime it was like a trench when they lay down an artillery barrage."[7]

It was the same on the streets. According to Gellhorn, you would walk along, hearing the normal city sounds of streetcars and automobiles, and suddenly would come the huge booming of a falling shell. "There was no place to run," says Gellhorn, "because how did you know that the next shell would not be behind you, or ahead, or to the left or right?" She noticed an old woman holding a terrified boy by the hand. "You know what she is thinking," writes Gellhorn. "She is thinking she must get the child home, you are always safer in your own place, with the things you know. . . . She is in the middle of the square when the next one comes. A small piece of twisted steel, hot and very sharp, sprays off from the shell; it takes the little boy in the throat. The old woman stands there, holding the hand of the dead child, looking at him stupidly, not saying anything, and men rush out toward her to carry the child."[8]

The Republican defenders of Madrid were undermanned and underequipped, and despite the help of American volunteers and the support of many American journalists, Madrid fell to the fascists on April 1, 1939. Just five months later, Hitler invaded Poland, and Gellhorn was in Europe to cover World War II. Despite her newly earned celebrity, Gellhorn was seldom given official access by the military during her reporting on World War II. She simply went out on her own. Victoria Glendinning, a friend and colleague, says, "She wasn't remotely interested in briefings from generals or handouts from governments or press kits. . . . She wanted to be on the ground, where the people were who were suffering the brunt of war. . . . I don't think she could have endured the kind of war reporting that people have been forced to do in, say, Afghanistan, where you can't get into the country, you can't get near it."9

In the winter of 1944, she covered the Eighth Army near Rheims just before the push to Berlin. She had installed herself in an empty house and went out on night patrols with a couple of sergeants. She was later found wandering around the area, out of uniform, with her notebook, but without any kind of press pass or military accreditation. She was picked up and taken to James Gavin, the divisional commander of the Eighty-Second Airborne. When she admitted to her lack of credentials, Gavin said her obvious talent for living off the land would make her a fine guerrilla fighter. He agreed to pretend that he had never seen her and said that she was "free to pursue her private war."10

Despite her fear of flying, Gellhorn had long sought an assignment on a bomber mission over Germany. Her requests had all been turned down, generally on the grounds that she was a woman. Finally, she talked her way on board a P-61 on a night flight over Germany. She was the first woman correspondent to do so. "Terrified beyond belief," clutching a poorly fitted oxygen mask to her mouth, she squeezed into a narrow spot behind the pilot. At the dinner after the mission, she wrote in her notebook, "Seven men down—no one spoke of it. Drinking and singing 'I want to go home.'"11

Years later, Gellhorn would cover the Vietnam War, and again her focus would be the human toll of war. Under a September 1966 dateline she described the civilian casualties treated in hospitals in South Vietnam: "[I]f any neutral harmless-looking observers went through the provincial hospitals and asked the people how they were wounded and who else in their family was killed, I believe that they would learn that we, *unintentionally*, are killing and wounding three or four times more people than the Vietcong do. . . . This is indeed a new kind of war, . . . and we had better find a new way to fight it. Hearts and minds, after all, live in bodies."12

Gellhorn would cover seven wars during her long reporting career. Shortly before her death, she made a simple judgment of her work: "War is always worse than I knew how to say." At the age of 81 she went to Panama to view the aftermath of the U.S. invasion, which had been hidden from on-the-scene press coverage. By examining the rubble, she discovered that the U.S. Army had lied about the munitions it had used. "Martha had the ability to smell out things that other reporters didn't see," said Jonathan Randall, who had worked with her in Vietnam.13

Martha Gellhorn died in 1998 at the age of 89. Bill Buford, a long-time friend, editor, and sometime agent for Gellhorn, had a decidedly unromantic view of Gellhorn's bold spirit. Late in her life, as Gellhorn continued to seek wartime assignments, Buford would sigh and say, "There's something wrong with somebody who wants to go where people are being shot. . . . The ones who are really weird, the real screwballs, are the ones who . . . keep going back for it and can't stop. In a way, that was what was so compelling about Martha Gellhorn. She was desperately trying to get a paper to send her to the Gulf War. She must have been eighty-six. Loopy."[14]

Ernie Pyle

Ernie Pyle was surely the first icon among war correspondents. His name became a household word because he dealt almost exclusively with feature stories, the "soft" stories of the war, the personal tales of GI Joe. He described the daily life of the "grunt," what he ate, how he slept, how he died. He put names, home towns, and family backgrounds to the young faces in the foxholes. The mythic nature of Pyle's reputation was perhaps best expressed in the 1945 Hollywood film, *Ernie Pyle's Story of GI Joe*, starring Burgess Meredith as Ernie Pyle.

Part of the myth of Pyle's reporting is that he wrote his stories in the foxholes. In reality, says Joseph Tobin, a Pyle biographer, Pyle wrote a story in a foxhole exactly once. In his introduction to *Reporting America at War: An Oral History*, Tobin realistically characterized the dangers faced by journalists during the "conventional" wars of the past. "Sometimes war correspondents are in danger," he wrote. "Mostly they're not. They seldom find themselves in the middle of an actual clash of arms, and when they do, it's more often by accident than by intent."

One such accident placed Pyle's life in danger from "friendly fire" during the allied bombing of Saint Lo, France. Pyle described the explosions and machine gun fire as "a sound deep and all encompassing with no notes in it— just a gigantic faraway surge of doom-like sound. . . . It is possible to become so enthralled by some of the spectacles of war that you are momentarily captivated away from your own danger."[15]

But Pyle was quickly brought back to reality. He wrote,

As we watched, there crept into our consciousness a realization that windrows of exploding bombs were easing back toward us, flight by flight, instead of gradually forward, as the plan called for. Then we were horrified by the suspicion that those machines, high in the sky and completely detached from us, were aiming their bombs at the smokeline on the ground, and a gentle breeze was drifting the smokeline back over us. An incredible panic comes over you at such times. We stood tensed in muscle and frozen in intellect, watching each flight approach and pass over us. . . . And then all of an instant the universe became filled with a gigantic rattling as of huge, dry seeds in a mammoth dry gourd. . . . It was bombs by the hundred, hurtling down through the air above us.[16]

Pyle crawled under a cart in a shed and awaited his doom. "The feeling of the blast was sensational," he later wrote. "The air struck you in hundreds of continuing flutters. Your ears drummed and rang. You could feel quick little waves of concussions on your chest and in your eyes."[17]

Eventually, the bombing pattern shifted forward again. No one in Pyle's little group had been hurt, but in the fields around them 111 men had died, including Bede Irvin, an Associated Press (AP) photographer. Almost 500 men were wounded. James Tobin speculates that such a horrific American blunder would have been treated less gently during the Gulf War or Vietnam War than it was by Pyle and the other reporters during World War II. Pyle wrote, "After the bitterness came the sober remembrance that the Air Corps is the strong right arm in front of us. . . . Anybody makes mistakes. . . . [T]he percentage of error was really very small compared with the colossal storm of bombs that fell upon the enemy."[18]

Pyle's other close call came at Anzio, the Italian coastal town where the Allies made an amphibious landing. On February 25, after the Allies had bogged down in a stalemate with the German defenders, Pyle visited the beach-head, which was regularly shelled and bombed. Correspondents were housed in a four-story villa on a bluff above the water's edge. Pyle chose a room on the top floor. On the morning of March 17, the reporters living on the first floor saw their ceilings crumble from a direct German hit on the villa. A succession of blasts followed, filling the first floor with bricks and plaster. The reporters on the first floor survived, but they assumed that Pyle had died in the rubble above. "Well," said one reporter. "They got Ernie."[19]

Moments later, Pyle came down the stairs, bloody from a small cut on his face, but otherwise unharmed. He wrote three columns on his narrow escape at Anzio.

Pyle made no pretense of objectivity. He and his beloved GIs were part of a team that shared a noble cause. In the process of writing about American soldiers, sailors, and pilots, Pyle developed a kind of aesthetic appreciation for war, what Tobin called "the comradeship that grows out of shared struggle; the sense that one is living and seeing life at its most intense."[20] This attitude was common among reporters covering World War II, and although in Pyle's case it seldom placed him in the heart of battle, it did put him at risk.

Pyle made his name covering the war in Europe, but as V-E day approached, he felt obliged to join the GIs fighting in the Pacific. But his heart was no longer in it. On his way to Okinawa, he wrote his wife: "I'd like so much to be home and not see any more war ever. I don't expect to see as much here as in Europe, but I'll have to see a little eventually, and I dread that."[21]

War correspondent Chris Hedges explains: "Once you can't make sense of the savagery of war, then it's like all the lights are flicked out. And that's probably why he [Pyle] didn't want to go back."[22]

Pyle told friend Paige Cavanaugh, "I wouldn't give you two cents for the likelihood of me being alive a year from now."[23] Despite his misgivings, Pyle decided to accompany a Marine landing on Okinawa, although not with the first waves. Okinawa seemed less perilous than many of the war zones he had covered. The one hundred thousand Japanese defenders of Okinawa had withdrawn inland, and as a result there was little Japanese resistance to the American landing on April 1, 1945. Pyle wrote, "The carnage that is almost inevitable on an invasion was wonderfully and beautifully not there. . . . I realized there were no bodies anywhere—and no wounded."[24]

Pyle was assigned to the Army's Seventy-Seventh Division, which was to take the ten-square-mile island of Ia Shima, a few miles northwest of Okinawa. Landings were set for April 16, and a day later Pyle went ashore. For the next two days he talked to infantrymen and ate cold C rations. On the morning of April 18, Pyle hitched a ride with Colonel Joseph Coolidge, who was crossing the island in search of a site for his regimental command post. Most of the fighting was inland, leaving the road from the beach quiet, but at about 10 AM a hidden Japanese machine gun began firing scattered bursts at their jeep. Pyle, Coolidge, and the others in the jeep dove out into a roadside ditch, where they were pinned down. Pyle raised his head, and one of the sniper's bullets hit him in the left temple.

The presence of the hidden sniper prevented anyone from reaching Pyle for four hours. Finally, a combat photographer crawled to Pyle's lifeless body and snapped a picture. Minutes later, Pyle's body was pulled out of the sniper's line of fire, loaded onto an open truck, and transported to the command post on the beach. An AP correspondent sent the first bulletin: "Ernie Pyle, war correspondent beloved by his co-workers, GIs and generals alike, was killed by a Japanese machine-gun bullet through his left temple this morning."[25]

Pyle was buried with his helmet on in a long row of soldiers' graves on Ia Shima. A crude marker on his grave read: "At this spot the 77th Infantry lost a buddy ERNIE PYLE 18 April 1945."[26]

Edward R. Murrow

Many journalists believe that the work of Edward R. Murrow marked the beginning of the modern era of war reporting. Before his time, the public depended solely on the printed word for information about military conflicts, and the communications technology of the day often imposed heavy delays on reports from the front.

Murrow was the first great news broadcaster. Indeed, he essentially invented broadcast journalism. Murrow's on-the-scene radio broadcasts introduced a dramatic new sense of immediacy and authenticity. He covered events live, with sound and later pictures, and he developed a team of talented innovators who would come to later prominence themselves. These included Eric Sevareid, William L. Shirer, Charles Collingwood, Howard K. Smith, and Daniel Schorr.

Richard C. Hottelet, another trailblazing broadcast journalist, said Murrow's great accomplishment was to invent broadcast news from abroad. Before that, says Hottelet, "broadcast news was somebody ripping wire copy off a teleprinter and reading it through a microphone." Murrow initiated reporting in the field and the hiring of reporters, not broadcasters. Of course, working in the field could be dangerous business. Hottelet recalls, "I remember some of the broadcasts we did from London [during the German Blitz]. He would always be the first to go up on the roof and see where the action was that night. As a matter of fact, he did things that he might not have given as an assignment. His bomber trips with the RAF went deep into Germany. We knew that he was the bravest of the lot, and that was part of the respect in which he was held."[27]

Joseph Persico wrote of Murrow: "He faced danger with stoicism, avoiding shelters, standing on roof tops, sketching word pictures of a man-made hell as it happened. . . . He never denied his fears. He particularly feared . . . being blinded by flying glass."[28]

Murrow had written to his parents, "This is the end of an age, the end of things I was taught to love and respect. And I must stay here to report it if it kills me."[29]

The German bombing of England initially concentrated on airfields and other military and shipping targets along the coast, but gradually certain civilian locations were considered appropriate targets for German bombers. Primary among them was Broadcasting House, the London location for BBC as well as CBS and NBC. Murrow and NBC's Fred Bates were in Broadcasting House when it took a direct hit from a bomb that lodged, unexploded, in the center of the building. It lay there for forty-five minutes. The bomb squad was at work when the bomb went off, killing seven, wounding many others, and destroying the BBC's program library. Murrow was on the air as they brought the dead bodies past Studio B-4 to the aid station. He knew most of them personally.

Another bomb nearly killed Bates outside Broadcasting House, tearing off part of his ear, embedding shrapnel in his head, and severing tendons in both legs. Despite his injuries, Bates, script in hand, attempted to drag himself into the building for his broadcast. Cooler heads sent him away. Murrow's office was destroyed in the same blast.

CBS, Murrow's network, suffered no casualties during the Blitz, but three successive Murrow offices were destroyed. Kay Campbell was blasted across the room on one occasion, and Ed and Janet Murrow had several close calls. Biographer Bob Edwards says, "Ed avoided bomb shelters except to report on them.

He was afraid he'd grow accustomed to them. Instead, he drove through London in an open car . . . or walked the streets."[30]

Murrow sailed home after the battle of Britain was won, but he returned to London in 1943. He was now offered the opportunity he had been seeking for a year, accompanying American bombers over Germany. On December 2, 1943, he was aboard a Lancaster code-named *D-for Dog*. Murrow wrote,

> Yesterday afternoon the waiting war was over; the target was to be the big city. . . . We were approaching the enemy coast. The flak looked like a cigarette lighter in a dark room. . . . Sparks but no flame. . . . We flew steady and straight, and soon the flak was directly below us. . . . Suddenly, the dirty gray clouds turned white. We were over the outer searchlight defenses. . . . We were flying straight toward the center of the fireworks. . . . And then, with no warning at all, *D-Dog* was filled with an unhealthy white light.

An antiaircraft search light had fixed on them, and *D-Dog* went into a dive. Murrow was on his knees as the plane corkscrewed, evading the lights and the flak. *D-Dog* returned unharmed that night, but fifty bombers were lost. Murrow recalled, "There were four reporters on this operation—two of them didn't come back. Two friends of mine—Norman Stockton . . . and Lowell Bennett."[31]

CBS's Paul White continually forbade Murrow from flying on combat missions, saying the network's European director was too valuable to take such risks. Even CBS owner William Paley pleaded with Murrow not to take such risks. Murrow repeatedly promised White that he had gone on his last flight, but he totaled twenty-five combat missions before the war ended. "There was no way to make him stop," said White, "short of firing him."[32]

Murrow's attitude was expressed in a letter to a friend: "In order to write or talk about danger, you must experience it. The experience teaches you something about what happens to fighting men, and perhaps more important, it teaches you something about yourself."[33]

Walter Cronkite

Walter Cronkite, anchorman for CBS Evening News from 1962 to 1981, was surely the most visible journalist of his generation. Widely regarded as the most trusted man in America during his tenure on television, Cronkite actually had established his career and reputation during his years as a print correspondent for the United Press during World War II.

Cronkite was working for United Press in New York at the time of Pearl Harbor, and he immediately decided he wanted to get into the war as a correspondent. Assigned to the Eighth Air Force in Europe during World War

II, Cronkite was part of a fabled group of correspondents dubbed by an Air Force public relations man as "The Writing Sixty-Ninth." In addition to Cronkite, the group consisted of Andy Rooney, Homer Bigart, Gladwin Hill, William Wade, Bob Post, Denton Scott, and Paul Manning. Their first mission was the American air raid on the German submarine base at Wilhelmshaven. Most of the reporters wanted to go with the fleet of Flying Fortresses, but Bob Post chose to go with a squadron of Liberators. His plane was shot down. Cronkite recalls, "He was lost—the only loss among the five of us who got over the target that day. Crews of other Liberators said they saw men bail out of Bob's stricken plane, but they came under heavy ground fire as they floated down."[34]

The planes carrying Cronkite and the other surviving reporters endured heavy attacks for two-and-a-half hours until they reached the English coast. On the plane, Cronkite was assigned to the plastic nose of the ship, along with the bombardier and navigator. There were three guns between them, so Cronkite manned the spare. "I fired at every German fighter that came into the neighborhood," he recalls. "I don't think I hit any, but I'd like to think I scared a couple of those German pilots."[35]

When the planes returned, Cronkite's colleague Homer Bigart asked him what the lead for his story would be. Cronkite said he would use, "I've just returned from an assignment to hell, a hell at 17,000 feet." Bigart who couldn't stand such purple prose, replied in his usual heavy stammer, "You-you-you wouldn't."[36] But Cronkite's story received heavy play in the U.S. and British papers.

In covering the ground war in Europe, reporters were assigned to armies, and the press set up somewhere around Army headquarters. They were briefed by the officers on where the action was going to be, and if the action was something they wanted to report on, they would get a jeep assignment—usually the same jeep each day—and off they would go to the front. They were given a chart and a map to locate the group they wanted to find, and they usually stayed with the soldiers. In the evening they went back to press camp and wrote their stories.

Cronkite recalls, "We were out there with the guys in the foxholes, in the airplanes, in the parachute jump groups, in the gliders. It was entirely voluntary, and the frequently asked question to the reporters from GIs was, 'What the hell are you doing here? Do you have to be here?' 'No,' we'd say, 'we don't have to be.' . . . They looked upon us as heroes, in a way, as we looked upon them."[37]

Cronkite was in Brussels covering the Twenty-First Army Group when Hitler sent 250,000 men to crash through the Ardennes Forest. Nineteen thousand Americans and forty thousand Germans would die in the ten-day Battle of the Bulge, and at the start of that bloody battle the United Press sent Cronkite a cable saying that they had lost touch with the First Army and asking Cronkite to get out there and write the story. To this day, Cronkite has saved the cable because he considered the request to be crazy. If the Germans had surrounded the First Army, how was a lone correspondent going to reestablish contact with the outside? Nonetheless, he joined an armored unit that had the best chance of breaking through to the beleaguered forces at Bastogne.

After joining the unit, Cronkite was approached by General Maxwell Taylor, commander of the 101st Airborne Division, who asked, "I'm going to Bastogne. Do you want to come?" Being the first reporter into Bastogne would have been a great story for Cronkite, but how would he get the story out? There was no communications link out of Bastogne, and by the time he had his story on the wires, the correspondents on the outside would already have reported the dramatic events. Cronkite gave this quite logical explanation to Taylor as he declined his invitation to go to Bastogne. "But I knew the truth, and I suspect he did," Cronkite would later admit. "Taylor's drive to Bastogne could well have been a suicide mission. A lot of glory, perhaps, for a career officer; simply a sad footnote for a war correspondent."[38]

In hindsight, Cronkite says, "I'm not sure that a little yellow streak didn't appear. . . . Many days, guys, including me, would simply say, 'Well, I don't see anything very different in that story. Why should I go up and get my ass shot off for another platoon action?' . . . Of course, if you don't go often enough, your company would presumably recall you. That's not the kind of war correspondent you want at the front."[39]

After the Germans surrendered in western Holland, Cronkite's car took a back road around the troops and entered Amsterdam first. From their open command car they received salutes from confused German soldiers lining the route as well as enthusiastic adulation from thousands of Dutch who jammed the streets. Cronkite recalls, "They pelted us with tulips until our car was fender deep in them. . . . The only blood I spilled in the war was that day—hit by a bunch of tulips tied together with a piece of wire."[40]

Despite his record of bravery and professionalism as a war correspondent, Cronkite was modest to a fault about his battlefield experiences. "People take a look at my record and it sounds great," he wrote in 1970. "Personally, I feel I was an overweening coward in the war. I was scared to death all the time. I did everything possible to avoid getting into combat. Except the ultimate thing of not doing it. I did it. But the truth is that I did everything only once. . . . If you go back and do it a second time, knowing how bad it is, that's courage."[41]

Andy Rooney

Andy Rooney's World War II assignments included the invasion of Normandy and the drive across France and Germany to Berlin. After the war, he worked as a freelance writer and then a newspaper columnist, and in 1976 he assumed the responsibility for which he is best known today: the curmudgeonly commentator on CBS TV's *60 Minutes*.

Rooney worked as a reporter for *Stars and Stripes*, the official newspaper of the U.S Army, during World War II. As just another army draftee, he was unique among war correspondents. He was initially assigned to England as a battery clerk, but due to some very imaginative resume writing, he managed to land a job as a reporter on *Stars and Stripes*. The London offices for *Stars and Stripes* were top rate because the *London Times* had evacuated them in favor of a safer location two stories underground, protected from German bombs. *Stars and Stripes* thus inherited the excellent, but vulnerable, plant.

During the German Blitz, virtually no area of London was safe. Even Rooney's lodgings were fire bombed. But by 1943, the American and British air forces were taking the war to German cities, and Rooney was assigned to the Eighth and Ninth Air Forces. Overall, about 5 percent of the planes were lost on every mission. A crew was committed to twenty-five raids before it was retired or reassigned. Rooney says, "It didn't take any mathematical genius to understand that if you fly twenty-five raids in a few months, and the loss rate was 5 percent, that's a loss of the equivalent of every crewman in the bomber group plus a quarter of the new replacements."[42]

The Eighth Air Force press group, which contained many prominent correspondents, decided it should go along on a bomber mission. Rooney says, "It probably grew out of that uneasy feeling we all had that we were watching too many young men . . . die while we were writing stories about them."[43]

The officers in charge decided that the reporters would first have to attend gunnery school. Those attending the school were Walter Cronkite, Homer Bigart, Paul Manning, Jack Denton Scott, Gladwin Hill, Bob Post, Bill Wade, and Rooney.

At 5:30 a.m. on February 3, 1943, the morning of the mission, Rooney and the others were allowed into the briefing at which the details of the mission were laid out. Reporters had never been allowed such access before. A map was displayed, and Wilhelmshaven, a heavily defended German port, was pinpointed. Rooney recalls that this was the first time he had seriously considered his own death. "I wondered what I was doing there. Was it really necessary for me to volunteer for a mission that could easily cost me my life simply to get a story? . . . The chance of being shot down was estimated to be something like one in five or one in six. About as good as Russian roulette with a six-shooter—which isn't very good."[44]

On the day of the mission, two of the eight reporters who were to go on the raid were sick and decided they couldn't go. Rooney recalls, "The thought crossed my mind that I didn't feel too well myself." But he went on the raid, sit-

ting on a small, makeshift seat behind the bombardier and opposite the navigator. "It's perfectly possible I'll never come back," Rooney thought. "There's a
good chance we'll be shot down or that I'll be seriously wounded. . . . This is a
silly, fake brave gesture I'm making considering the high risk it involves."[45]

Once Rooney boarded his bomber he began to think, "Why am I doing
this? I'm scared to death. The plane was a perfect target for the gunners under-
neath, and that was the frightening part of it."[46]

Rooney was aboard the *Banshee*, one of forty-three bombers in the formation. When they approached Wilhelmshaven the flak began. Some of the bombers were hit and were unable to keep up with the formation, but the *Banshee*
continued on, dropped its bombs, and turned to head home. At this point, German planes attacked, hitting several B-17s and sending three down in flames.
Suddenly, there was an explosion in the *Banshee's* nose compartment. A shell
had blown off the tip of the Plexiglass nose, leaving a jagged hole about the size
of a man's hand. The navigator took off his gloves and tried to shove one of them
into the hole, but the cold air at 18,000 feet froze his hand and pieces of flesh
were scraped off on the jagged edges. Meanwhile, the navigator's oxygen tube
had been severed, causing him to quickly lose consciousness.

The captain told Rooney to take some deep breaths, remove his oxygen
mask, and go to the back of the plane to retrieve an emergency oxygen bottle.

"I felt inadequate," says Rooney. "They'd forgotten I was a reporter."[47]

Rooney did as he was told and tried to remember the few things he had
been taught about the use of oxygen masks. "I didn't know how to do any of
this," recalls Rooney, "and here I was, with somebody's life at stake, and I didn't
know how long you lasted once you took your oxygen mask off."[48]

He succeeded in fitting the bombardier with the emergency mask, allowing
him to regain consciousness. Meanwhile, the German planes continued their
attacks until the *Banshee* reached the safety of the British coast. Five of the six
reporters who had gone on the mission returned safely. Bob Post, a thirty-year-
old reporter for the *New York Times*, was lost in action.

Not all of Rooney's wartime experience was with the air war. Several days
after the D-Day assault of June 6, he arrived on Utah Beach. By that time the
grave registration unit had collected countless bodies and laid them out on the
beaches. But the fighting was far from over. Rooney says, "When I came in, row
on row of dead American soldiers were laid out on the sand just above the high-
tide mark. . . . It's not possible for anyone who has been in a war to describe the
terror of it to anyone who hasn't."[49]

After D-Day, Rooney worked alongside foot soldiers crossing France. "The
difference between my life and theirs was that I could walk among them . . . with
notebook and pencil in hand, get names and stories—and then leave. I had the

same uncomfortable sense of copping out that I'd had covering the Eighth Air Force. What I did was marginally dangerous because there were always artillery and mortar shells coming in, but when the dreaded whisper 'Move out' was passed down the line, . . . I didn't have to move out."50

Rooney says the Allied breakthrough at Saint-Lo was one of the handful of events that dominates his memory of the war. Early in the morning of July 18, Rooney picked up a colleague, Bob Casey, in his jeep and headed for Saint-Lo. Along the way, mortar shells dropped regularly around them and they could hear machine gun fire and shells whistling through the air. Rooney says, "We rolled slowly toward town in low gear, weaving our way down the road strewn with dead bodies and tanks, trucks, half-tracks, and German command cars." Rooney stopped his jeep, got out, and walked down the road. "It was a mindless thing you wouldn't do if you considered the risk," says Rooney, "but I was interested, curious, and somehow oblivious to danger. . . . I didn't get hit and I got a story."51

The end of Rooney's Saint-Lo story would come several months later when he returned to Paris. Colonel Ensley Llewellyan called him into his office and displayed a box containing a medal and a citation. "I see we have another hero with the paper," said Llewellyan without enthusiasm. Rooney took the box and saw the Bronze Star. He had already received the Air Medal for the five trips he had made on bombing raids. The citation with the Bronze Star commended Rooney for having "penetrated to the heart of Saint-Lo under small arms and open range artillery fire and gathered, without regard to his own safety, first hand [sic] descriptive material for a complete and accurate story."52

Rooney says he was simultaneously pleased and embarrassed.

Ward Just

Ward Just's reporting from Vietnam was as influential as that of any other correspondent in convincing the American public and American political leaders that something had gone awry in our attempt to win the hearts and minds of the Vietnamese people. Just was not so much a critic of the war as a scrupulous observer. He had been trained as a *Newsweek* reporter covering the war in Cyprus in 1966 and would later be sent to Vietnam by the *Washington Post*. His writing never descended to cynicism, and he always identified with the American troops.

Just's experiences under fire in Vietnam were chronicled in stark prose. While accompanying an American patrol deep inside North Vietnamese lines, he found himself facing attack from all sides. "There were literally hundreds of them, and there were, you know, 40 of us," recalled Just. "There was a captain with us and he gave me this .45 caliber pistol. . . . I wanted to disappear. You can talk about the public's right to know and the First Amendment all you want, but this is serious business. People were dying."[53]

The Vietcong attackers did not have mortars, but they had grenades, small arms, automatic weapons, and good cover to shoot from. Just's 1968 book, *To What End: Report from Vietnam*, described the experience in brutally realistic terms.

"You picked a great patrol," Captain Higinbotham told Just sarcastically.

"Mr. Reporter, how much you get paid for this?" asked one of the soldiers.

"Not enough," answered Just.

Just recalled his brush with death: "I . . . reflected on the similarity of the soldier and the war correspondent, the basic text for which comes from the Joseph Heller novel, *Catch-22*. On the one hand, no one wants to get ambushed. . . . On the other, if nothing happens there is no story."[54] This was what Just called Catch-23.

As it turned out, something did happen. Something terrible. "At two thirty in the afternoon the first grenade crashed down the ridge line," wrote Just. "In the first fifteen minutes, three died and six fell wounded. The firing came from three sides, hitting the Americans at all points on the trail." After two hours of enemy fire, the situation was almost lost and Captain Higinbotham radioed for reinforcements: "If you don't get up here soon, we're all gonna die."[55]

A wounded infantryman was calling out from the left flank, his voice cracked with agony. Just wrote, "As he screamed and moaned, I moved forward. . . . I had the idea that I might save his life. I looked around at the others and then the wounded man screamed, and was silent. . . . Now I didn't have to think about it. He was dead."[56]

Then someone shouted, "Grenade!" There was a flash and a burst of fire, and Just screamed, "I'm hit!"

"You're OK," said Higinbotham.

"The hell I am," responded Just. "Christ almighty there's blood everywhere."

His arms and legs were shaking uncontrollably. A medic scrambled up and gave him a shot of morphine, restoring some control of his limbs.

"Where are the VC?" he stammered.

"We stopped the bastards," Higinbotham said.

Just recalls, "I thought that line was in the best MGM tradition, and told Higinbotham so."[57]

"Where's that newspaper fella?" asked a trooper.

"He got hurt," Higinbotham said.

"Hurt? Sonovabitch," said the trooper.[58]

Just took more than thirty pieces of shrapnel in that attack and declined to be evacuated until dozens of wounded enlisted men were airlifted out. There was no landing zone for the helicopters, so they hovered at about 100 feet and lowered a T-bar to a strobe-lit area. One by one, men were strapped to the T-bar and lifted 100 feet to the copter. "You ascended alone into the eye of the light, and heard the crack and thwup of bullets, and realized that the enemy, still entrenched on the ridge line, were shooting," wrote Just. "They were shooting at the wounded men being pulled into the helicopter."[59]

Ward Just was flown back to the United States for medical treatment, but he soon returned to Vietnam to complete his assignment there. More recently, he has turned his attention to fiction writing, producing short stories and novels such as *A Dangerous Friend* (1999), *Echo House* (1997), and *Ambition and Love* (1994).

Peter Arnett

Peter Arnett's long service as a foreign correspondent bridges the conventional wars and the modern warfare that makes journalists legitimate military targets. Among the many countries in which he has covered armed conflict are Cyprus, Thailand, Cambodia, Laos, Vietnam, Chile, El Salvador, Nicaragua, Panama, Iran, Indonesia, Afghanistan, and Iraq. His decade-long reporting in Vietnam established his credentials as a bold and gifted correspondent, not intimidated by battlefield danger or Pentagon bureaucrats.

Arnett began his Vietnam assignment for the AP on June 26, 1962, and quickly formed a close relationship with the legendary AP correspondent Malcolm Browne, who ran the Saigon bureau like a drill sergeant. Browne gave Arnett a copy of his *Guide to News Coverage in Vietnam*, which, among other things, recommended that correspondents carry a pocket pistol: "If you are with a government operation you will be the target of enemy fire, exactly as if you were a combatant. If you are wounded in a convoy or in a position that is overrun, you probably will be shot to death."[60]

The guide explained that most war correspondents in Vietnam carried pistols in order to have some chance of shooting their way out of such situations, but it warned that carrying weapons was not condoned officially by Vietnamese or American authorities.

Arnett's first combat operation came on August 28, 1962, when he accompanied the U.S. Marine Corps's 163rd Helicopter Squadron to a small village named Ca Mau. Despite Malcolm Browne's advice, Arnett did not carry a pistol. Arnett and AP photographer Horst Faas traveled with Vietnamese troops aboard a helicopter and were delivered to Ca Mau. They were immediately greeted by Vietcong sniper fire. Bullets whizzed around them, causing the unit to return fire and call for air support. A T-28 aircraft soon began to bomb, strafe, and napalm the area for nearly an hour, but when it departed, the snipers, undeterred, resumed their fire. The Vietnamese soldiers were too tired to bother responding.

In May, Arnett had another close call near Song Be, where a number of U.S. military "advisors" had been killed by Vietcong just few days earlier. When Major Mitchell Sakey was informed that Vietcong were massing on the slopes below for another attack, he told Arnett and Faas, "I'll need you two to assist in the defenses tonight." The major gave Arnett a carbine and told him to go protect the mortarman on the western berm. When Arnett asked about the Geneva Conventions prohibiting civilians from carrying weapons, the major responded, "You want to believe the VC are going to respect your civilian status tonight, fella?"[61]

Arnett stuffed his shirt and trouser pockets with ammo clips and stumbled off to the mortar position he was to defend. Soon, C-47 gunships appeared in the sky and began firing at the dark landscape in front of Arnett. The mortarman fired repeatedly at the shadows before them as Arnett laid prostrate, rifle at his shoulder, waiting for the Vietcong ground assault to begin. It never came.

A later incident near a Vietcong base north of Saigon proved even more dangerous. Arnett accompanied the First Battalion in an assault in which Vietcong machine gun fire cut down the first seven Americans in the patrol. Arnett hit the dirt as bullets thudded into nearby tree trunks. When the captain moved forward, Arnett followed. They came across the bodies of many dead Americans and quickly slid back down the hill to join their unit. Helicopters were called in to evacuate the wounded, and Arnett took the last copter out.

After a few more such incidents, AP chief Wes Gallagher wrote to Saigon complaining that firsthand reporting on patrol action was taking unnecessary risks. He concluded, "The lives of Peter and Horst are much too valuable to take a chance on the patrol type of reporting. . . . I want Horst and Peter to know that I feel they should pull their horns in a bit and not be pushing the percentages."[62]

But among the war correspondents in Vietnam, competition, not caution, was the watchword. As Arnett pointed out, you not only had to be first with a story, you had to be first every day. Despite the attempts of the AP and other news organizations to reign in its more adventurous reporters, fatalities among correspondents began to mount. Arnett says, "There were no flags for the journalists who died in Vietnam, and not much glory. We gathered up our own dead and sent them home by air freight. . . . Only the combat soldiers we traveled with, and whose dangers we shared, took our real measure, always curious as to why we chose such dangerous company."[63]

Arnett would later explain why he continued to seek out dangerous assign-ments. "I sort of have a genetic tic that allows me to go into dangerous areas without too much concern," he said.[64]

The November 13, 1965, issue of *Editor and Publisher* displayed a picture of Arnett in combat boots walking along a bomb-cratered road in Vietnam with a company of Vietnamese soldiers. The caption read, "Peter Arnett went to Vietnam in July 1962 to cover a dirty little war. It's bigger and deadlier now. In October it took the lives of two photographers . . . , Bernard Kolenberg and Huynh Thanh My. In a thousand days, Peter Arnett has personally gone through a hundred battles, from the ambush-ridden delta to isolated outposts in the highlands. . . . Peter Arnett like other AP men in Vietnam believes the place to get the story and the picture is with the fighting troops. In doing this he has displayed courage and shown initiative and reporting skill in the highest tradi-tion of his profession."[65]

In November 1967, Arnett joined an AP reporting team in Dak To where three U.S. paratrooper companies were surrounded after suffering heavy casual-ties. A relief mission was assembled, and Arnett volunteered to go along. As the relief column crept through the tangled underbrush, hidden gunners opened up with antitank rockets that exploded overhead, forcing the column to hit the dirt. When the rocket fire subsided, they pressed on, soon noticing dead bodies in the shadows around them. Then they came upon mounds of dead paratroop-ers and behind them scores of wounded. One of them told Arnett he had been there for thirty-six hours and that eleven of the twelve battalion medics had been killed trying to help the wounded.

Arnett began to dig himself a foxhole in which to spend the night, but his shovel hit human flesh, a body buried by a bomb explosion earlier in the day. "I recoiled in horror and stepped back on something soft and discovered it was a detached arm from another corpse," wrote Arnett.[66] That night, Arnett slept in a shallow hole. He awoke to the sound of mortar tubes followed by violent explosions. A group of soldiers nearby writhed wounded in the dirt. The lieu-tenant radioed for an air strike which soon dropped napalm and bombs on the enemy position. A U.S. Navy A-3 jet followed, dropping two projectiles from its bomb rack. "I waited for them [the projectiles] to fly overhead, but they kept coming in toward me and I knew right then that I was looking death in the face and I didn't have time to be frightened but wondered what my corpse would look like, splintered into a thousand pieces by the explosions."[67]

One of the projectiles landed far to the right of Arnett, exploding harm-lessly in a bunker. The other embedded itself just fifteen yards in front of him, but, miraculously, it did not explode. Later in the afternoon, helicopters came in to take away the dead, the wounded, and the newsmen.

In addition to his regular assignments on patrol, Arnett was an eye witness to the Tet Offensive in Saigon. "I opened the window and watched the war come to the capital," he wrote. "Red tracer bullets zipped through the sky near the presidential palace and the American embassy and the muffled roar of hand grenades or rockets or both vibrated through the night."[68]

Arnett was, of course, battle-tested, but many of the reporters in Saigon were seeing war firsthand for the first time. "It was a watershed in how the press covered the war," recalls Arnett, "because suddenly the capital city, where hundreds and hundreds of reporters were based, was under attack. . . . Suddenly, all of these reporters were war reporters, right in the middle of it."[69]

Arnett tried to drive around the city, but automatic weapons fire forced him to stop and climb under the car for protection. He later learned that Vietcong guerrillas had driven unchecked through the city and stormed the American embassy, killing five guards. The Tet Offensive was, of course, only a brief display of Vietcong power, but it was the handwriting on the wall. On April 30, 1975, Arnett witnessed the fall of Saigon. He recalls, "My feeling at the fall of Saigon . . . was what a wasted effort. . . . [N]ot only of the journalists, over 60 dead, but all the other casualties, all the efforts at nation-building. . . . All of it ended one sunny morning."[70]

There were many more adventures ahead for Peter Arnett, including his first overseas assignment for CNN in El Salvador in the autumn of 1981. But his departure for Iraq in 1990 marked the beginning of his most controversial work as a correspondent. The American invasion—Gulf War I—was imminent, and CNN producer Robert Wiener told him that "staying behind when the war began would be suicidal." Pilots with the U.S. Navy carriers in Gulf waters were quoted as saying that the al-Rashid Hotel, where Arnett and most other journalists stayed, would be used as a landmark for the bombing campaign. When Arnett tried to reassure Wiener by pointing out that the U.S. "smart" bombs knew the difference between a strategic installation and a hotel, Wiener responded, "But what if they're one and the same thing."[71]

When Saddam Hussein failed to withdraw from Kuwait by the U.S. deadline, the press corps in Baghdad began leaving. The White House issued warnings for journalists to leave Iraq. Even Walter Cronkite, appearing on the air from Washington, emphasized the risks of remaining. "I think the decision to stay in a place that is clearly a major danger zone where one's mortality has to be considered on the line is probably the toughest decision any newspaperman ever had to make," he said. Cronkite concluded with some friendly advice for Arnett: "Peter, you're a very valuable asset to courageous reporting around the world. . . . [S]ave your skin, boy."[72]

Arnett remained in Baghdad, the lone Western newsman covering the American bombardment. His regular broadcasts for CNN gave the entire world a dramatic picture of unrelenting destruction by the most sophisticated military technology ever seen. Arnett's hotel was hit and devastated, but neither Arnett nor his CNN staff were injured. The last bombing of Baghdad occurred in the early hours of February 28, 1991, and within an hour President Bush would announce that the war was over. The attacks had gone on for forty-three days.

Arnett would go on to cover hot spots like Afghanistan, before the American invasion, but his controversial solo reporting from Baghdad had permanently defined his popular image.

Chapter 2

Journalism and the New Face of War

Current Violence against War Correspondents

In June, 2004, Philip Bennett, the *Washington Post's* assistant managing editor for foreign affairs, visited the *Post's* Baghdad bureau and discussed the problems of covering the war in Iraq. The five correspondents seated around the table with him had covered nearly the entire map of conflicts since Vietnam. From his conversations, Bennett concluded, "Iraq is different." Kidnappings and ambushes had driven most foreign civilians out of the country or into fortified bunkers guarded by the U.S. military. "For journalists, the familiar rules of engagement have been stripped away," wrote Bennett. "Gone is the assumption that correspondents are more valuable as witnesses than as targets, and that they share only the risks that all civilians face in wartime. To insurgents, foreign journalists are . . . just another element of an occupying force to which we don't belong."[1]

ABC-TV News anchor Peter Jennings says he heard talk on the streets of Baghdad about bounties offered for kidnapped foreigners: $2,000 for a journalist, $3,000 for a U.S. soldier. "It's very intimidating," he said.[2]

In September 2004, the Overseas Press Club in New York hosted a panel discussion by editors who oversee foreign correspondents. In a sober introduction, the audience was told, "In the three years since the [9/11] terrorist attacks, journalists reporting from abroad have faced sinister new dangers, kidnapping, assassinations, death by friendly fire. Some of our best journalists are literally risking their lives to bring us the news."[3]

Panel member Adi Ignatius, executive editor for *Time* magazine, told of correspondent Michael Weiskopf, who was traveling in a truck with U.S. soldiers when an insurgent threw a grenade in the back of the truck. "Michael had the quick thinking to grab it and try to throw it out of the truck. It went off before he could throw it. He probably saved everybody's lives. He lost his hand. He's now fitted with a prosthetic hand."[4]

Susan Chira, *New York Times* foreign editor, described a harrowing 48 hours during which *Times* correspondents Jeffrey Gettleman and John Burns were captured by insurgents in separate incidents. After his release, Burns concluded, "In the end, you're faced with an irreducible risk because there is nothing that will protect you against a rocket-propelled grenade someone fires at a motor vehicle. Nothing will protect you against hostage taking. Nothing will protect you against roadside bombs."[5] Chira concluded, "So we are facing every day the question of whether one can travel. I have gotten phone calls in the middle of the night and we have talked about whether it's safe to go down X or Y road. And one day when we all agreed to wait, two Polish journalists were killed going down the same road."[6]

In October, 2004, Terrence Smith, media correspondent for public television's Lehrer News Hour, introduced a panel of war correspondents by declaring, "The security situation in Iraq has grown so perilous in recent months that several areas of the country are virtually inaccessible to western reporters. . . . Covering Iraq has proven to be a deadly job. In all, 46 reporters have been killed in the 19 months since the start of the war. Reporters from many European countries have packed up and left, fearing for their safety. They have good reason."[7]

Since the fall of Baghdad to Coalition troops in April 2003, *Washington Post* reporter Robin Wright has accompanied the U.S. Secretary of State on three official visits to Iraq. Her accounts of those visits reveal the steady deterioration of security in Iraq and the increasing isolation of reporters. "On our first trip, in mid-September 2003, the State Department entourage and diplomatic press corps stayed for two nights at the legendary Al Rashid Hotel," wrote Wright. "Back then we could tool around the Iraqi capital. With a *New York Times* colleague I walked through the concrete barriers down the lonely lane that linked the protected Green Zone to the rest of Baghdad. . . . Back then, [Secretary of State Colin] Powell would leave the Green Zone—surrounded by a 'security bubble'—for meetings with Shiite, Kurd, and Sunni government officials."[8]

Wright's second trip to Baghdad, on July 20, 2004, was a closely guarded secret. Members of the press corps traveling with Secretary of State Powell could not reveal their travel plans until after their arrival in Baghdad. They traveled from the airport to the Green Zone in Black Hawk helicopters as U.S. troops manning machine guns watched from open windows on both sides of the road.

"The route was so dangerous that we were all given flak jackets and helmets for the short trip," said Wright. "This time, Powell's bubble—and ours—was much smaller. America's top diplomat didn't leave the Green Zone and U.S. security wouldn't let the press out, either. . . . There was no connection with ordinary Iraqis or the real Baghdad."[9]

Wright's most recent trip to Baghdad, on November 11, 2005, was kept secret even from members of Secretary of State Condoleezza Rice's staff. The members of the traveling press were summoned to the State Department the day before they were scheduled to leave on a routine trip to the Middle East and were sworn to secrecy after a briefing about an unannounced stop in Baghdad. "We could tell an editor and a family member, but we were asked not to mention it to anyone else," recalls Wright. "If word got out, the trip would be canceled. . . . On this latest trip to Baghdad, the bubble shrank even more. No roaming the Green Zone."[10]

The press corps was sequestered in Saddam Hussein's old palace for most of their seven-hour stay. "All we saw were new barricades trimmed with barbed wire, concrete blast walls, roadblocks and time-consuming identity checks," said Wright, who described their nervous departure from Iraq. "The pilot of the C-17 military transport that flew us out of Iraq did not turn on the interior lights until we had reached a safe altitude—and were well out of Baghdad airspace."[11]

As we saw in Chapter 1, reporting on war has always been a dangerous business. It is the purposeful targeting of journalists by combatants that is new. The abduction of the *Chicago Tribune*'s Philip Caputo by Fedayeen in Lebanon in 1973 should have been a wake-up call for news organizations, but it was over ten years before another high-profile journalist was kidnapped, again in Lebanon, when CNN's Jerry Levin was taken by Hezbollah, a radical Shiite group. A year later, Terry Anderson, Middle East correspondent for the Associated Press, was grabbed in Pakistan and held for almost seven years, making him America's longest-held hostage. In between these abductions were periodic acts of violence against reporters. In today's Middle East, such acts of violence are *daily* occurrences, whereas abductions and murders are *weekly* events. What has changed in the nature of war and journalism, and when did the change occur?

Terry Anderson says, "Today, journalists are targeted, which we never were. During most of the war in Lebanon you could go and talk to anyone, including the most radical groups. I was picked up by Abu Nidal one day, along with my photographer, in the Bekaa Valley, which scared the crap out of us. But all they wanted to do was give us an interview and send us on our way. I would go and talk to just about anyone during those days, and while it was dangerous—you could get beaten or thrown in jail for a while—the presumption was that you were there to tell a story, their story as well as anybody else's.

That changed at the end of the Lebanese war when Hezbollah came in. They didn't care who you were. If you were a westerner, particularly an American, you were dead meat."[12]

Clearly, Hezbollah's early attacks on Americans in Lebanon included journalists, but the systematic targeting of journalists began, ironically, with the war on terrorism. The 2001 invasion of Afghanistan began the process. Within months of the invasion there were more foreign journalists in Afghanistan than at any time in its history. After Johanne Sutton of Radio France Internationale (RFI), Pierre Billand of RTL, and Volker Handloik of *Stern* were killed in Afghanistan, anxieties among the press corps were high. In late 2001, Scott Peterson of the *Christian Science Monitor* wrote, "With eight journalists killed . . . Afghanistan is now the deadliest place in the world to practice this profession. . . . The risks are rising now, in part, because the battle lines are vague. . . . Most journalists feel a professional competitive pressure to test the limits of safety to get a story . . . sometimes crossing the line between observer and combatant."[13]

Patrick Cockburn, veteran correspondent for the London *Independent*, wrote, "It's more dangerous here for foreign journalists than in Lebanon or Kurdistan, because the anarchy is worse, and there's more pressure on journalists to get the story."[14]

On November 18, 2001, three more journalists from RFI were attacked along a road in Kabul province by young bandits armed with Kalashnikovs. On that same day, Filipino journalists were robbed on the way to Kabul. The very next day, an eight-car convoy of journalists left Jalalabad for Kabul without the usual armed escort. The convoy, which included journalists from the *Washington Post, Los Angeles Times, Baltimore Sun*, and a number of European publications and broadcast outlets, became separated between cars by as much as one hundred yards as it climbed the steep Kabul River gorge toward the capitol. Suddenly, a group of at least six men armed with Kalashnikov automatic rifles appeared and stopped the second and third cars in the convoy.

The second car held Maria Grazia Cutuli, a reporter for the Italian daily *Corriere dela Sera*, and Julio Fuentes from Madrid's *El Mundo*, along with their driver and translator. The third car held two Reuters journalists, Harry Burton, an Australian cameraman, and Aziz Haidari, an Afghan-born photographer, with their driver and translator.

The attackers ordered everyone out of the cars, told the Afghan drivers and translators to turn back, and took the four foreign journalists away. "They hit them with their rifle butts," recounted one Afghan driver. "One man took a stone and threw it" at the journalists while another shouted, "What do you think? It's the end of the Taliban? The Taliban are still here!"[15]

One of the translators for the journalists recalled, "I tried to move away to save myself. . . . I heard a Kalashnikov three times, maybe four times." Another of the drivers said, "They shot the people and I ran away."[16]

After being beaten and pelted with stones, two of the journalists were killed at the site of the abduction and the other two taken away and killed later. All four bodies were dumped on the road from Kabul to Jalalabad. The postmortem examination revealed that the bullet-riddled bodies had first been stoned.

The day after the murders, three more journalists, Matthew MacAllester and Moises Saman from *Newsday* and Larry Kaplow of the Cox newspaper chain, were robbed and threatened with death on the same road where the others had been killed. The attackers ordered them to empty their bags, took $120, and threatened them with their weapons, saying that the mullahs had ordered them "to kill as many foreigners as they can." Their Afghan translator convinced the attackers not to kill the journalists.[17]

As the frequency of such attacks on journalists grew, the BBC and several major U.S. television networks pulled their correspondents out of northern Afghanistan, and by early 2003, the U.S. invasion and occupation of Iraq had shifted the focus of media coverage from Afghanistan to Iraq. As a result, Iraq has become the most dangerous assignment for journalists today. Bill Katovsky begins the introduction to his book *Embedded: The Media at War in Iraq* (2003) with the statement, "Let's start with one simple fact about the war in Iraq: Statistically, journalists were ten times more likely to die than the 250,000 in American or British soldiers."[18]

Veteran *New York Times* correspondent John Kifner says, "It [Iraq] is absolutely the worst war I've ever covered. [In Lebanon] you had a much better physical sense of where danger could come from, whereas in Iraq it's just all over."[19]

Sarhaddi Nelson, Middle East bureau chief for Knight Ridder, told of being abducted by Shiite militiamen on suspicion that she was a CIA agent. She was eventually released after convincing her captors that she was not a spy, but she says, "There is no sense of safety anywhere in Baghdad. Journalists have become targets."[20]

It is not the location of the war that has determined press casualties. After all, only four journalists died in Iraq during the first Gulf War. The fatal count had reached thirteen by the end of the third week of Gulf War II, and the death rates continue to rapidly accelerate. It is the nature of war and the ways of covering it that have changed.

Iraq is flooded with journalists. By late 2004, more than six thousand journalists had registered with the U.S. military's press office in Baghdad's heavily fortified Green Zone. This downtown enclave of several square miles contains offices and living quarters for American administrators attached to the Coalition

Provisional Authority (CPA). It is encased in concrete barriers, razor wire, sandbags, and warnings in English and Arabic that "deadly force is authorized." Foreign journalists who live outside the Green Zone have constructed their own mini–Green Zone, either in leased homes with private security guards or in hotels, the latter protected by U.S. forces *if* they also house foreign contractors. This retreat into isolated and protected zones has compromised the scope and quality of reporting in Iraq.

In December 2005, investigative journalist Seymour Hersh described the continuing security problems in Iraq: "You're locked into Baghdad if you're a reporter," he said. "You don't get to report on much. I was talking to somebody in the CIA who said that even within the station there were very few people who got out of the Green Zone. He told me about a wonderful shirt they wear there which says: Welcome to the Green Zone, Our Ultimate Gated Community. So even our intelligence operatives can't get out because of security."[21]

Most correspondents currently live in the Sheraton Hotel or the adjacent Palestine Hotel, which have become fortresses, surrounded by concrete barriers, a U.S. guard post, and a perimeter that keeps traffic away.[22] But even these security precautions have been unable to protect the scores of journalists housed there from deadly attacks by both insurgents and coalition forces. The most publicized attack came on April 8, 2003, when an American tank fired upon the Palestine Hotel, killing Reuters cameraman Taras Protsyuk and Spanish cameraman Jose Couso (see Chapter 4). The tank attack came just hours after American planes destroyed al-Jazeera's Baghdad offices near the Monsur Hotel.

More recently, the insurgents have begun coordinated attacks on the hotels housing journalists. On October 24, 2005, a car loaded with explosives blasted the wall surrounding the Palestine Hotel, allowing armed insurgents to drive a cement truck refitted as a suicide vehicle into the hotel compound. The truck detonated in a giant fireball, after which insurgents armed with rockets and bombs killed 16 people and wounded 22. Three Associated Press Television News staff were among the wounded. Iraq's national security adviser, Mowaffack Rubaie, said that the journalists inside the hotel were the target of the attack and that the insurgents had hoped "to take Arab and foreign journalists hostage."[23]

A Western journalist staying at the hotel said, "The lobby of the hotel is completely trashed. Even by the standard of Baghdad car bombs, this was a large one."[24]

Less than a month later, an almost identical suicide bomb attack on the Hamra Hotel, which housed many Western journalists, killed eighteen Iraqis. An initial explosion crumbled the concrete wall surrounding the hotel, allowing a larger vehicle bomb to enter the complex. The second blast sent body parts flying around the hotel courtyard. Part of an arm cleared the twelve-story hotel, landing hundreds of feet away.

Correspondents venture out of their protected areas at their own risk. In Iraq, there is little distinction made between combatants and noncombatants. Even the American occupation forces have, by accident or design, turned their guns and missiles on journalists, who now find themselves at increased risk and with no protection provided by Coalition forces. It is understandable, therefore, that many reporters have chosen to "embed" with the military. Embedded reporters eat, sleep, live, and travel with the troops. Such a status offers them relative safety and immediate access to the troops, but it only gives one side of the picture: the military side.

Those reporters who chose not to embed were dubbed "unilaterals." They were exposed to much greater danger but had much greater freedom of movement and access to the civilian population. Most, but not all, of the harrowing stories of attacks on journalists contained in this book come from unilaterals. Their descriptions of the grinding tension of reporting in Iraq make one wonder why they are willing to endure it. Many say they will not return when their tour ends.

Adi Ignatius, executive editor of *Time* magazine, has noticed the same phenomenon. "Things changed a lot after April [2004], since the uprising," he said. "Now it's very hard to find people who want to be in Iraq for the long term."

Susan Chira, foreign editor for the *New York Times*, added a sober footnote: "I don't want to go into detail on this, but [the danger for reporters] has made us think really hard about such things as insurance policies, the equity of what provisions we make for people and their families. That's terrain that has taken on a new dimension in urgency."[25]

Throughout most of 2004, the American press covered the deaths and abductions of journalists selectively. As we shall see in Chapter 3, the U.S. government frequently pressures the families of hostages to avoid public comment lest they compromise official efforts to free the captives. Similarly, the press has been urged to restrain its coverage of attacks on journalists and thus deny the publicity sought by the insurgents. This strategy of silence was never very popular with the families of hostages, and press editors often chafed at such restrictions, but more often than not they dutifully complied. Then came an Internet breakthrough that seemed to trigger more outspoken press coverage of the plight of journalists.

On or around September 28, 2004, Farnaz Fassihi, a *Wall Street Journal* war correspondent in Baghdad, sent a candid e-mail to friends, describing the pervasive security problems that prevented journalists from doing their jobs in Iraq. Somehow, this private e-mail reached the Internet, where it bounced around and soon became common knowledge to both the public and the news organizations.

Fassihi's e-mail began, "Being a foreign correspondent in Baghdad these days is like being under virtual house arrest. . . . I am housebound. . . . I avoid going to people's homes and never walk in the street."[26] Fassihi listed some of the things she can't do: grocery shopping, eating in restaurants, conversing with strangers, looking for stories, driving in anything but a full armored car, going to the scene of breaking news stories, getting stuck in traffic, speaking English outside, taking road trips, admitting to being American, lingering at check points, and being curious about what people are saying, doing, and feeling.

"There has been one too many close calls," she said, "including a car bomb so near our house that it blew out all the windows. So now my most pressing concern every day is not to write a kick-ass story but to stay alive and make sure our Iraqi employees stay alive. In Baghdad I am a security personnel first, a reporter second."[27]

Fassihi said the dreadful turning point for journalists in Iraq came with the wave of abductions and kidnappings. She described a frantic phone call from a female journalist friend late one night telling her that two Italian women had been abducted from their homes in broad daylight. Then came the news of two Americans who were captured and beheaded. "I went to an emergency meeting for foreign correspondents with the military and embassy to discuss the kidnappings," said Fassihi. "We were somberly told our fate would largely depend on where we were in the kidnapping chain once it was determined we were missing."[28] The correspondents were told that criminal gangs usually do the kidnapping and then sell the captives to Baathists in Fallujah who in turn sell them to Al Qaeda.

After Fassihi's e-mail became public, the broadcast media seemed more inclined to express their concern over the plight of reporters in Iraq. On January 11, 2005, the PBS TV news series Frontline examined the dangers of reporting from Iraq and opened the show by stating, "In Iraq, 54 journalists have died since the war began, nearly the number of reporters killed in Vietnam."[29]

The sense of foreboding for reporters covering Iraq begins even before they land in Baghdad. The flight from Amman, Jordan, used to be filled with reporters, but the Frontline documentary showed reporter and film maker Nick Hughes as virtually the only one on the plane, along with a couple of security contractors and a few Iraqi businessmen. Hughes is somewhat agitated as he remarks, "Insurgents surround the Baghdad airport. They will fire rockets and missiles at planes attempting to land. A gradual descent would make us an easy target. A corkscrew dive is our only way in."[30]

The plane descends eight thousand feet in thirty seconds and lands safely. Hughes goes directly to the Al Hamra Hotel, one of three hotels in Baghdad that house journalists. There he runs into an old friend and colleague, Scott Peterson, who has just returned from an embed assignment in Fallujah. Peterson shows Hughes a number, X-96, that he has inked onto his wrist, his helmet, and flak jacket. "They call this the Kill Number," he says, "so that if something happens to you, instead of calling in and saying, 'Scott Peterson's been blasted,' they can say, 'X-96 has been wounded.'"[31] Thus the Kill Number avoids confusion of identities when journalists are killed or wounded.

Peterson warns Hughes that the Al Hamra Hotel is a dangerous place. Just a few months earlier, rockets were fired at the hotel and two journalists were kidnapped on the very doorstep. "It really raised tensions a lot," says Peterson. "It means that we were making decisions every single day about how far we go, who we talk to, . . . where we meet people. So every day is high risk and high tension."[32]

Peter Spiegel, defense correspondent for the *Financial Times*, has recently returned from Iraq, and he told me that the risks for reporters do not end when they get settled in their hotels. "Our representative in Baghdad now is staying at a hotel named Al Hamra," says Spiegel. "He sees guys standing across the street taking down license numbers of journalists and things like that."

I asked Spiegel who would be doing that and why?

"The current theory is, it's basically thugs, guys in the street who capture journalists and sell them on to the insurgents. Usually Baathists and such people who sell them on to [Abu Musab] Zarqawi and his group. Our security consultants have told us, 'In order to be rescued from the kidnappers, we have to get to you early on in that chain, while it's still a matter of money, not religion or ideology.' These criminals who are doing the actual muscle work know that the journalists stay at the Al Hamra. They're looking for American faces or western-looking faces. The problem is, after having talked to friends and colleagues who are there now, there is a lot of nervousness that journalists are being targeted because, as Danny Pearl proved [see Chapter 3], there's more media attention when you kidnap a journalist."[33]

In response to the growing danger, many individual journalists and news organizations are pulling out of Iraq. But even the act of departure is fraught with peril. Armed guards must escort anyone traveling the road to Baghdad's airport. CNN's Anderson Cooper told his viewers about the harrowing ride along the airport road: "There's the fear of suicide car bombers, of snipers, of improvised explosive devices. And on that road, I can tell you, when a car pulls up alongside you, you were checking them out several times to make sure that they're not bad guys looking to blow you up."[34]

Dexter Filkins of the *New York Times* was filmed recently as he traveled the dangerous road to the airport. "It's about a mile long, this little block of road," Filkins tells the camera, "and it gets attacked every day. This is really the worst stretch of the road right here . . ." Suddenly, the armed guard sitting next to him interrupts anxiously as they approach what looks like a possible car bomb. "Watch this BMW on the right side!" shouts the guard. "Go to the left!"[35]

The guard sitting next to Filkins is paid about $2,000 a day to protect him. This is serious business, given the fact that there have been fifteen suicide bombings on this stretch of the road in the past month. After swerving around the suspicious car, Filkins breaths a loud sigh of relief. "Whew! The other day my colleague . . . went to the airport, and I think he had to drive through one car bombing and then through a gun battle. They tried once [to get through to the airport], came back, and then tried again. They got through, but it took a long time. That's what you go through every day on this road. It's just a measure of how troubled this whole enterprise is that 19 months into this thing we can't really drive into the airport with any degree of assurance, and it's only a couple of miles down the road."[36]

Such constant danger gives even the boldest correspondent pause. Terry Anderson, former Associated Press correspondent who was abducted and held in Pakistan for almost seven years, recently told me, "I don't know how I'd cover the story in Iraq today. I'd like to think I'd be brave enough to get out there and actually cover it from the point of view of the ordinary people. I can't promise you I would. . . . That's dangerous, really dangerous, and at this stage of my life I wouldn't do it. I might have 20 years ago, but I wouldn't do it today."[37]

Committee to Protect Journalists

There are a number of professional organizations devoted to the protection of a free press and support for journalists worldwide. These include, Reporters sans Frontieres, the International Federation of Journalists, and the Committee to Protect Journalists (CPJ). None is more aggressive in seeking safety for foreign correspondents than CPJ. Founded in 1981, this independent, nonprofit organization defends the right of journalists to report the news without fear of reprisal. The organization was created by a group of U.S. foreign correspondents in response to the often brutal treatment of their foreign colleagues by enemies of independent journalism. Currently, CPJ has a full-time staff of twenty at its New York headquarters, including area specialists for each major world region. It also has a representative in Washington, D.C. A thirty-five-member board of prominent journalists directs CPJ's activities, and its two honorary co-chairmen are Walter Cronkite and Terry Anderson.

CPJ investigates and documents attacks on the press, classifying cases in the following categories: ABDUCTED; ATTACKED (journalists wounded or assaulted); CENSORED; EXPELLED; HARASSED (access denied or limited; detained for less than 48 hours); IMPRISONED (arrested or detained by a government for at least 48 hours); KILLED (murdered or missing and presumed dead, with evidence that the motive was retribution for news coverage or commentary; includes journalists killed in crossfire); LEGAL ACTION; MISSING (kidnapped or detained by nongovernment forces for at least 48 hours; disappeared); THREATENED (menaced with physical harm or some other type of retribution).

In early 2005, I interviewed CPJ's Middle East and North African specialist, Joel Campagna, and asked him about CPJ's focus of concern. Every topic he addressed is analyzed in depth later in this book.

"Obviously, our current attention is directed on Iraq, which, in our opinion, is the most dangerous place in the world for journalists," Campagna told me. "That's borne out by the statistics, which show 43 journalists killed in action and another 19 media support workers killed since March 2003. We break it down between reporters, news gatherers, and support staff, which includes fixers, drivers and interpreters. The threats in Iraq are quite unpredictable, ranging from insurgent attacks, bombs, missile attacks and suicide bombers to U.S. troops and Iraqi police. Collectively, they pose unique threats to the various journalist constituencies that are out there, from western reporters to Iraqi journalists and fixers. We just put out a release on our web site indicating that 56 journalists were killed in the line of duty during 2004, and that was the highest number we've accounted for in a decade. The war in Iraq had a lot to do with that alarmingly high number."[38]

I asked Campagna what had changed to cause such a rise in fatalities during the Iraq conflict.

"We're looking at a conflict that brought thousands of media personnel to Iraq and the region, where they encountered an array of threats both during the war and in its aftermath to the present day. The so-called 'unilaterals,' those who were not embedded with the military during the war, were operating in very unpredictable conflict areas where there were many casualties and deaths. But we also had a number of casualties among the embedded reporters traveling with front line U.S. troops. In the post-war [occupation] environment we're seeing an anarchic situation where there is very little rule of law, criminal gangs and insurgents roam the streets and prey on journalists and other civilians operating in Iraq. So the combination of the high media presence and the anarchy has produced these chilling media casualties."

Campagna noted that the real-time technology of modern journalism may be increasing the risks for reporters. "What's interesting in Iraq is that many of the journalists who have been killed, injured, or harassed are part of the so-called 'front line' reporters, including cameramen for some of the Arabic satellite stations who have been providing a lot of the hard news on things like combat operations, militant attacks on U.S. troops and on-the-scene coverage of explosions. People who are working to report hard news in Iraq rank high among the casualties. Part of the problem with the broadcast media in Iraq has been the fact that they often travel quite conspicuously. They have to haul around a lot of equipment and that has hindered their mobility compared to the print reporters. When they do go out, they have the added vulnerability of being noticeable as members of the press."

I asked whether this new vulnerability was likely to be the permanent face of war and journalism.

"What's been troubling in recent conflicts has been the erosion of the perception of journalists as neutral observers, people who can easily maneuver between both sides of the front, so to speak, and not be harmed by participants to the conflict. This traditional image of the neutral observer has been eroded, not only in Iraq, but in places like Afghanistan and Pakistan as well. The combatants are no longer recognizing the neutrality of journalists, and the Daniel Pearl case showed journalists just how vulnerable they are. It extends beyond western journalists to Iraqis working for foreign companies, including media organizations, making anyone fair game who is perceived to be participating in the occupation."

Since most journalists abducted in Iraq have been charged by their captors with being spies, would it help reporters if the CIA unambiguously renounced its policy of using journalists as agents?

"I don't know how much that would qualitatively affect the situation for reporters on the ground in Iraq today, but that's a position that we strongly support," said Campagna. "We believe that any time the government recruits journalists or uses journalistic cover for espionage, it's detrimental to the safety of journalists world-wide and undermines the perception of journalists as neutral observers, rather than combatants. In 2002, our Washington representative, Frank Smyth, gave Senate testimony on our position against the use of journalists for espionage."

How can individual journalists, news organizations, and professional organization like CPJ minimize the risks for foreign correspondents?

"By making sure that reporters and news managers are prepared as much as possible for dangerous assignments," said Campagna. "In 2003, we published a journalist safety guide which provides useful background information for journalists preparing to work in hostile environments. As of last month, the guide is available online in both Arabic and Spanish. But no guide or level of preparedness can ensure a journalist's safety, especially in a war zone or hostile area. The key is to mitigate risk as much as possible and constantly assess and reassess your situation. Obviously the news organizations have to take into account the safety of their journalists, and that entails never forcing a journalist to take a dangerous assignment. It involves ensuring that all newspaper staff, reporters, fixers, whatever, are properly equipped from a safety perspective when covering a dangerous assignment. That might include everything from armored cars to bulletproof vests. In places like Iraq, I'm sure the journalists themselves are quite aware of the risks they take. They are constantly calculating every move they make to ensure that they survive each day. But it is also up to the news managers to recognize when an assignment becomes too dangerous or when the risks outweigh the importance of the story."

The issue of journalists in Iraq being killed by "friendly fire" from American troops is a matter of concern to Campagna and CPJ. "The record shows that U.S. forces have not taken adequate precautions to ensure that journalists can work safely in Iraq," he said. "When journalists are killed, the military often seems indifferent and unwilling to launch adequate investigations or take steps to lessen risk. At least 9 journalists and two media workers have died as a result of U.S. fire in Iraq.

"Looking at some of the deaths at the hands of U.S. troops, we believe many of those were avoidable. Journalists who were operating very openly as press should never have come under fire. In our report on the Palestine Hotel incident in Iraq on April 8, 2003 [see Chapter 4] we concluded that the deaths of journalists were 'avoidable but not deliberate.' Things could have been done to avoid the incident. The hotel was a very well known journalist location in the center of Baghdad, arguably one of the best known civilian locations in the entire city. The international media were based there and western news organizations were filing their reports from there, so why were the troops on the ground not aware of such a press center at a time when the Pentagon was priding itself on protecting civilian sites like mosques, schools and hospitals? The evidence that we were able to gather showed that it was not a deliberate act. It was a mistake, but one that should have been avoided. The military's own investigation left unanswered the central question of why U.S. troops on the ground were not made aware that the Palestine Hotel was full of journalists.

"We have met with Pentagon officials and worked with other media organizations to make our concerns known to the Pentagon and to military commanders. We have submitted recommendations including: making U.S. troops mindful of the presence of journalists in combat zones; recognizing that journalists have the same protected status as civilians; and that when conducting armed operations, the military must do everything in its power to protect civilians. We have also called on U.S. officials to conduct credible inquiries into journalist deaths at the hands of U.S. troops, including the April 8, 2003 air strike on al-Jazeera's Baghdad bureau that killed reporter Tarek Ayyoub—an incident which, according to the Pentagon, has yet to be investigated.

"There have also been a number of cases where journalists have been detained by U.S. troops. We've repeatedly expressed our concern to U.S. military officials regarding the numerous cases of journalists—mostly Arab or Iraqi—who have been detained without charge and harassed while working near or in the vicinity of U.S. troops. In some cases, they alleged they were abused by U.S. troops. One such case involved three employees of Reuters News Agency who were detained last year near Fallujah. The military's inquiry, which absolved troops of any wrongdoing, fell well short of being credible."

I asked whether CPJ had received a sympathetic response from the Pentagon.

"This year, the Pentagon turned down a request from CPJ's board of directors to meet with Secretary of Defense Donald Rumsfeld to discuss our concerns about the U.S. military and journalists' safety," said Campagna. "The message has been heard and, interestingly, the CENTCOM itself has actually put forward some very sensible recommendations on how to better protect journalists. Regrettably, the Pentagon has, to our knowledge, failed to take action to implement its own recommendations concerning the safety of journalists working in areas of conflict. Those recommendations include: improving communication between military units about the presence of journalists in operational areas; assessment of the rules of engagement for U.S. troops; and improving communications between the military and news bureau chiefs in places like Baghdad. The problem is, how do you get these things implemented? We need to keep reinforcing the idea that the Pentagon has a credibility problem on these issues."

Selective Snapshots of Attacks on Journalists

On The Road Again

Jeffrey Bartholet, foreign editor of *Newsweek*, tells of his concern upon receiving a call from one of their photographers early in the Iraq war. In hurried fashion, the photographer said he and *Newsweek* reporter Scott Johnson "had been ambushed and had abandoned their cars and were on foot, running, so he had to go now." Before ending his message, the photographer told Bartholet that he had seen Johnson's car "get hit by an RPG [rocket-propelled-grenade] and roll over a couple of times," but he had to abandon Johnson and keep running "because they were still under attack."[39]

A few minutes later, Bartholet received a call from an American military official saying he had found an empty car with blood in it and he was calling one of the numbers on the cell phone found in the car. It was, of course, Johnson's cell phone and the number called was *Newsweek*'s news desk. The military official said all he had was a bloody car and a cell phone, and he did not know what happened to Scott Johnson. Bartholet says, "As it turned out, Scott was unbelievably fortunate. He crawled out of the broken windshield, played dead as the bad guys raced by, and then an American convoy followed up . . . and he waved them down."[40] The details, as subsequently provided by Johnson, are as follows.

Having crossed into Iraq from Kuwait in separate cars during the first few days of the American invasion, *Newsweek* reporter Scott Johnson and French photographer Luc Delahaye were traveling along a desert road. Although they were "unilaterals" (unembedded reporters), they frequently came upon slow-moving U.S. Army convoys, which they simply leapfrogged. "I was terrified," recalls Johnson, "because we were the only journalists around. We were far from any towns, and there were no people."[41]

In their separate cars Johnson and Delahaye passed one convoy, then actually joined another, but when Johnson's car got stuck on a hill, the whole convoy ground to a halt. From that point on, the two journalists were forced to follow the convoy from behind. Everything went fine until that night when the convoy's commanding officer came over and told them that they could no longer follow the convoy. "If you try to follow us," said the officer sternly, "we'll. . . ." He didn't finish, but it was a clear threat.[42]

So the two journalists headed off to the northwest. They would occasionally come across formations of American tanks, which would swing around and point their turrets at them. Clearly, they were not welcome. Other times, troops would jump out of U.S. Army trucks, hit the ground, and point their guns at them, forcing them to get out of their cars, hands held high, until they were identified and sent on their way again. Despite the less-than-friendly reception they received from each convoy, the journalists did not want to get ahead of the forward line of U.S. troops and into the midst of the fighting.

They followed Route 1 until it hit Route 8, a modern, paved, four-lane superhighway. They had barely eaten or slept for three days. The highway was filled with military vehicles as far as the eye could see: tanks, Humvees, supply trucks, and Bradley fighting vehicles. There were scores of children jumping frenetically beside the tanks. Johnson and Delahaye proceeded along Route 8 and came to one convoy after another. The convoys appeared to be about five miles apart, but after passing one convoy they drove for several miles without reaching another one.

They noticed a small shack in the middle of the road with several soldiers standing nearby. Luc drove on past the shack, and as Johnson drove by he noticed a man standing on the median with a large caliber machine gun. The two journalists did not realize it, but they had crossed an invisible border. They were no longer in U.S.-controlled territory. Suddenly, Johnson heard Luc's voice on the radio shouting, "Weapons, weapons," and then bullets began hitting his car. He ducked down, losing control of the car, slamming into a light post and flipping the car on its right side. "I could hear the bullets going ping, ping, ping. . . . I concluded, 'Okay, I'm going to die here.'"[43]

Bullets continued to rain on the car as Johnson kicked at the windshield, eventually breaking a hole large enough to crawl through. When he climbed out, he was fortunate to find that the car was now between him and the shooters. He crawled on his belly and lay in a hollowed base between the two sides of the median. "Every once in a while I could hear the bullets pop right over my head," he recalls. "It was the most terrible, horrifying experience I've ever had. I felt completely vulnerable, with no recourse."[44]

After about ten minutes of lying in the dirt ducking bullets, Johnson heard a rumbling on the road. It grew louder and louder. It was the convoy he had passed some miles back. As the first vehicles started to roll by, Johnson put his hand up and waved. Some of the soldiers waved back, but no one stopped. He started yelling, but either the troops couldn't hear him or they didn't care. He was reluctant to get up and expose himself to the shooters, but finally he rose from his protected spot.

"I started running as fast as I could. . . . I was shouting and waving and running alongside the tanks, but the soldiers just looked at me. It was like a nightmare." Eventually, Johnson ran out of breath and slowed to a walk. Finally, a Humvee stopped, and Johnson shouted, "I'm an American. I was attacked."[45]

The soldier in the driver's seat told him to get in. When Johnson told them he was a *Newsweek* reporter they looked at him like he was a Martian. "Then I started trembling," says Johnson, "not screaming, but yelling, hyperventilating and wheezing."[46]

Later, Johnson would learn that Luc Delahaye had endured his own nightmare, chased on foot through the desert by Iraqis for several hours. Despite the fact that everything turned out well, Johnson says, "I am much more conflicted now about war. There's something very profound and disturbing about being in an environment where matters of life and death are an issue, not just for the people you're writing about, but for yourself."[47]

Jeff Bartholet, Johnson's editor, says the terrifying incident was ironic as well. "Just a week before that, I had ordered Scott out of Baghdad," he recalls. "We thought, Baghdad's not going to be safe during this 'shock and awe' campaign, . . . so we told Scott to get out of Baghdad and get over to Kuwait, . . . and [look] what happened to him."[48]

Better French Than Dead

One attempted attack on an American journalist in Iraq was thwarted by a simple ruse: pretending to be French. Peter Spiegel, an American working as a defense correspondent for the London-based *Financial Times*, told me of an unusual incident in early December 2004 in the Iraqi city of Samara. "It was the first major insurgent attack on U.S. forces in Samara," he said.[49]

> We woke up the next morning, heard about what had happened and drove up to Samara from Baghdad. We were making the rounds when we came across a large crowd near a mosque. The mosque had apparently been hit by an American tank, or so they said. We were there interviewing several of the people, and, as always with such incidents, the tensions got very frayed. So it was a rather tense situation to begin with, but I didn't feel threatened at the time because everyone just wanted to tell their story.
>
> Then, halfway through, after we had finished perhaps 20 minutes of interviewing, my translator, Wa'il, came up to me, and though he doesn't speak English very well, he signaled that "we have to leave now, have to leave now." I didn't particularly want to leave, because I thought the interviews were going well and I couldn't figure out why he was gesturing so frantically. In any case, we quickly got into the car and started driving off without Wa'il, so I shouted to my driver, Haider, "Stop the car, stop the car, we've got to go back and get Wa'il." So we went back and picked up my translator, and as we drove off once more, a red car began to follow us. It pulled up along side of us, and though it didn't force us off the road, it started edging in front of us and, let's say, encouraged us to pull over. Our driver pulled over and an older gentleman came up to us with two younger men trailing him.
>
> A heated conversation ensued in Arabic, so I couldn't exactly figure out what was going on, but toward the end of the conversation, the older man turned to me sitting in the back of the car and said, "Chirac, Chirac [the French Prime Minister]," holding his thumbs up. I just responded in kind, saying, "Chirac, Chirac," putting my thumbs up as well. We were then allowed to drive off. I wanted to go someplace else in Samara, but my driver, Haider, said emphatically, "No, we're going back to Baghdad."
>
> I asked Wa'il what had happened and he explained that while we were doing the interviews near the mosque, two young men walked up to him with AK-47s and said, "You'd better take the American away from here or we'll kill him."

I asked Spiegel how they knew he was American.

> I guess because I was speaking English. That's my assumption. Also, as we were talking, people were asking, "Are you American?" and that kind of thing. There was a lot of, "Oh, you're CIA," because they see an

American with a notebook taking names down and they're all accusing us. This would happen repeatedly. My translator was very good at explaining, "No, he's a journalist," but in this case, the two young men told him, 'Get the American out of here, we're going to kill him."

Wa'il thinks they chased us away in order to separate us from the larger group so they could take care of us in an isolated area. It turns out that the older man was the father of the two young men, and he told Haider, "My sons were ready to kill the American, but I told them, let's first go and find out what he's doing here." At that point, Wa'il assured the old man that I was French, and that's why he responded with the "Chirac, Chirac" thing, and I played along with it. Luckily, we were able to drive away.[50]

This was not the only time Wa'il saved my life. There were other less dicey situations where people were questioning me and nerves were very riled. He would put his arm around me and explain to them, "He's with us, he's just telling your story," and that kind of thing. I've had several other dicey situations in Afghanistan and Iraq, but this is at the top of the list.

Being French Is Not Enough

On August 20, 2004, two French journalists, Georges Malbrunot of the daily *Figaro* and Christian Chesnot of Radio France Internationale, were abducted on the road from Baghdad to Najaf. Their Syrian driver was also taken, but later released. The last time the journalists had checked in with their news organizations was in Baghdad, but they had been subsequently sighted on the road to Najaf, about twenty miles outside of Baghdad.

A group calling itself the Islamic Army in Iraq claimed responsibility for the abduction. On August 28, the al-Jazeera satellite channel broadcast a tape from the group, saying the journalists were being held to protest a French law banning head scarves in schools. The tape gave the French government forty-eight hours to overturn the law, seen by many Muslims as directed against the traditional head garb worn by Muslim women. The warning on the tape was considered ominous because just a few days earlier al-Jazeera had broadcast a tape from the same group showing Enzo Baldoni, an Italian freelance journalist, being beheaded.

The two French journalists were moved around Iraq in various cars, forced onto the floor, and covered with blankets. Even when a tire blew during one transfer, the kidnappers remained calm, warning the journalists not to move under their blankets until the tire was changed. The kidnappers appeared to be able to move their captives around with little difficulty, from south of Baghdad to an apartment in the suburbs to a base north of the city. They carried a variety of weapons, plenty of money, and had no fear of the U.S.-trained Iraqi police, whom they claimed to have infiltrated.

The journalists were held in five different locations, bound and gagged, sometimes placed in cardboard coffins. They were later tried by a self-styled Islamic court. Militants came and went with ease, suggesting wide sympathy for the insurgents among the local population. The chief of security for the Islamic Army had been trained in Saddam Hussein's intelligence services. His behavior toward the captives varied from blunt to cajoling, from threatening to concilia-tory. "He was a professional, an ex-Baathist, a follower of Islam, but not a fanatic," said Malbrunot.[51]

Another man, called "boss" by the kidnappers, told Malbrunot about the connections between his group and the Jordanian militant Musab al-Zarqawi. "He said they would cooperate on certain tactical missions, but maintained sep-arate organizations and overall strategies," said Malbrunot.[52]

The captives often feared for their lives, even after the security chief told them that if they had been American or British, they would have been beheaded. They were told that they had become a "political card" in intermittent negotiations with the French government and that an Islamic court had decided, for now, to spare their lives. But repeated promises of imminent release always proved false, and their spirits were flagging. Malbrunot recalls, "Christian was talking about Christ-mas, and I started thinking about my girlfriend, . . . I just burst into tears."[53]

About a week later, on November 8, the security chief told them that the French authorities were being stubborn and that their lives were now in danger. In early December came another turnaround, as they were allowed to speak on a new videotape, on which they stated that the U.S. invasion had been illegal and that France had opposed it because it better understood Iraq, Islam, and the Middle East. Finally, on December 21, they were stuffed into the trunk of a Mercedes and delivered to French intelligence agents on a road near Baghdad airport. They were free.

The release of the two journalists was greeted with jubilation in France. An indication of the importance of the event to French national pride was seen when the journalists were greeted upon their arrival in France by the French president, the prime minister, and much of the cabinet.

"We're fine," said Malbrunot at the airport. "We survived a difficult experi-ence, at times very difficult. But we never lost hope, and we always had confi-dence in the actions of the French authorities"[54]

In a nod to French policy on Iraq, Malbrunot added, "I think we are alive today because we are French."[55]

Speaking in French, Christian Chesnot said, "We understood that the kid-nappers didn't want to kill us straight away, so we tried to talk to them. Then in

November, one of the leaders came, looking quite nasty. He said our situation had become quite critical, that France was refusing to meet their demands, and that our lives were now in danger. Psychologically, that was hard."[56]

Malbrunot concluded, "We are very happy to be home, because when you are a hostage, you don't know what you will be tomorrow. You can be released, you can be killed, you can wait for two weeks, you can wait for six months, you can wait for two years. So, you know, there is pressure. So it's a very tough situation when you are surrounded by people with guns, masks. It's a tough experience."[57]

Ambush Zone

During the summer of 2004, *Washington Post* correspondent Dan Williams wrote of looking into the face of would-be assassins who shot bursts of AK-47 fire into his SUV on the superhighway from Fallujah to Baghdad. "[T]he first thing that came to mind was the likely headline in the next day's paper: 'Post Reporter Dies in Hail of Bullets,'" said Williams.[58]

Williams and his driver, Falah, were driving through Fallujah, the heart of rebellion and bloodshed in Iraq's Sunni Triangle, when they found themselves blocked at every exit by masked insurgents. This was the town where just a few months earlier four American contractors were ambushed, killed, and mutilated, two of the burned bodies hung from a bridge over the Euphrates. Neither Williams nor his driver were armed.

Suddenly, a car painted like a taxi pulled up behind Williams and began firing at the bullet-proof rear window, leaving the tell-tale spider-web cracks where the bullets hit. After the opening fusillade, the taxi pulled alongside Williams' car. Fire was directed at the front wheel and then at Falah in the driver's seat but it missed the tire and only grazed the bullet-proof windshield. Then the taxi dropped back again, and two shooters popped their heads out and fired their AKs from both sides of the car. One tire was flattened, and the SUV began to wobble. "It's alright," said Falah, "we can keep going."[59]

Now the taxi roared past them and parked ahead on the road, waiting in Ambush. When Falah reached the ambush point, bullets rained on the car, one hitting just above Williams's head.

"They're going to shoot until they kill us," he shouted.

"Yes, maybe they wanted to kidnap before, but now they want to kill," said Falah as he sped by.[60]

Having failed to stop the determined Falah, the insurgents pulled back onto the road and renewed their pursuit. The taxi continued to fire from behind, causing the spider-web pattern on the rear window to grow until it finally burst. Now, with the bullet-proof rear window gone, the attackers really let loose their fire power. Another tire was flattened, causing the SUV to spin out of control. Williams thought, "That's it, we're done."[61]

When the SUV skidded to a stop, Williams wanted to jump out and run for the reeds in a nearby canal, but Falah told him, no, we're better off in the battered armored vehicle. The taxi sped by them and, to their surprise, continued on. As the taxi disappeared down the road, highway traffic that had been held up during the fire fight began to reappear. Falah tried to wave one of the cars down, but no one would stop. Finally, Falah got the SUV started again, and the car slowly limped forward on two wheels. When they reached the safety of Abu Ghraib prison, the American soldiers there let them take refuge. When Williams recounted his story to the marines, one of them said calmly, "A lot of that goes on out there."[62]

In retrospect, Williams asks: "Why am I still alive? All told, the circumstances favored death over survival. If they had shot out the front wheels, if they had come to finish us off, if the SUV had flipped we would have been killed."[63]

That night back in Baghdad, Williams's article about the violence in Fallujah was bumped from the *Post* by stories about Ronald Reagan's death. "So goes the newspaper business," said Williams, who fantasized about a headline, "Reagan Dead, But Williams Still Alive"[64]

Saved by Sadr

On August 13, 2004, Micah Garen, American journalist and founder of the Four Corners Media company, was abducted in Nasiriya, Iraq, while investigating the looting of ancient artifacts that date to the Sumerian civilization as many as five thousand years ago. Garen and his Iraqi interpreter were taken at gunpoint from a crowded shop. The shopkeeper confirmed that two armed men entered his shop that evening and quickly dragged Garen and his interpreter into a car.

Several days later, the al-Jazeera TV network aired a video tape showing Garen kneeling in front of five masked men armed with rifles and rocket-propelled grenade launchers. A voice on the tape identified the kidnappers as a group called the Martyrs Brigade and said Garen would be killed within forty-eight hours if U.S. forces did not leave Najaf, where they had been fighting the Mahdi Army militia of Shiite cleric Moktada Sadr. Similar videos in the past had been followed by beheading of the hostages.

Garen's family said they had received information that he was still alive, but would say nothing more, believing that his well-being required their silence. Garen's father, Allan Garen, said his son "went to Iraq fully aware of the dangers, but determined to alert the world to the tragic loss of an irreplaceable archeological heritage. . . . He refused to turn aside in the face of injustice and inhumanity even from those with the power and responsibility to provide protection, and he is now in mortal danger."[65]

Things were looking desperate for Garen until details of his work in Iraq became known to the kidnappers. Moktada Sadr himself discovered that Garen had helped expose the killing of Iraqi civilians at the hands of Italian troops in Nasiriya, and he promptly issued a plea for Garen's release. The kidnappers then delivered Garen to Sadr's office, and Sadr turned him over to Iraqi government officials and then to the Americans.

"The kidnapers were responding to the calls they heard from Sadr's office," said Aws al-Khafaji, the local representative for Sadr. "Moktada's personal appeals had a very heavy impression on the abductors."[66] Al-Khafaji said the kidnappers originally believed Garen was working for U.S. intelligence services. An American close to the negotiations confirmed that Sadr had sent public and private messages to the shadowy group of kidnappers to set Garen free.

Upon his release, Garen told the Associated Press Television Network, "I'd like to thank the Sadr office for its help in securing my release and I'm very happy to be free."[67]

Garen said he was abducted while using a small camera to photograph scenes in a busy market. "I think that they did not like it when I was taking some photos," he said. "There were many people in the marketplace. I cannot tell who they were. . . . I think they considered me to be a suspicious person and, therefore, there was a misunderstanding."[68]

Despite his terrifying experience, Garen said he hoped to stay in Iraq to continue working on a documentary project on the looting of archeological sites. "The experience hasn't made me want to leave at all," he said. "I feel like I have lots and lots of friends here and I hope that I can continue to work here."

Women Journalists Attacked from All Sides

Women have not been spared the violence against journalists in Iraq. Florence Aubenas of the French newspaper *Liberation* and Giuliana Sgrena of the Italian daily *Il Manifesto* were prominent among the abductions during 2005.

Aubenas was kidnapped, along with her fixer/interpreter Hussein Hanoun, on January 5, 2005. No insurgent group claimed responsibility, and no information on her circumstances was made public for almost two months. Finally, in late February, a video of Aubenas was released showing her seated on a floor, pleading desperately for help. After giving her name, Aubenas said, "I'm French. I'm a journalist with *Liberation*. My health is very bad. I'm very bad psychologically as well. Please help me."[69]

The press organization Reporters Without Borders said, "We found the video of Florence Aubenas and her appeal to be very disturbing. . . . The exhaustion and anxiety on her face is extremely worrying. . . . We solemnly call on the kidnappers to release Florence and her assistant, Hussein Hanoun. . . . [O]ur organization appeals to the news media of the entire world, especially the Arab world, to help Florence and Hussein, as well as the kidnapped Italian journalist Giuliana Sgrena."[70]

Aubenas was kept blindfolded in a basement cell measuring thirteen feet by six feet. She was often told that her release was imminent, only to have her hopes dashed. Finally, on the morning of June 11, a man opened the door to her cell and said, "Today, Paris."

Aubenas and her interpreter were led into an adjoining room where their personal belongings were returned to them. They were later blindfolded and taken to a waiting car, which quickly sped away. Aubenas was told to pretend she was the driver's wife. When the car eventually stopped, she was pulled out of her seat by a French security agent who told her, "It's over, it's over."[71]

Aubenas was flown to a military airfield outside Paris, where she was greeted by French President Jacques Chirac and by family and friends. She told the assembled reporters, "I wish to thank the French people, the president, the ministers and all of those who have helped me return to France."[72]

When asked how she felt, Aubenas answered, "Well, much, much better. When you are there, you do what you can. I was held in a basement with Hussein, under very severe conditions."[73]

On February 5, 2005, one month to the day after Florence Aubenas had been abducted, Iraqi insurgents kidnapped Giuliana Sgrena, the Middle East correspondent for the Italian daily, *Il Manifesto*, after she had completed two hours of interviews with refugees from Fallujah.

On that afternoon, a minibus blocked Sgrena's car as armed men took her away in a hail of gunfire, leaving her driver and an Iraqi journalist behind. Sgrena had not followed the cautious protocol of most Western journalists. She had no bodyguards, and she had spent almost three hours in the same place, uncommon for journalists who try to stay on the move to make kidnapping more difficult.

A little-known group, the Islamic Jihad Organization, took initial responsibility for the abduction and set a seventy-two-hour deadline for Italy to remove its troops from Iraq. However, just two days later, the group released a statement on the Internet saying that Sgrena would soon be released because it had been determined that she was not a spy.

"Since it has become absolutely clear that the Italian prisoner is not involved in espionage for the infidels in Iraq . . . we in the Jihad Organization will release the Italian prisoner in the coming days," said the statement.[74] As so often happens in Iraq, things were not as rosy as they appeared.

Sgrena had visited Iraq many times, documenting the death and destruction caused first by the lengthy embargo and then by the invasion and occupation. Nonetheless, her captors either decided to hold her or passed her on to another more radical group. About a week later, a video tape aired on Italian television showing Sgrena, frightened and desperate, pleading for her life.

"I beg you, put an end to the occupation," she said in Italian, holding her hands together as if in prayer. "I beg the Italian government and the Italian people to put pressure on the government to withdraw. I beg you to help me. I beg my family to help me, and all those who stood with me to oppose the war and the occupation."[75]

She then began to cry. An offstage voice was then heard speaking to her, and she repeated her message in French. At the top of the TV screen, written in Arabic, was the name "Mujaheddin Without Borders." Sgrena then concluded with the warning, "No one should come to Iraq any longer, because all foreigners, all Italians, are considered enemies. Please do something for me."[76]

Italian Foreign Minister Gianfranco Fini, a supporter of the war on Iraq, gave no indication that Italy would reduce that support in exchange for Sgrena. He issued a public statement saying, "I tell the kidnapers that all the Italian people ask for her release, independent of our well-known position on Iraq."[77]

Weeks went by with no further word from Sgrena or her captors. There were rumors of a deal in the works, possibly involving ransom. Then, on the night of March 4, she was released into the custody of an Italian intelligence agent, Nicola Calipari. Sgrena's ordeal was over. Or was it?

As the car containing Sgrena, Calipari, and another Italian agent approached the Baghdad airport, American troops attacked in force. In a fusillade of bullets, Calipari was killed and Sgrena and the other Italian agent were seriously wounded. Calipari, who had negotiated Sgrena's release, had thrown his body over her as protection when the car came under fire. Sgrena was later taken to a Baghdad hospital, where shrapnel was removed from her shoulder.

Sgrena recounted the shooting as follows:

The driver had notified the embassy and Italy twice that we were heading to the airport, which I knew was controlled by the American troops. It was less than one kilometer . . . when. . . . I remember only fire. At that point a rain of fire and bullets came at us, forever silencing the happy voices from a few minutes earlier. The driver started shouting, . . . "We are Italians". . . . Nicola Calipari dove on top of me to protect me . . . and immediately I felt his last breath as he died on me. . . . I recalled my abductors' words: They said they were deeply committed to releasing me, but that I had to be careful because "the Americans don't want you to return."[78]

Italian Prime Minister Silvio Berlusconi summoned the American ambassador for an explanation, demanding that someone "take responsibility" for the shooting. He said "disquieting questions" needed to be answered. But U.S. military officials said they had not been informed of Sgrena's release and that soldiers "fired on a vehicle approaching a checkpoint in Baghdad at a high rate of speed." A later statement said the soldiers "attempted to warn the driver to stop by hand and arm signals, flashing white lights, and firing warning shots in front of the car."[79]

But Sgrena's own account cast doubt on the military's version. "We weren't going very fast, given the circumstances," she said. "It was not a checkpoint, but a patrol that starting firing right after lighting up a spotlight. The firing was not justified by the movement of our automobile. . . . We thought that the danger was finished after my handover. Instead, suddenly, this shooting. A rain of fire came. Nicola folded himself on me, probably to defend me and then he collapsed. I saw that he was dead."[80]

Italian Prime Minister Silvio Berlusconi, a key U.S. ally in Iraq, agreed to conduct a joint investigation with the United States to determine the precise circumstances of the tragic incident. However, after five weeks of work, the cooperative venture collapsed, with Italy unable to accept the American account. Italy's foreign minister, Gianfranco Fini, told reporters, "Respect for the memory of Nicola Calipari, as well as for our national decorum, could only prevent the government of Italy from assenting to a reconstruction of events that does not correspond with what happened that evening."[81]

Prime Minister Berlusconi challenged the U.S. account in a speech to Parliament, saying U.S. military officials had approved Calipari's mission to free Sgrena and were expecting her arrival at Baghdad's airport. Foreign Minister Fini provided details on the negotiations for her release and said the information was shared with the U.S. Embassy's hostage working group in Baghdad. According to Berlusconi and Fini, Calipari and his colleague arrived at the Baghdad airport on the day of Sgrena's release and spent forty minutes notifying U.S. military authorities in charge of the airport of their mission and acquiring a safe-conduct document. Calipari "therefore warned the American military officials of their immediate arrival in the airport zone," said Berlusconi.[82]

As for the shooting itself, Fini said Sgrena's car was traveling at no more than twenty-five miles per hour as the driver carefully steered around concrete blocks. He said the driver was applying the brakes when the car was hit by gunfire that lasted ten to fifteen seconds.

On May 2, 2005, Italy released its own sixty-seven-page report on the incident. Although they declared that there was insufficient evidence to conclude that the shooting was "willful," the report said, "It is likely that tension, inexperience and stress led some of the U.S. troops to react instinctively and with little control."[83] The report dismissed U.S. claims that the car containing Sgrena was speeding and said U.S. authorities knew of Calipari's mission.

The ambiguities surrounding the attack on Sgrena made conspiracy theories unavoidable. Sgrena herself called the shooting an ambush, saying, "I don't see why I should exclude having been a target of the United States." She later modified her comments by stating, "You could characterize something as an ambush when you are showered with gunfire. If this happened because of a lack of information or deliberately, I don't know. But even if it is due to a lack of information, it is unacceptable."[84]

Adding to the controversy, Sgrena described a warning given to her by her captors as they released her: "They declared that they were committed . . . to freeing me but I had to be careful [because] the Americans don't want you to go back."[85]

Canadian journalist Scott Taylor, who was himself abducted and tortured by Iraqi insurgents (see Chapter 3), brought some calm analysis to the tragic incident in an article for al-Jazeera: "It is unfathomable that the Pentagon would have ordered the deliberate assassination of a Western reporter under such high-profile circumstances," he wrote. But he noted that

> the US has completely lost control of the security situation in Iraq and, as a result, allied governments have no choice but to take matters into their own hands to protect their nationals. . . . The most ironic thing about those partisan . . . statements that challenge Sgrena's story is that the US soldiers unquestionably proved the insurgents' prophecy. They warned her to be careful of the Americans, and they were right. Did US Secretary of Defense Donald Rumsfeld specifically target a journalist in this instance? Absolutely not. He didn't have to, as his policies have already turned all of Iraq into a deadly free-fire zone.[86]

The First American Journalist Murdered in Iraq

On the night of August 2, 2005, American journalist Steven Vincent and his Iraqi interpreter Noor al-Khal were abducted in the southern Iraqi city of Basra. Vincent's bullet-riddled body was found the next morning, his hands tied with plastic wire and a red piece of cloth tied around his neck. Al-Khal, seriously wounded, was hospitalized.

Vincent became the first American journalist to be murdered by insurgents in Iraq. No organization claimed responsibility for his murder, and Reporters Without Borders said this could be a sign that Sunni rebels did not do it, because they usually claim responsibility when they kill foreigners in Iraq. A witness to the abduction said that "a white pickup pulled alongside Vincent and his interpreter, Noor al-Khal, then four gunmen got out, grabbed them and bundled them into the pickup."[87]

In the wake of his killing, Vincent's wife speculated on whether any of his writings had led to his death. He had been a vocal cheerleader for the war in Iraq and an aggressive critic of Islam. "I figured our enemy was Islamic terrorism— and I wanted to do my part in the conflict," Vincent earlier explained. "[S]o I decided to put my writing talents to use. The results were numerous articles supporting the war." In his writing, Vincent stressed "how important it is that we refer to American 'liberation' rather than 'occupation'. . . . Instead of saying that the Coalition 'invaded' Iraq and 'occupies' it today, we could more precisely argue that the allies liberated the country and are currently reconstructing it."[88] His recent articles had described the growing influence of Shiite militias in Basra, and Shiite cleric Moqtada Sadr was one of his frequent targets.

Vincent lived and worked largely outside the protected enclaves into which most foreign journalists have retreated. He had recently moved to Basra where he survived "by slipping below the radar screen, so to speak, blending in with the Iraqi people, sometimes disguising myself, keeping as low-profile a presence as possible."[89] He began dressing as a Shiite in order to pass unnoticed, and the day of his murder he was wearing a black T-shirt with a picture of Imam Hussein and black prayer-beads around his neck—the distinctive mark of the Shiite.

Vincent's wife said she and her husband had agreed that if anything happened to him, she would not talk about him with the news media. "He had a disgust for anyone who had suffered a bereavement and went immediately to the cameras," she said.[90]

Chapter 3

Personal Stories of Abduction, Torture, and Death

Philip Caputo: An Early Hostage (May 7, 1973–May 12, 1973)

Long before America's War on Terrorism made war correspondents in Afghanistan and Iraq targets for abduction and murder, Philip Caputo was kidnapped and tortured in Lebanon as he attempted to cover the conflict there for the *Chicago Tribune*. Caputo won the Pulitzer Prize in 1972 as part of an investigation team for the *Tribune*, and his coverage of his experience as a captive in Lebanon won him the Overseas Press Club's George Polk Citation. In his book *Means of Escape* he wrote of war, insurrection, revolution, and the struggles of the people in places from the jungles of Vietnam to the mountains of Afghanistan to tragic Beirut. Since his harrowing experience in Lebanon, Caputo has characterized our era as "The Age of Terrorism."

On Monday, May 7, 1973, Caputo was in Beirut covering the Lebanese civil war. He hired a driver and translator named Zouhair Zakhreddin, who said he could take Caputo to a Lebanese army position near the airport that was shelling Palestinian guerrillas in the Sabra camp. Caputo agreed, hoping to get a firsthand look at the fighting and interview a few soldiers. Things didn't work out so well.

In a recent interview, I asked Caputo whether, in retrospect, he felt he could have avoided the abduction and brutal confinement that befell him that night in Beirut:

> With a little bit more, call it common sense, I might have avoided it. I
> was very new to Beirut when that happened and I was really not as
> familiar with the conflict there as I should have been. That was 1973,
> and the tense situation that existed there between the Palestinian gueril-
> las and the Lebanese authorities resulted in a lot of fighting between the
> two forces, along with pervasive civil violence. I was pretty green as far
> as the situation in Beirut was concerned. I should have taken at least
> two or three days to get a sense of what was going on. Also, I could
> have made better local contacts.
>
> I went in there cold. I was a young hard charger. I remember my
> motto then was Winston Churchill's old adage that it was the war corre-
> spondent's job to go as far as he can as fast as he can. I was following
> that axiom, quite forgetting that when Churchill was covering the Boer
> War, he was reporting on something quite different from the conflict I
> was assigned to. I didn't realize that you can go too far, too fast, and
> that's what I did.[1]

Both Caputo and his driver, Zouhair, went a bit too far, too fast that night in
Beirut. Zouhair couldn't find the army position they sought, and he ended up driving
aimlessly through dark and nearly deserted Beirut streets. They came to an intersec-
tion and Zouhair pointed to a dark block of buildings. "Fedayeen," he said. "We can't
go near there. . . . They would hold you for ransom or kill you if they caught you."[2]

Zouhair was confident that the army camp was nearby, and he felt that a
lone car at night would be a prime target for a sniper or ambush. So they got out
and began walking. Almost immediately they were approached by three
unarmed teenaged boys. Zouhair asked them where the army position was, and
the boys asked for their IDs. Caputo showed them his Rome press card, and
they beckoned for them to follow. They walked a short distance in the dark until
Caputo bumped into the muzzle of an automatic rifle resting on a sandbagged
bunker. Voices came from the darkness and Zouhair whispered, "Oh, my God,
they are Fedayeen."[3]

Two more youths with AK-47s appeared. "One of them took me by the
wrist," Caputo later recounted, "and I thought, well, this is it. I'm a prisoner of
war."[4] They led Caputo and Zouhair into an alley where a dozen armed men
crouched behind a wall. A hundred and fifty yards away one could see armored
cars and bunkers. It was the army post—they had missed it by a block.

Automatic weapons fire rang out from the army position, and the Fedayeen
returned fire. Another guerrilla appeared and led the two captives into a courtyard that was out of the line of fire.

"Who are you and what are you doing here?" the Palestinian asked in good
English. Caputo said he was a correspondent for the *Chicago Tribune* and

showed him his press card. The guerrilla put the card in his pocket and said, "Okay, Mister Journalist. Come with me. You are a journalist for the fedayeen."[5]

Caputo knew what that meant. He was a prisoner. He and Zouhair were led into a low cement building to a room about twelve feet square. Dirty cockroaches crawled about, illuminated by a single bulb hanging from the ceiling. Another man, medium height and bald, came in and told them to empty their pockets. He asked Caputo what he was doing in the fedayeen positions at night. Caputo explained he was trying to report on the fighting and stumbled upon their positions by accident. Asked how many times he had been to Israel, he answered, just once, three years ago as a tourist. But when the Palestinian searched Caputo's wallet, he found two Israeli business cards. It looked like he was lying.

"They think I'm a spy for Israel," he thought. "It's just a matter of time till I die."[6]

Caputo and Zouhair were moved to another building and placed in a makeshift cell with steel bars on its lone window. They were told to knock if they needed to use the toilet. The next morning they were awakened by heavy mortar fire that sent smoke through the window bars and plaster dust falling as a heavy mist from the ceiling. For much of the day, they huddled on the floor, waiting for the ceiling to cave in on them. That night, Caputo's intensive interrogation began.

A man with blue eyes, speaking impeccable English, began asking him everything about his life, when and where he was born, where he had lived, where he went to school, what he did during his three years of military service. This detailed autobiography took two hours.

Now, Mr. Blue Eyes, as Caputo called him, began exploring more sensitive matters. "If you don't tell the truth," he told Caputo, "things will not stop with me. You'll go higher, and things could be worse."[7] He asked once more what Caputo was doing inside fedayeen lines. Caputo repeated that he was a correspondent.

"What else are you?" shouted Mr. Blue Eyes.

"That's all."

"Agents use journalism as a cover, don't they?" the interrogator shouted.

When Caputo continued to insist he was a journalist, Mr. Blue Eyes yelled, "Very well, Philip. I hoped we could do this quickly."[8]

He picked up Caputo's phone book and vowed to quiz him on every one of the two hundred or more names in it. Caputo knew that at least twenty of those names were Israeli. There was bound to be trouble. After seven or eight hours of explaining names, Caputo was asked about Charlie Weiss, a *Tribune* stringer in Jerusalem and a *Voice of America* correspondent in Israel. His answers were greeted with suspicion.

Mr. Blue Eyes closed the phone book, said he would return the next day to continue the interrogation. Caputo asked, "Are you going to shoot me no matter what I say?" Mr. Blue Eyes smiled and said, "In spite of whatever you have heard about us, we are not murderers."[9]

He left the room. Zouhair was brought in and they were both bound, wrists lashed behind them and then wrists tied to ankles. They slept fitfully that night, bound and contorted.

The next morning, Mr. Blue Eyes resumed his interrogation, seeking hidden meanings in every name, every number. The he began asking about two men who he said were working with Caputo the night he was captured. Caputo said he and his driver were the only ones there.

"I want the truth," shouted Mr. Blue Eyes. "There were two men in a car behind you. They got away but we got you. Who were they?"[10]

Caputo recalled that he had heard a car speeding down the street half an hour after he was captured. That must be what Mr. Blue Eyes was referring to. He said he had no idea who was in that car, but Mr. Blue Eyes kept repeating the question, over and over. And Caputo kept saying he didn't know who was in the car. Eventually, the questions turned to Israel: When had he last visited there, whom had he seen, why did he have two Israeli business cards in his wallet? The questioning continued all day.

At one point, Caputo broke down and shouted, "You want me to tell you I'm a spy. . . . Will that make you happy?"

"No," he answered. "Only if that's the truth."[11]

At the end of the day, Caputo was returned to his cell. Lice were crawling through his hair, and the stench of urine permeated the room. A guard aimed his rifle at Caputo and said, "You work for the CIA, don't you?" Caputo offered his regular denials and then said with bravado, "When are you going to shoot me? Today or tomorrow."

The guard answered, "[I]f you are our enemy, then we'll shoot you."[12]

Caputo would later recall, "The helplessness, the filth, the sound of shells being hurled back and forth—now louder, now softer, like the footsteps of some monster pacing back and forth through the night—filled me with despair."[13]

After more than three days in captivity, continuous interrogation, and confinement in a dark cell, Caputo was taken out into the street. Two armed fedayeen tied a blindfold over his eyes and prodded him forward with a rifle poked in his butt. After walking about ten minutes, Caputo was pushed up against a wall and his guards stepped back. Caputo awaited the sound of rifle bolts signaling his execution.

"I surrendered all hope," recalled Caputo. "Now I knew what was going to happen and was at peace." But nothing happened. Caputo called out the name of one of his regular guards, Mahmoud, and asked if he was going to be shot. "Don't worry," answered Mahmoud. "We won't shoot you."[14]

Caputo was led down the stairs into a tiny windowless cellar, less than a yard deep, a little over five feet high. The stone wall dripped dirty water. Roaches scurried past his feet. The wooden door was slammed behind him and Caputo was left in this dank, airless hole. He could stand only if he bent down. He could lie only if he pulled his knees tightly against his chest. The only ventilation came from a tiny crack between the door and the floor.

"I had difficulty breathing. Claustrophobia closed in upon me. Is this how a man feels when buried alive?" he wrote.[15] "I put my face against the crack and tried to suck in fresh air. Some cinders stuck to my lips. . . . They crumbled in my fingers and the smell told me they were droppings. . . . *Rat shit.*"[16]

Then came a scratching at the cellar door, a squealing and scratching. It was a pack of rats clawing at the door. Caputo stuffed his blanket into the crack under the door, but it soon became almost impossible to breath. He removed the blanket, deciding to let the rats come in if they wanted to. He recited the Lord's Prayer over and over, and eventually fell asleep, legs propped against the wall. When he awoke, he felt prepared for the next interrogation. He thought, "[I]f that man thinks he can break me, he is wrong. . . . [I]f he decides I am to be sentenced to death, I don't care. Death is better than this."[17]

Caputo called out for water—he had had nothing to drink for thirteen hours. He continued to call for half an hour, but no one came. He had to go to the bathroom, but again his calls were unheeded. He eventually had to urinate on the floor. He aimed for the crack under the door, but the urine puddled and soaked his blanket. "I tried to get a grip on myself but failed," Caputo recalls. "I banged on the door, screaming the way a man would if his guts were being torn out. The scream of a lunatic."[18]

Some time later, his door opened and two men took him out, blindfolded him and led him back up the stairs. "The odors of mud were as lillies," he wrote later. "The reek of open sewers as jasmine. I sucked in deep, deep breaths, like a drowning man shot back to the surface."[19]

When the blindfold was removed, Caputo found himself back in the interrogation room.

"Well, Philip, I now believe you are a journalist," Mr. Blue Eyes told him, but quickly followed with, "But what else are you?"[20]

Once more came the same questions and answers, the charge that he was a spy, the denials.

"What happened to you last night is *nothing* compared to what we can do. Believe me, please, *nothing*. Now, I want you to convince me you are a journalist only."[21]

Caputo broke into sobs. Mr. Blue Eyes took hold of his face and told him that what he had endured the night before was something he had learned from the Israelis when they arrested him on the West Bank. He had been confined in the same kind of hole for eighteen months, not eighteen hours, he told Caputo. He said he would refer Caputo to a fedayeen court if he thought he was guilty, and a jury would then make the final determination. He concluded, "Convince me, Philip. Carefully but quickly convince me you are a reporter only."[22]

Caputo composed himself and began to recount his every movement since arriving in Lebanon. He spoke for only a half an hour. When he finished he said, "That's it. . . . [Y]ou can stick me back in the hole for the next year and you'll never hear me say anything other than what I've just said."[23]

Mr. Blue Eyes stared at him, expressionless. Then he asked Caputo if he wanted a shave. He said yes, and was brought a blade, hot water, and soap. Was this the last shave for the condemned man? When Caputo finished, Mr. Blue Eyes told him that the Algerian ambassador to Lebanon would come to pick him up in about an hour. Apparently, Caputo had been convincing.

Zouhair had already been released. Now it was Caputo's turn. One of his regular guards told him that now he had a great adventure to write about. Caputo said he didn't regard it as an adventure. He was taken back to fedayeen headquarters where his money, wallet, passport, and all belongings were returned to him. A limousine pulled up with the Algerian flag flying from its front fenders. In a few minutes, Caputo stepped out of the limousine at the entrance to his hotel. "I had to face a battery of cameras and microphones," he recalls. "I was a newsman who made news, and I was embarrassed."[24]

Caputo is now a writer of fiction, quite a successful novelist. In his 1991 autobiographical account of his adventures as a war correspondent, he wrote: "I am nearing fifty now, and I'm not looking for any more visas except the tourist kind, nor do I seek terra incognita. . . . The world, which seemed in my boyhood full of beauty and mystery spiced with a bit of danger, has in my manhood lost most of its beauty and mystery while gaining more than a seasoning of danger."[25]

Jerry Levin: A Decade Later in Lebanon (March 7, 1984– February 14, 1985)

In March 1984 Jerry Levin, a prominent foreign correspondent for CNN and its Middle East bureau chief stationed in Lebanon, was kidnapped in Beirut, Lebanon, and held in brutal captivity for almost a year. I recently asked Levin if he thought there was anything he could have done to avoid his ordeal.

"Yes," he told me. "Number one, I shouldn't have thought it couldn't happen to me. So I ignored the advice of the embassy in Lebanon at the time by doing such things as walking to work. I also should have varied my route on the way to work. Because I wanted to be free to live the way I wanted, I ignored the embassy's advice, which was relevant and pertinent. Allowing my kidnapers to know when I would be walking and the route I would be taking made it easier for Hezbollah to plan on picking me up. I was a target, and I allowed myself to be staked out. They knew our routines. They wanted us, so they got us. At that time, clearly, if they wanted you, they were eventually going to get you.

"It wasn't a random act. The tragedy for all of us who were kidnapped was that we were in jobs that usually required us to be out in the streets. Our work obviously required that. So the work we were doing absolutely laid us open to danger, but in my case as with some of the others, we were taken because we didn't follow wise advice. Ignoring that was crucial. And I don't just mean advice from our government. The night before, Fahd, my driver, said, 'I'll pick you up in the morning,' and I said, 'No, Fahd, I'm going to walk.' He said, 'Don't do it, Jerry. That's what I'm here for. Let me pick you up. It's too dangerous.' And, of course, since I was the boss, I ignored his advice."[26]

Indeed, in what was to become a common occurrence in the Middle East for the next twenty years, Jerry Levin was kidnapped on the morning of March 7, 1984, as he was walking toward the CNN offices in Beirut. He felt a tap on his shoulder and a heavily accented voice said, "Excuse me." When Levin turned, a man pushed a small handgun into his stomach and demanded, "You come."[27]

Soon, Levin's wife, Sis, was told that Jerry was missing. No one was yet sure of what had happened, but the British Ambassador suggested that Sis talk to Nabih Berri, the leader of the Lebanese Shiite faction Amal. She asked Levin's Lebanese driver, Fahd, "Can you take me to Nabih Berri . . . now?" Fahd agreed to take her to Berri's military headquarters. When they arrived, Dr. Ghassan Siblani, Berri's right-hand-man, greeted Sis and said, "We abhor kidnapping. Jerry is our brother. He has been reporting our story fairly."[28] Sis had been told that Amal was the enemy, but she left the meeting with a new sense of hope.

Meanwhile, Levin lay in a bed, blindfolded, in a house not far from where he was kidnapped. Over and over he was accused of being a spy.

"I am a TV journalist. I am not a spy," he would respond.

"No. You are a CIA spy," came the reply.

"I am not a CIA spy," insisted Levin.

"Then you're an Israeli spy."[29]

Finally, a gag was thrust into Levin's mouth and he was wrapped head-to-foot in brown wrapping tape, so tight that he could feel the circulation cut off. He was lifted and thrown into some kind of truck, which then roared away, traveling on bumpy mountain roads for a couple of hours. The truck eventually reached a level highway, and Levin concluded that he was in the Bekka Valley, home of the Iranian-backed Hezbollah. Levin was dragged into a building where chains were attached to his wrists and then to the floor of a tiny room.

Meanwhile, CNN had called Washington, sent people to the Syrian and Lebanese embassies, and talked to the United Nations (UN) delegates from Saudi Arabia, the Palestine Liberation Organization (PLO), and Libya. They also called contacts in Beirut, checking out earlier brief detentions of newsmen, many of them never made public. Sis found out that the group holding Jerry was motivated by reasons far beyond what CNN could handle.

By April [1984], Jerry remained in the same tiny room in solitary confinement, chained night and day to a radiator. Because the chain was too short to allow him to stand, his leg muscles had begun to cramp horribly. The bare room had a single window, painted over. He was warned not to try to look out of it. Levin had not seen a human face since his abduction. He had been instructed to pull his blindfold on whenever his captors entered the room. One man repeatedly stuck a gun to his temple and pulled the trigger. He heard the click of an empty chamber. "Blindfold okay, you okay," said the gunman. "You see out, we kill."[30]

Despite the admonition, Levin had a tiny slit of vision at the bottom of the blindfold, enough to see the feet of his captors, or their hands when they unchained him. From this he could tell that they were young. One of them liked to jump heavily on his legs. The others slapped him around.

As the days passed in solitary confinement, time was blurred, so Levin began to scratch a tally on the wall. By the time his tally reached twenty-eight days, the solitude and silence were taking a toll on him. He feared that he might be losing his mind. When the guards reappeared, he asked them why they were holding him.

"You spy," they repeated.

"You know that's not true," Levin responded. "I'm a TV journalist."[31]

Levin was moved to another "safe house," but conditions remained much the same. He was chained to the floor of a solitary room with a single window, this one shuttered rather than painted. The unbearable silence was causing him to talk to himself. The constant lying or sitting position he was forced into caused severe stiffness and pain. Otherwise, he lay in motionless silence. He had lost a lot of weight.

One time each morning he was unchained and led to the bathroom. On one occasion, alone in the bathroom, he lifted his blindfold off and moved to the bathroom's window. It was painted over, but he scraped a small opening and looked through it. He could see mountains. He stared at the sight until he had taken enough time. Then he replaced his blindfold and knocked on the door. A guard came and led him back to his room.

Later, he heard others being led to the bathroom. The guard spoke to them in English, and Levin concluded that the other captives were Americans.

Meanwhile, Sis Levin continued to seek any information she could on Levin's condition. George Malouf had confirmed that Jerry was kidnapped by Hezbollah, the radical Shiite group which advocated Iranian-style fundamentalist rule in Lebanon. Hezbollah was apparently warehousing Americans to exchange for the seventeen Shiite prisoners held in Kuwait for bombing the U.S. and French embassies there. The State Department continued to tell Sis that Jerry was alive and well, but they warned, in no uncertain terms, that if she did not keep quiet and leave the entire matter to them, she would "get the hostages killed." Sis noticed that media editors around the country had taken the same advice, and they gave very little space to the hostage crisis. She wondered how not allowing the public to know what was going on could help Jerry and the others.

Then came some bad news. Jay Parker, her State Department contact, told her that Kuwait had set a date for the execution of their Lebanese prisoners. Both the Reuters and UPI wire services ran stories saying that Hezbollah had promised to execute their hostages if Kuwait executed their prisoners. Fortunately, the Kuwaitis later agreed to delay the executions indefinitely, at least until Jerry's release could be secured.

Back in his cell, Jerry had developed an intestinal virus that left him weak and dispirited. He heard a knock on the door and reflexively replaced his blindfold. But the guard told him to take his blindfold off and look straight ahead. A piece of paper was thrust into his hands, and he found himself looking into a video camera lens. He read a prepared statement: "I am Jeremy Levin. My life and freedom depends on the life and freedom of the prisoners in Kuwait."[32] Finally, Levin knew why he was being held.

The videotape would eventually reach the U.S. State Department, and Terry Arnold, Sis's contact there, gave her a personal screening after warning her that it was Top Secret. She was appalled at Jerry's weak voice and appearance. He looked ill. When he identified himself as Jeremy Levin, she knew that the text had been written for him. He never used the name Jeremy. Terry Arnold told her that the State Department was in touch with the Algerian government, which had agreed to intercede on Jerry's behalf. But Arnold warned her once more not to let this leak out, or the plans could be aborted.

Sis now realized that the Reagan administration was more worried about its image in the hostage negotiations than it was about the hostages themselves. Public awareness of the plight of the hostages could be devastating. Sis was willing to keep quiet, for now, but not to do nothing. George Malouf and Lebanese Ambassador 'Nsouli arranged a meeting with Sheik Mohammed Hussein Fadlallah, the spiritual leader of Hezbollah, who then put them in touch with the group that abducted Jerry. George and 'Nsouli were shown a Polaroid photo of Levin, and they heard the soundtrack from Levin's video. At a subsequent meeting 'Nsouli made a humanitarian plea for Jerry's release, but it became clear that the captors were counting on a more material offer from the American government.

By now, Levin's virus was making him weaker by the day. A doctor saw him and assured him that he would be given medicine, but it never came. His condition worsened, and the doctor came again, asking if he had taken his medicine. When Levin said he never received it, the doctor barked orders to the guards and promised that the medicine would be brought promptly. "We have nothing against you as a person," the doctor told him. "We just hate . . . America for bombing us and killing our people."[33]

Levin was beginning to assume that he would die in captivity, unless he could escape.

On the outside, Sis was becoming similarly desperate. She knew there were three American captives in Lebanon, probably held by the same people and for the same reason, yet the Reagan administration had failed to condemn the abduction or even admit it. She wondered, "Why *couldn't* we deal with the Arab countries in a more civilized way? Why *couldn't* we try peaceful dialog and negotiations for a change?"[34]

In September 1984, Sis began calling television networks, making it clear that she was available for interviews. On the *60 Minutes* show she told Mike Wallace that the American public remained ignorant of the hostage situation, including the captors' demands. She concluded, "Maybe we have to learn to talk to all of the factions about our desire for a peaceful dialog."[35] After the show finished taping, Mike Wallace and everyone on the set congratulated Sis for a job well done. But the show never aired. To this day, the public has never seen the *60 Minutes* tape.

On the *Today Show* she told Bryant Gumble, "We need to look at the causes of Arab hostility toward us."[36]

Soon, the families of the other hostages began contacting Sis, and it quickly became clear that they were all disappointed with the government's lack of support for them and the State Department's demand that they keep silent. Landrum Bolling, president of the Ecumenical Institute, operated by the University of Notre Dame on the outskirts of Jerusalem, offered to assist Sis. Bolling was a former college professor and foreign correspondent known for his work on behalf of peace and reconciliation. He urged Sis to focus on Syria as the key player in Lebanese affairs, and the two of them agreed to meet in Damascus in late October 1984. Bolling would arrange a meeting with Syrian Foreign Minister Farouk Al Sharaa. "And also we can see some of the Damascus-based PLO people," he told Sis. "They just might have some interesting information and advice."[37]

At the meeting with Foreign Minister Sharaa, Bolling calmly told Jerry's story and explained the important contribution that Syria could make. At the conclusion of the meeting, Sharaa promised nothing specific, but said, "Let me make my inquiries with the security authorities and with the [Syrian] president. I will be in touch with you again."[38]

By November 1984, Jerry had been moved to still another building, this time in a room with no heat. He was still weak from recurring bouts of intestinal virus, and the constant cold made things worse. His captors no longer beat him, sometimes airing their grievances before Levin, who listened silently, blindfolded, curled into a fetal position to conserve body heat. By late December the temperature in his room had dropped to the point where he feared he would soon die of exposure.

As Christmas approached, a guard brought him a bowl of oranges, grapes, and chocolate. For some reason, thoughts of Sis rushed to his mind, and he asked the guard about his wife. Surprisingly, the guard answered, and with apparent knowledge of her activities: "Your wife went back to America, but she was here a few weeks ago talking about new ways to achieve peace." The guard then asked Levin if he would like anything for Christmas. Levin asked for a Bible and was given a pocket-sized version of the New Testament. As the guard left the room, Levin could hear a voice say, "Joyous Noel."[39]

Back in the United States, Sis continued to assemble powerful supporters for the cause of the hostages. Reverend Jesse Jackson invited her to a Rainbow Coalition press conference followed by a private luncheon. "We are all held hostage as long as our sister here is suffering," he told his group.[40] He then promised Sis that he would check with his contacts in London, and if they thought the possibilities for success were good, he would travel to the Middle East.

Another unexpected supporter surfaced when Susan Baker, wife of President Reagan's Chief of Staff Jim Baker, suggested that an ecumenical prayer service be held at the National Cathedral to highlight the plight of the hostages. Baker, an Episcopalian like Sis, said such a service had been held during the Iranian hostage crisis, and all that would be required would be the approval of the bishop of Washington, something that should have been routine. But, to the surprise of all, the bishop turned down the request. When Susan Baker contacted a friend in the White House for an explanation, she was told that the Reagan administration had directed the bishop to cancel the service. Once more, Sis had discovered that the administration would do anything to inhibit public knowledge of the plight of the hostages.

Meanwhile, Jerry Levin's routine in captivity continued. On February 13, 1985, after he was taken on the usual morning trek to the bathroom, he pulled the blindfold down and peeked out of the bathroom window, recognizing the highway in the distance. He was in Baalbeck. When he was brought back to his room, the guard secured him carelessly, making it possible for him to work his way loose. Later, near midnight, he got up, removed his blindfold, and, unobserved, he went to the room's lone window. After tying his blankets together, he opened the window and attached the makeshift rope to the balcony railing, lowering himself silently to the ground below.

Barefoot, he ran down the mountainside. Dogs were barking and howling, but he made it to the highway, and followed it toward the city. When he heard voices coming toward him, he threw himself under a parked truck. Lights shone on him, and he heard warning shots fired. Someone shouted an order in Arabic, and Jerry crawled out from under the truck, holding his arms out imploringly and saying in French, "Aidez-moi." Help me. A man wearing the red beret of the Syrian army approached and smiled.

Jerry Levin was free. His first press contact was with Agence France Presse (AFP) in Damascus. "I escaped Wednesday at around midnight from a two-story villa where I was being held," he told AFP. "I walked for two hours in the [Bekaa] plain before hearing dogs barking and human voices. Thinking my assailants were following my tracks, I hid under a truck. However, as soon as I saw that they were Syrian soldiers, I turned myself over to them."[41]

In a subsequent interview with CNN, Levin said, "I was treated miserably. . . . They could have been 100 percent better to me and I still would have been treated miserably. They were rough on me the first six months and then not really rough the second six months." He said they would hit him, swat him around, slap him, pound his back, and pound his shoulders, the object being to teach him obedience. "[O]bedience for them was, 'Don't ever look at our faces or we'll kill you; don't ever look out the window or we'll kill you, don't even stand up or we'll kill you.'"[42]

AFP said the pajama-clad Levin appeared to be in good health but fatigued by his detention and long trek. Expressions of relief and elation poured in from around the world, but there was considerable confusion over how Levin had gained his freedom. On the day of his release, a telephone call claiming to be from the Islamic Jihad group said, "We released . . . Levin after many approaches by some brotherly and effective sides . . . after our investigations established he was not involved in espionage or subversion against Islamic forces."[43]

The call seemed to suggest that pressure may have been exerted by Syria to effect Levin's release. The *Washington Post* quoted a senior U.S. official, who asked not to be identified, saying that there were some indications that Levin had been allowed to escape, and that Syria might have had something to do with it. "What one has there is a process in which undoubtedly the Syrians must have played a role, but it is a complicated process, and we don't know what roles different parties played."[44]

At a briefing for reporters, State Department spokesman Ed Djerejian said simply, "We are appreciative of the Syrian government's role in this matter." When pressed on the question of whether Levin had escaped or been released, he said, "You will have to draw your own conclusions."[45]

Interviewed on NBC's *Today Show*, Levin's wife said she was more inclined to believe he had been released than that he had escaped. "I don't think that's what happened," she said. "I think this is a message from the Middle East, a desire for peace. . . . It'd be awfully strange for him to escape after being held for a year, but these things have happened before, and it may be their way of making a gesture."[46]

Regardless of how it came to pass, Jerry Levin was free. Now came the problem of picking up his life where it had been before his captivity. First he had to make sense of a harrowing experience. Levin recently told me, "During my captivity, I always kept telling myself, 'Nobody made you come here Jerry. You wanted to be a big-shot correspondent. *You pays your money and you takes your chances.*' I was, however, angry at the circumstances of the U.S. involvement in the Lebanese war that created the conditions that led to my kidnapping and the kidnapping of the others. I was also angry about the way our government patronized and lied to my wife, keeping her and rest of the American public in obfuscating dark. My differences with the government had to do with the lies they were telling about the circumstances of our captivity, but never did I blame them for my being a captive. It wasn't their specific fault. In broad, existential terms, perhaps it was, but in personal existential terms, it was my decision to take the Middle East bureau job. Nobody made me take it. I was ambitious. I wanted to be a foreign correspondent, so it was my choice."[47]

Perhaps Levin's candid acceptance of responsibility for his painful experience in Lebanon helped him to adjust in the aftermath. "I never did have bad dreams about my captivity once I escaped and reached freedom," he told me. He continued,

Thereby hangs a little tale. There are two types of post-incident reactions that people have to a traumatic experience like that. The sad and tragic response is when the experience was so traumatic that the person's present is ever after literally haunted by that traumatic past event. That would include nightmares and what have you, forming what is usually called post-traumatic stress disorder. The other response comes when a person is blessed with a constitution that allows them to withstand as well as endure the privation. My situation was pretty diffi-cult, but, for one reason or another, once I got home I was so elated and delighted to be free that the past miserable experience didn't haunt me. I've had no nightmares since then. As bad as the experience was, it wasn't enough to break me down physically and emotionally. Indeed, during my captivity I had a profound spiritual awakening, something that is not all that unusual under these circumstances. It changed my ambi-tions and redirected my life, as you know, so that I really had something to work for after I got out. I was no longer motivated by just my own interests and ambitions, but was driven to be of service to others' needs and no longer for position and power for the sake of both. It's a blessing not everyone has been able to receive, and for that I'm very grateful.[48]

Terry Anderson: America's Longest Held Hostage (March 16, 1985–December 4, 1991)

Terry Anderson was a U.S. Marine correspondent during the Vietnam War and later an Associated Press (AP) reporter in places such as Tokyo, Johannes-burg, and Beirut, where he was AP's chief Middle East correspondent. He was abducted on a west Beirut street on March 16, 1985, and held for 2,454 days before being released on December 4, 1991.

Could Anderson have done anything to avoid that brutal fate? "Sure," he told me recently. "I could have got the hell out of there. Most of the other jour-nalists had already left. In retrospect, I should have also, but I convinced my boss that I should stay, and he has regretted that ever since. You know, they tried to kidnap me the day before they actually got me. If I had been smart or paying attention at all, I would have left, as most of the journalists had. There were only two or three western journalists left in town when I was taken."[49]

I asked Anderson what he believed was the real reason he had been kid-napped.

"I was available," he said simply.

You know, journalists don't have body guards and they have to be on the streets if they're going to do their job. Second, I was an American, and reasonably prominent as the Associated Press's chief Middle East correspondent, so they knew they'd get publicity out of it. And their pre-conception was, they assumed I was a spy. They were from a country without a free press where journalists usually are. So I fed all their pre-conceptions and was available. And remember, most of the people they kidnapped were not their enemies. People like Father Jenco and [Ben-jamin] Weir, David Jacobsen, Tom Sutherland, and myself. We were all there doing at least as much for the Shia as anyone else.

My assumption was that I would not get kidnapped because I spent most of my time in those days reporting from South Lebanon on the Israeli occupation. And I was not gentle with the Israelis. They did not like me at all because of my reporting. So I assumed, hell, they're not going to take me because I'm telling their story. But, of course, we're dealing with radicals who don't think in any rational or logical way.[50]

I suggested that perhaps his captors were unaware of his evenhanded writing on the Middle East conflict.

"Well, they certainly knew who I was," said Anderson, "and they did target me. Whether they paid any attention to what I was writing, I don't know. I don't think it was important to them."[51]

In any case, Anderson's captors carefully planned his abduction. It began at about 8 A.M. on that March morning as Anderson dropped off AP photographer Don Mell at his apartment after an early tennis game. Anderson noticed a green Mercedes approaching, and suddenly three unshaven young men leapt out holding nine-millimeter pistols, pulled open Anderson's car door and ordered him to get out or be shot. Anderson was forced into the Mercedes, pushed to the floor, and covered with an old blanket. The car then sped away, leaving Don Mell frozen with shock on the street.

"Don't worry. It's political," said one of Anderson's abductors in a strange attempt to reassure him.[52] Anderson immediately thought of other Americans kidnapped in Beirut for political reasons: William Buckley, missing twelve months; Reverend Benjamin Weir, missing ten months; Father Lawrence Martin Jenco, missing two months.

Anderson's captors certainly didn't treat him gently as they whisked him away. A foot pressed his head into the car floor, a gun was poked into his back, and the rough blanket covering his head made breathing difficult. The speeding car turned off the main highway and into what Anderson thought was a garage. The car doors were opened, and Anderson was pulled out. The blanket was replaced with a dirty cloth around his face, secured with plastic tape wrapped tightly around and around. His shoes were yanked off, as was his watch, his gold bracelet, and the gold chain around his neck. More tape was wrapped around his wrists and arms, and his legs were taped tightly around the ankles, knees, and thighs. Anderson was then guided across the floor and placed in a chair.

"What is your name," a heavily accented voice asked.

"Terry Anderson," he answered. "I am a journalist."

When asked what company he worked for, Anderson told them it was the Associated Press, a wire service.

"You are a spy," the questioner declared.

"No. I am a journalist," said Anderson, explaining his duties at AP.[53]

The interrogation continued with repeated accusations and repeated denials. Anderson was asked for the names of the others who worked in his office, and then for the names of all Americans that he knew. He refused.

"We can make you," he was told sternly, but Anderson insisted he could not provide the names of his friends.[54] Eventually, the interrogation was halted, and Anderson was taken to an apartment building where he was dumped on a steel cot and had heavy chains attached to both feet with a large padlock on each ankle. Other chains were attached and padlocked to his wrists, and all chains were fastened to the walls, leaving insufficient length to allow Anderson to sit up.

The passage of time, hours, days, was a blur to Anderson. He recalls waking up at dawn one morning to find that his blindfold had slipped slightly from his eyes. He had been told that if he attempted to see anything around him he would be killed instantly, so he cautiously tried to pull the blindfold back into place. He felt the barrel of a gun touch his neck and heard a voice admonishing him.

"It slipped," Anderson explained.

"Careful," said his guard.[55]

Over time, Anderson was taught the rules of his new existence by means of slaps and punches when he did something wrong. Even rolling onto his side to relieve painful muscle cramps would bring a slap or a poke with a gun.

In his book *Den of Lions*, Anderson describes the deadening passage of time in captivity: "Blank nights. Gray dawn after dawn." One day, an English-speaking man appeared in Anderson's room, gave him a pen and paper, and dictated a short letter. From the text Anderson was able to get his first glimpse of the official reason for his kidnapping. The dictated letter, purporting to be from Anderson, began, "I am fine," and then proceeded to tie Anderson's freedom to the release of Arab prisoners in Kuwaiti prisons. The letter ended, "Please do your best and move very swiftly to end my detention because I cannot take it anymore."[56]

The words suggested that Anderson's captors would release him only as part of a swap for Kuwaiti prisoners, something that could only happen if the U.S. government brought pressure to bear. Anderson knew that would not happen, and he concluded that he would remain a captive for a long time. His days settled into a routine: sleepless nights, bedridden days causing constant stiffness and pain, roaches two inches long, occasional sandwiches of Arabic bread and dry cheese, brief trips down the hall to a filthy bathroom, and then back to the cot. The guards were uniformly surly and often threatening, but, so far, there was no systematic violence.

One day the guards showed up carrying several large sheets of plywood and some two-by-fours and began constructing a wooden cell just wide enough to hold Anderson's cot. Soon he was chained to his cot in this small closet. Around this time, a new hostage was brought in to join Anderson. His name was David Jacobsen, the administrator of the teaching hospital at the American University in Beirut. He was placed on a mattress just outside the plastic curtain of Anderson's cubicle and chained to the wall. A week later, Anderson and Jacobsen were moved to another building and chained to a wall in the same room. They were aware of other prisoners in an adjoining room, and a guard told them that they were a priest, Father Martin Jenco; a pastor, Ben Weir; and a professor at the American University, Tom Sutherland.

Shortly thereafter, all of the prisoners—Jacobsen, Jenco, Weir, Sutherland, and Anderson—were brought together in a room and told that one of them would be released, and that they were to decide among themselves which one would go. The Hajj, as the current leader was called, then specified that it cannot be Sutherland or Anderson.

The prisoners conferred and quickly decided that, whatever their choice, it must be unanimous and by secret ballot. They also decided to ignore the restrictions announced by the Hajj. After a few rounds of voting, the count was four for Anderson and one for Jacobsen. The next round gave all five votes to Anderson.

They called the guard and told him the choice. He laughed and said, "We have already chosen."[57] Then the Hajj entered the rooms and told Ben Weir that he was the one to be set free. Weir turned to the other prisoners and said he was sorry. The date was September 18, 1985.

The American public would later learn that Weir's release was the result of President Reagan's secret "arms for hostages" deal with Iran. As American officials continued to insist publicly that the United States would never negotiate with terrorists, they were doing just that behind the scenes. But Anderson would not benefit from the deal. In his book *Den of Lions*, Anderson explains that the original Iranian promise to free all of the hostages "melted down to their freeing one"[58]: Ben Weir.

Upon his release, Weir held a press conference in Washington, D.C., at which he told questioners that the other prisoners were well, but, "If something isn't done soon, the captors are going to execute the hostages. They have released me to urge the administration to act immediately, . . . or the consequences will be fatal."[59]

Indeed, reports of the death of all the hostages began appearing in the media. Soon thereafter, Anderson and the others were allowed to write letters to President Reagan, members of Congress, and the archbishop of Canterbury, but they were required to include a denial of the media reports of their deaths. The letters were all delivered to the local AP office, and the captives were hopeful once more. Anderson wrote, "It's incredibly strange to sit here in our underwear, blindfolds perched on our foreheads, absorbing the abuse and petty humiliations of these young men, then listen to our letters being read and reacted to in Washington and New York by the world's mighty."[60]

By now, Oliver North had negotiated a detailed package of weapons and missiles for Iran and had skimmed millions of dollars off in what would become known as the "Iran-Contra scandal."

On July 26, 1986, Father Jenco was released, but Anderson was losing hope and feared that he was losing his sanity as well. David Jacobsen's subsequent release made Anderson wonder whether he was marked for indefinite captivity, or worse. The release of Ben Weir and Father Jenco seemed to be on the basis of how long they had been held, meaning Anderson should have been next. As it turned out, no more hostages would be released for nearly four years. "I'm afraid I'm beginning to lose my mind, to lose control completely," wrote Anderson. "This solitary confinement is killing me."[61]

Meanwhile, back in the United States, sympathy for the hostages was growing. On March 16, 1987, the American Baptist Church held a prayer ceremony for Anderson and the other hostages. Other churches quickly followed suit. Some of Anderson's colleagues and friends organized the Journalists' Committee to Free Terry Anderson. Even the powerful New York Senator Daniel Patrick Moynihan joined the crusade by vowing to place Anderson's name in the *Congressional Record* every day until he was free. He kept his promise. For example, the March 20, 1990 *Congressional Record* contained the following entry:

TERRY ANDERSON BEGINS SIXTH YEAR OF CAPTIVITY

Mr. MOYNIHAN. Mr President, I rise today to remind my colleagues that Terry Anderson is entering his sixth year of captivity in Lebanon. . . . Today marks his 1,830th day of captivity.

Mr. President, during that time, Terry Anderson has lost his father and his brother. His daughter was born. She is now 4 and has never seen her father.

When Terry Anderson was taken hostage on March 16, 1985, Ferdinand Marcos was in power, Solidarity was struggling against martial law, and the Iran-Contra affair had yet to make headlines. . . . And Terry Anderson has remained chained to a wall in a basement, somewhere in Beirut.

I would like to recall today the sad and sobering words of French journalist and former hostage Jean-Paul Kauffman, who wrote on the fourth anniversary of Terry's captivity:

"The truth is that the hostages in Lebanon today have become the damned of the West. Without hope of being saved, imprisoned in silence and darkness, deprived of the sight of the world of the living, forgotten, they no longer represent anything. . . . The most tragic thing is that his torment is administered as much from the outside by countries and people indifferent to their fate as on the inside by their captors."

Mr. Kauffman's poignant thoughts struck me then, as they do now. The plight of the hostages in Lebanon requires our constant care and attention. We must do all we can to convey to Terry Anderson and the others that we have not forgotten, that we are not indifferent, and that we will not stop fighting for their release until they are resting safely in their homes. Captivity is a day-to-day ordeal for them; it has to be for us as well.[62]

Anderson and the others were moved frequently, and their treatment became more brutal with the passage of time. Tom Sutherland was badly beaten after he was caught trying to look out of his cell window. Anderson writes, "It is impossible to describe how it feels hearing someone being beaten like that. To hear the ugly dull thumps and slaps and the shouting, and be able to do nothing."[63]

With the collapse of the now notorious Iran-Contra scheme, the most promising initiative to free Anderson was being pursued by Giandomenico Picco, the assistant UN Secretary General. Picco met with Iranian representatives in Beirut, offering them neither money nor weapons, but good public relations, including a United Nations finding that Iraq, not Iran, was primarily to blame for the bloody Iran-Iraq war. Eventually, Picco was able to meet directly with the kidnappers. Arrangements were made for him to be picked up on a Beirut street, where he was pulled into a car, blindfolded, and taken to a house where he met for several hours with some of the kidnappers. At a second meeting, he was allowed to see one of the hostages. Picco did not reveal which one.

On December 4, 1991, Anderson's 2,454th day of captivity, Anderson was told that he would be going home that night. Two new leaders told him that their group realized this had all been a mistake and that they had gained little from it. They asked Anderson to make one last videotape, telling the world their view of the entire episode. Anderson agreed, so long as he could specify that it was their statement, not his. He was then given a new shirt, trousers, some shoes, and left alone in his room. Finally, several guards came in and blindfolded him, this time without using tape. He was handed a small bouquet of carnations and told, "Give this to your wife, and tell her we're sorry." He was then taken outside to a waiting Mercedes, identical to the one that had taken him almost seven years before. After a short ride, the car stopped and a Syrian colonel greeted him, declaring, "You're free."[64]

Daniel Pearl: Abduction and Murder in Pakistan (January 23, 2002–January 31, 2002)

Daniel Pearl began working for the *Wall Street Journal* in November 1990 as a reporter in Atlanta and then moved to the paper's Washington, D.C., bureau in 1993. He assumed an important position in London in 1996, where he reported on the Middle East, and then on to Paris where he covered the Balkan crisis. "If you were in the field, you wanted to be with Danny," says Craig Copetas, a former *Journal* correspondent who worked with Pearl in Kosovo. "He was very prudent, very cautious."[65] Other colleagues at the *Journal* say Pearl did not fit the stereotype of the bold and swaggering correspondent running off into harm's way. In late 2001, when other big media correspondents were clamoring to go to Afghanistan to cover President Bush's initial front in the War on Terror, Pearl declined, saying, "It's too dangerous. I just got married, my wife is pregnant. I'm just not going to do it."[66]

How, then, did this prudent and cautious reporter come to place himself in circumstances that led to his cold-blooded murder? Pearl decided to cover the War on Terror from Islamabad, Pakistan, away from the fighting in Afghanistan, but plagued by its own dangers from local assassins and kidnappers. On January 6, 2002, Pearl read a story in the *Boston Globe* about Richard Reid, the accused "shoe-bomber" who allegedly tried to blow up an American airliner. The story said Reid had studied under a Pakistani Islamic leader named Sheik Mubarik Ali Gilani. Pearl decided to seek an interview with Gilani, and he contacted a man who called himself Arif who agreed to set up a meeting with a friend of Gilani's. Pearl had no way of knowing that "Arif" was actually Hashim Kadir, an operative of Harkat ul-Mujahedin, a radical Kashmiri group with a history of kidnapping Westerners.

Pearl sensed that he was onto a good story, but he was uneasy. He consulted with a local antiterrorist group called the Citizens Police Liaison Committee about the advisability of a meeting with an associate of the sheikh of an Islamic extremist group. Pearl received the same advice from the committee that he had received from his colleagues in the press: Don't go, but if you do, don't go alone, and make sure you meet your source in a public place. Pearl chose to disregard the advice. He had agreed to meet his source at the Village Restaurant at 6:30 P.M., and by the time he arrived, darkness had fallen and the restaurant was almost empty.

A single unarmed kidnapper awaited Pearl at the restaurant, with one or two accomplices waiting out of sight on a motorcycle. The unsuspecting Pearl climbed into the man's car and was driven for about forty minutes to the northern outskirts of the city. The car followed the motorcycle into a small compound containing a two-room building. When Pearl stepped out of the car he was approached by the motorcycle driver, a man named Naeem Bukhari, leader of the militant group Lashkar-e-Jhangvi. Bukhari put his arms around Pearl's shoulders as though in friendship, but with his other hand he pushed a gun into Pearl's ribs. "Now you are kidnapped," Bukhari said. Initially, Pearl thought the man was kidding, but he was roughly handled, strip-searched, and left in his underwear.[67]

Pearl's tragic journey into Karachi's shadowy Islamic kidnapping network had begun.

By dawn, when Pearl had not returned home, his wife Mariane was filled with dread. A journalist herself, she knew full well the dangers her husband faced. She and her Indian-born Muslim friend and colleague Asra began calling anyone who might know of Danny's fate. Among their calls was one to Khalid Khawaja, former ISI (Pakistani intelligence) agent who claimed to be a friend of Gilani and of Osama bin Laden. Asra reached Khawaja by phone and said, "You know my friend Danny Pearl. He was scheduled to meet Sheikh Gilani last night at seven, and he never returned."[68] Khawaja said it must have been a setup, perhaps by the CIA, because Gilani would never agree to meet with a journalist, particularly not a foreigner.

When Khawaja dismissed Asra's concern for Mariane and her unborn child by launching into an extended lecture on innocent women and children killed by American bombs, Asra hung up.

None of the "authorities," Pakistani or American, seemed to have much to offer Mariane, so she and Asra turned to street connections, trying to reconstruct the chain of contacts that Pearl had used in his attempt to interview Sheikh Gilani. They began with Asif, known as Asif-le-fixer, a journalist for the local publication *Jang*, who had frequently arranged interviews for Pearl and other Western journalists. Asif, who has good contacts with fundamentalist groups, sent Mariane to Jaffar, another journalist for *Jang*, who introduced her to a key player who called himself "Bashir." But Bashir was in fact Omar Ahmed Saeed Sheikh, a British-reared Pakistani who had lured four Westerners into a kidnapping in India in 1994. He had deceived Daniel Pearl and now he was deceiving Mariane. Even so, Mariane's meeting with Bashir provided some crucial details on Pearl's abduction.

Pearl had asked Bashir to arrange an appointment with Gilani. Bashir agreed, but said Danny would first have to prove himself by submitting a selection of his articles. If the articles passed muster, a meeting with Gilani would be arranged. Danny e-mailed the articles to Bashir, setting in motion a series of communications between the two. On January 19, Danny received a message from Bashir saying Sheikh Gilani "has read your articles" and "you are welcome to meet him."[69]

The following day, Danny and Bashir made plans to meet with the sheikh in Karachi. Bashir's e-mail to Pearl said, "When you get to Karachi please contact Mr. Imtiaz Siddique [at] 0300-2170244 who will arrange to meet you and take you to Gilani."[70] But of course, Danny was never taken to Gilani, and the entire process was undoubtedly a ruse used to lure him into captivity. Bashir (Omar Saeed Sheikh) would later tell police that he did not originally intend to abduct Pearl, but when "Arif" (Hashim Kadir) told him that an American journalist was seeking an interview with Gilani, he decided to meet Pearl himself. Their series of e-mails followed, which Bashir later admitted was simply a way to trap Pearl. As the process proceeded, Bashir concluded, "I might as well do it," because the abduction of an American journalist would receive wide attention and strike a blow against the United States.

Bashir then assembled a team and devised the kidnapping. The plot involved independent cells of people who communicated largely through mobile phones. Like Bashir, everyone involved used false names. Bashir assigned one person to buy a camera and scanner, another to photograph Pearl in captivity, and a third to deliver the photos to a person who would scan and transmit the material to media organizations. Finally, he recruited a friend whom police call "Haider," a longtime militant who formerly trained radical fighters in Afghanistan, to do the actual kidnapping.

Even as Mariane began to assemble these pieces of the puzzle, she received the first of a series of chilling e-mail messages containing photos of Pearl bound with chains, a nine-millimeter pistol held to his head. The attached message from "kidnapperguy" began: "The National movement for the restoration of Pakistani sovereignty has captured CIA officer Daniel Pearl who has [sic] posing as a journalist of the Wall Street Journal."[71] The e-mail made a series of demands, including the release of the former Taliban ambassador to Pakistan, now held by the United States; the release of Pakistani detainees held at the American naval base at Guantanamo, Cuba; the provision of lawyers for Pakistanis arrested in law enforcement sweeps in the United States; and the expedited delivery of F-16 fighter planes to Pakistan. The e-mail stated that Pearl would be held in "very inhuman circumstances" until the Americans improved the treatment of their detainees.[72]

On the morning of January 30, another e-mail from Pearl's captors arrived containing two photos similar to those in the first e-mail. The new message read, "We have interrogated mr.D.Parl and we have come to the conclusion that contrary to what we thought earlier he is not working for the cia. in fact he is working for mossaad. therefore we will execute him within 24 hours unless amreeka filfils our demands."

The message concluded, "We warn all amreekan journalist working in pakstan that there are many in their ranks spying on pakstan under the journalist cover. therefore we give all amreekan journalists 3 days to get out of pakstan. anyone remaining after that will be targetted."[73]

Within twenty-four hours after the e-mail was made public, the media had made six hundred inquiries of the *Wall Street Journal*, asking for information and offering support and assistance. Prominent celebrities offered their help. Muhammed Ali submitted a powerful statement that began, "I pray this message reaches those who are detaining Daniel Pearl. . . . Daniel is a professional journalist. . . . Treat him as you would wish all Muslims to be treated by others. . . ."

Another Muslim celebrity, pop musician Cat Stevens, his name now changed to Yusuf Islam, wrote a statement ending, "As a message to those who are holding the journalist Danny Pearl: If justice is your goal, the cause of justice will not be served by killing an innocent man who has nothing but a pen in his hand."[74]

Paul Steiger of the *Wall Street Journal* also issued a statement that seemed aimed at the kidnappers: "The world now knows, and you seem to know, that Danny is a journalist, nothing more or less. Journalists are, by definition, trained messengers. Danny can be your messenger. . . . A captive or killed Danny cannot speak for you, cannot help you or your cause."[75]

On February 5, Mariane received a phone call from the trusted Pakistani police officer she calls Captain, who excitedly told her that his computer expert had traced the route of the e-mails from Bashir, who police had confirmed to be Omar Sheikh, to Danny, leading to the arrest of three men and the discovery of further details on Danny's abduction. Omar Sheikh had used the three men to set the trap for Danny. Mariane would later describe the situation as follows: "Omar Sheikh was probably looking for someone to kidnap. . . . He's a psychopath, but he's also a very bright man in his evil way. . . . He set the plans—the plan to trap—and, of course, Danny never got to meet this Gilani; he was just brought into a place where he was kept in captivity."[76]

Omar Sheikh himself was soon in custody, but it immediately became clear that Omar did not know where Danny was being held. Omar was just one link in a complicated chain. He was a tool, the lure, while others were the captors. In court, Omar shocked everyone by declaring, "As far as I understand, he [Danny] is dead."[77]

Mariane refused to believe it, but over the next few days evidence surfaced that Danny had indeed been killed. Captain told her there was a video showing his execution. Mariane, who is a filmmaker herself, said film could easily be faked, but Captain was firm. "Mariane," he said. "Danny is dead. . . . They had a knife, and they used it in such a way that there is no doubt. . . . He was beheaded."[78]

The struggle was over. Daniel Pearl was dead. Further detail on the circumstances of his abduction and murder surfaced in the testimony of suspects in police custody. Pearl was held in an isolated shack in a compound on the outskirts of Karachi, far from any roads or passersby. He had tried to escape by shimmying through a vent in the bathroom, but he was caught, brought back, and chained to a car engine. Another time, he tried to break loose while walking with his guards in the compound. He had also tried shouting to door-to-door vendors, but to no avail.

The men guarding Pearl spoke little English, preventing any real communication between them, and Pearl was apparently unaware that he was marked for death. Around February 1, three new men—Arabic-speaking, probably Yemenis—were brought to the compound and left in a room with Pearl and one guard. The guard who remained later told police that at least one of the visitors communicated to Pearl in a language the guard didn't understand. According to the authorities, "Mr. Pearl, who could speak French and Hebrew, responded with an angry outburst, his first conversation of any length since his capture. After the interaction calmed, one of the visitors turned on a video camera, and another asked Mr. Pearl questions about his religious background. . . . After the videotaped statement by Mr. Pearl, . . . [he] was blindfolded and killed."[79] Not until months later was Pearl's body found, cut into ten pieces and dumped in a four-foot-deep grave in the compound where he had been held.

Meanwhile, Omar Saeed Sheikh and his three accomplices were tried in a Pakistani court. The three accomplices were found guilty and sentenced to life in prison. Omar was sentenced to death by hanging, but his sentence is on appeal. Testimony in the trial clarified the elaborate cell structure involved in Pearl's abduction, detention, and murder. The first cell was that of Omar Sheikh and the three men who kidnapped Pearl. The second cell, responsible for holding Pearl and burying him after his murder, was headed by the man police called "Haider," who belongs to the Harkat-ul-Jihad-i-Islami group. Omar had called Haider and asked him to find a safe house for their use. All of these men are linked to the wealthy Karachi factory owner Saud Memon, who still evades police custody. Memon, who owned the compound where Danny was held, brought the three Arab executioners who comprised the third cell.

Memon drove the Arab speakers to the hideout on Pearl's eighth or ninth day of captivity. They bought the video equipment and ordered all the guards out of Pearl's room except Fazal Karim, who had been at the shack since Pearl's arrival. With video camera running, Pearl was blindfolded and murdered.

Police have never determined who actually ordered the murder, although Omar Saeed Sheikh and Saud Memon are the leading suspects. Saeed Sheikh continues to claim that he never meant to harm Pearl, and Memon remains at large. Meanwhile, fringe players in Pearl's murder are still being pursued by Pakistani police. Amjad Farooqi, a Pakistani militant with ties to al-Qaeda, has been declared "the most wanted man in Pakistan," partly because he was present when Pearl was beheaded, but mostly because he has been implicated in two failed attempts to assassinate Pakistan's president. Farooqi was one of the seven Pakistanis originally indicted in the Pearl case.[80]

Another accomplice in Pearl's kidnapping and murder, Asim Ghafoor, was killed in November 2004 as Pakistani agents tried to arrest him at a hideout west of Karachi. In July 2005, Hashim Kadir (alias "Arif") the man who lured Pearl into the hands of his kidnappers, was arrested in Gujranwala, Pakistan, in the province of Punjab. He subsequently confessed to working for two al-Qaeda-linked operatives.

Scott Taylor: Nightmare in Iraq (September 7, 2004–September 11, 2004)

Scott Taylor is a former soldier, well-traveled war correspondent, and publisher of *Esprit de Corps*, a prominent military magazine in Canada. He is a Canadian citizen, but as a freelance reporter he writes a syndicated column published in newspapers around the world. In Canada he is under contract to the *Halifax Herald*, the *Windsor Star*, and the *Pembroke Observer* as a weekly columnist, but he does print, broadcast, and film assignments for several international news organizations, including al-Jazeera, the most influential and respected Arab news network.

Just before dusk on September 7, 2004, Taylor and his translator, Zeynep Tugrul, a prominent female Turkish journalist, arrived by taxi at the outskirts of the northern Iraqi city of Tal Afar. The city is inhabited almost entirely by Turkmen, and Taylor had just finished a book about the history of these Turkish-speaking indigenous Iraqis. As a result, he had good contacts in Tal Afar, and although he knew that American forces were about to attack the city, he planned to observe the fighting from a safe house that had been arranged for him.

In a telephone interview, Taylor told me, "The Americans had not announced that they had lost Tal Afar to the mujahedin, and now the Americans were poised to retake it, sort of a prelude to Fallujah. The Americans shut off the water and the power, and the residents fled. About 150 to 200 thousand people fled from Tal Afar, but there were no media cameras, no hype prior to this. Very low key. Very few journalists have been to northern Iraq, and none have been in Tal Afar. None. It was an isolation area where the American forces could do a little practice run and see what they could get away with."[81]

When Taylor's taxi reached a police checkpoint, he asked to be taken to Dr. Yashar, the prominent local official who was his contact. Taylor and his Turkish colleague were then transferred to a nearby car containing four masked gunmen, one of whom said, in excellent English, "We will take you to Dr. Yashar—please do not be afraid."[82]

Taylor assumed the masked men were part of a special police force, but when he saw the streets of Tal Afar lined with similarly masked, heavily armed fighters, he knew he had been delivered into the hands of the resistance at the police checkpoint. How could that have happened? Taylor told me, "The police actually put us in the car, and at two other checkpoints these mujahidin drove us through the police in broad daylight. We were visible, yet these heavily armed mujahidin drove straight through police checkpoints. The police are working with the resistance anywhere they are unsupervised by the Americans. I was a witness to this while I was being held. That's why, when you see these police stations being overrun in places like Mosul and Baiji, there are no police killed, and the rebels have been able to seize all the weapons, ammunition, and flak jackets, which aren't readily available. Those police stations are fortified like Fort Knox. How do you overrun them without taking a single casualty?"[83]

Taylor and his translator were taken to a two-story home where the leader of a half dozen armed men told them, "You are spies . . . and now you are prisoners." The leader then left, saying he was going to fight the American invaders. Four more gunmen entered the room, forced Taylor against the wall with his hands on his head. He heard a Kalashnikov being cocked behind him, but before a shot could be fired, Zeynep screamed, "Don't shoot him . . . he has a son."[84]

While the gunmen were discussing Taylor's fate, the original captor returned, and the would-be-executioners departed. Taylor was promptly blind-folded, tied up, manhandled, and taken to a second house where his money (seven hundred dollars) was taken. Hours later his interrogation began. He was asked what intelligence agency he worked for, and over and over he explained that he was a journalist, not a spy. Finally, the "Emir," as the leader was called, agreed to check Taylor's story. "If you are telling the truth, we will release you," he said. "If not, you die."[85]

The next morning, Taylor and Zeynep were transported to a third house where the Emir told them that their stories checked out and they would be released.

When I asked Taylor about the ethnicity of his abductors, he said, "They're Wahabbists, an extremely fundamentalist chapter of the Sunni religion. Not your moderate Sunni. They were actually Turkmen, but part of the Ansar al

Islam group, which is affiliated with Al Qaeda and Osama bin Laden, also Wahabbists. These groups are pretty damn extreme. . . . No westerner other than myself had visited Tal Afar since the intervention, and probably not for the last dozen or so years, given the sanctions and the conditions in Iraq. I had been there in June, and I knew a prominent politician whom I had stayed with. I was trying to get to his house where I felt I would be safe. I did not realize that the fundamentalists were as strong and as well-organized as they were."

I asked whether being a journalist gave him a free pass with the mujahidin. "No," he said. "A guy shows up who's a military expert, a former soldier, looks like an American, is carrying a camera and is coming in on the eve of battle in the chaos of the main checkpoint. This is not going to look right. Remember, people were pouring out of the city, and we show up in a taxi trying to enter at dusk. I would have had my suspicions if I was the local mujahidin commander. Still, when they did check out our press credentials, we were told that we would be set free the next day. But unfortunately, the American air strikes started that night, the night of the 8th. That was the big battle, and the leader who agreed to let us go was actually killed that night, and all of our cameras and equipment were destroyed. So we started negotiating from scratch the next day. Some fifty Iraqi fighters had been killed, which is a lot if you compare it even to Fallujah. So, 50 killed, 120 wounded, a very big battle, and there we were, now with no identification, no cameras, and new leaders asking, 'Who are these prisoners?' The man who had interviewed us was now dead, and these guys were not just suspicious of us, they wanted revenge."[86]

When I asked if his abductors assumed he was American, Taylor answered, "Oh, absolutely. An American, a Jewish spy. A 'kaffir,' that's what they called me, which means an infidel. The main allegation was that I was a spy. They suspect journalists, they suspect Red Cross workers, and with some degree of reason. I think anybody crossing the line on a regular basis is assumed to be a spy. It's a modern phenomenon. Having these unembedded journalists is something which is really incomparable to, say, the World War II experience. We didn't have Swiss journalists going to the German positions one day and crossing in the night to visit the Allies, but we have that now. It's something that emerged basically around the time of the war in Bosnia and the breakup of Yugoslavia. There was sort of a mixed playing field and journalists found themselves crossing not just one set of lines, but many lines. That's when this whole unembedded phenomenon started to take place."

During his captivity in Tal Afar, Taylor, although blindfolded, could hear the noise of battle and the screams of Iraqi casualties. "You could hear kids crying in the other building adjacent to us," he recalled. "You could hear other kids in the street still playing after the huge air strikes. They didn't flee. I guess their belief in Allah is such that it's a very fatalistic society. But that doesn't mean it's right to start dropping huge bombs on them."[87]

Taylor said that, for the most part, his captors did not distinguish between the various Western nationalities, between the governments that supported the war and those who opposed it:

> The 38-year-old emir, the leader who first captured us, was fairly smart, spoke good English and had lengthy conversations with me. During my interrogation he clearly understood the difference between Canada and the United States, but not much beyond that. This was a pretty remote enclave. These young guys are unschooled and pretty much under the guidance of the clerics. This place was sort of the high water mark of the Crusades, and a Crusade-era fort still dominates Tal Afar. So they knew that the kaffir, the infidels, had come, and what had been done earlier was all very real to them. Then suddenly the kaffirs come back, much as had been predicted by the clerics, acting very much as you would expect infidels to act, driving around in great big vehicles, crushing cars, acting in a very arrogant manner. It made everyone believe that what the clerics had told them was true. That's what I think fleshed out the ranks of the mujahidin in the last few months. And of course, the biggest thing that contributed to that was the appearance of the photographs from Abu Ghraib. The mujahidin couldn't have bought that kind of propaganda.
>
> At first, I thought that I might face such abuse during my captivity, but my captors quite seriously explained to me that they might cut my head off, but "no, no Abu Ghraib," meaning they were not going to rape me or sexually abuse me. Only kaffirs would do that. So they claim a higher moral compass, which is interesting. American officials like Rumsfeld and Wolfowitz will point out, "We don't cut off heads." But the mujahidin see the separation of the head from the body as a sacrificial part of Islam. As grotesque as it seems to us, it's a quick and painless death, as opposed to being raped and humiliated.[88]

The possibility of ransom was never mentioned, and Taylor said there was clearly no way to buy your way out of captivity. "That would be ridiculous," he said, "because all they want to do is die. These guys were mujahidin. They were the real McCoy. What would they do with money? The only fortunate thing for me was being grabbed by a unit that was about to fight a major battle, so their only concern was, if you are spies, we'll kill you. If you're not spies, we'll let you go. But in the end, they turned us over to these other Arab guys who were a little bit sleazier. They were the ones that tortured me."[89]

I knew Taylor had received brutal treatment from his various captors, but I wondered if it had reached the level of systematic torture.

"Yeah, I was tortured by the Arabs, yeah," he said. "First, I was roughed up, as soldiers would do when taking anyone prisoner. In some ways, the worst thing was when they would put the hood on me to move me. You can't see and they're banging you around, and you don't know what's going to happen. Every time you were moved there was that uncertainty."[90]

In the course of five days of captivity, Taylor was repeatedly passed from house to house, group to group. His worst treatment came on the fourth day when he was delivered to a group of Arabs, not Turkmen. On his Web site, Taylor describes the physical ordeal he faced after the Turkmen leader left:

Within minutes of his departure, the Arabs burst into the room and roughly blindfolded me. As I tried to protest, I was kicked in the ribs, knocking the wind out of me. "Shut up American spy!" shouted my assailant. For the next hour I was interrogated. . . . Although intense, I was relieved when the questioning ended without any physical force being used. . . . I had barely removed the blindfold and taken a sip of water when five men rushed back into the room. I could see the batons and ropes, but I had no time to react before I was pulled to my feet. When I attempted to resist, my feet were knocked out from under me, and I was savagely kicked. They blindfolded me and gagged me with a headscarf. My hands were tied behind my back and I was rolled over with my feet up in the air—tied to a pole. Two men held the pole up when two other began beating my feet with straps and batons.

At first I could see no blows coming. In his pent up fury, one of my attackers struck my face several times with his fist knocking my blind-fold aside. I mentally promised myself not to give them the satisfaction of hearing me scream until after the 20th blow. . . . I kept my promise, but on the 21st strike I screamed out, "F--K!" the cloth muffling the sound somewhat. They deliberately hit the same spot on my thigh repeatedly. For the first four or five blows the pain would increase incrementally and then the final strike would force an involuntary convulsion. I could feel the pain explode in my head, and my body jack-knifed upwards reflexively . . .

I lost all track of time—I could have been tortured for 5 minutes or 25—I have no real conception of the actual duration. I do remember that despite the excruciating pain in my legs, I kept fearing that the next blow would be to my genitals. With my legs splayed apart and upended I felt incredibly vulnerable"[91]

When the beating finally ended, Taylor's feet were cut loose and he was roughly pulled upright. The interrogator handed him a pen and paper and told him to write down all the Web sites that might confirm that he was a Canadian journalist. He was told that if the information checked out, he would live. If not, he would die. Taylor was then forced to lie on the floor, a gun held to his neck, while Zeynep was beaten. As she cried out in pain, the guard repeatedly told Taylor that he could spare her the pain by simply confessing to being a spy. Each time Taylor denied the charge, the guard spat upon him.

Eventually, the interrogator returned and told Taylor that he had failed the test on the Internet and would therefore die—that night.

> When they told me I was going to die, and they meant it, they really became nervous about even letting me go to the bathroom. I couldn't get up to go pee, so they would just give me a bottle. When I had to take a dump, I told them, look, unless you want me to mess up your bed, you've got to let me go. The guy was still very nervous, but he took me to one of these Moslem-style toilets. I couldn't bend my knees, so I had to lean against the wall and try to aim this thing while the guy's got a gun to my head.
>
> There was a tremendous sense of curiosity about the foreigner. They had never seen a kaffir. I was like the big white monkey. They were very curious about how I would behave, and for that reason, because of my military training, I kept myself as clean as I could. I always tried to hold myself with an air of dignity, because station is a big thing for them, as far as whether you are subservient. So if I had been groveling in my own filth, weeping and rolling around, I would have been a despicable piece of filth to them. But I always made sure that I never gave them the satisfaction of so much as a grunt if they hit me. You know, just looking defiant. I kept my jacket and my shoes as clean as I could and my shirt tucked in. I would wash, and if I could find a razor, at least scrape away at the sides. Just a bit of aloofness. From the military point of view, if a prisoner is a wailing lump of crap he's not going to be given any respect. If your captive is stoic and he's taking it the way you would want to see yourself take it, you're going to ease up on him. I mean, if a guy would come over and punch you in the head, the other guys would say, take it easy, because it was no fun. But if you're crying and pleading and trying to offer them money, then it becomes a game with them.[92]

After Taylor's torture at the hands of his Arab captors he was taken to still another house, and the nightmare continued with a new set of tormentors. One man said, "We know you are a Mossad spy. . . . You have 24 hours to decide whether to tell the truth and die with a clear conscience . . . or go to your death as a liar."[93]

Many hours later, another interrogator arrived and assured Taylor that he would not be tortured this time. "It is either life or knife—with each answer that you give us," he said calmly. Taylor answered the usual questions in the same direct manner he had done with a succession of interrogators, but he no longer expected to be believed. To his amazement, during one of his lengthy answers the interrogator suddenly declared, "Stop. Get your things. You will live. You are free."[94]

Was this just another round of psychological torture, raising his hopes only to dash them once more? His handcuffs were removed, his shoes and jacket given to him, and, with his eyes still taped shut he was taken to a taxi and sent off to freedom.

In retrospect, Taylor thinks the decision to release him was probably made before his final interrogation even began. Perhaps his chances of being released improved when his captors did an Internet search and found several of his articles on the Web site of the Arab news network al-Jazeera, but Taylor thinks there were other forces involved:

> The Google searching for my al-Jazeera articles and so on did help keep me alive, but honestly, I think it was the intervention of the Turkish government that played the largest part in my release. They have a large presence in the north, as you can imagine, in terms of intelligence resources and, of course, the Iraqi-Turkmen Front, which is sort of the eyes and ears of the Turkish government inside Iraq. These are the guys I knew. They're not agents, but they have their own vested interest, their big brother in Turkey. And Turkey has its own interest in Iraqi oil and keeping the borders intact. They have a huge foothold in the north, and the girl who was abducted with me is well known as a Turkish journalist, as a foreign affairs columnist for the Sabah. The whole international community knows her.
>
> When they did let the girl go, that's when the negotiations for my release began in earnest. She was informed that I had been beheaded, but when she reached the Iraqi-Turkmen Front office in Mosul she insisted that they should at least negotiate for my body. Apparently the Turks and the Turkmen were still looking for us in the chaos that was Tal Afar. When she was released and showed up in Mosul, that told them, "He's here in Mosul too." It took about 27 hours after that before I was released. Whoever they were negotiating with, no one was exchanged for me, but in that huge milieu of intrigue that is northern Iraq, between the Turkmen and the Arabs and the various groups going back and forth, it was made known that I was important to them, and I was released. And, of course, I'm a good guy, right? They were going to cut my head off, but they were going to be sorry about it.[95]

After his release, Taylor spent one night with the Iraqi Turkmen Front office in Mosul, but they had no phones, and he was unable to contact his family. In the morning, Turkish intelligence officers came and picked him up and drove him to Irbil, where he contacted Canada. "I was in rough, rough shape at this point," he recalls. "I could barely move. But I was able to speak to my wife. Once the adrenaline was gone and I knew that I was going to live, the pain was excruciating. It was just unbelievable."[96]

I asked if he received an apology upon his release.

"From whom?" he asked incredulously. "No. One of the guys who finally released me, an Arab, was very disappointed. He wanted to cut me. He was looking forward to doing the deed. He was a son-of-a-bitch. There was actually a funny moment just before I was released. I was chained to the bed. My captors locked the doors and windows and left, so only the man who owned the house remained. Then he went outside to work on his car, and only his wife was left in the house with me. I guess he never told his wife what was going on with me, because while she was washing the floor she backed into the room and found me chained to the bed. She screamed, and the man came rushing back in. I could hear him screaming at her in Arabic and she kept yelling back at him. He struck her a couple of times, but she didn't stop screaming. You can imagine her wondering, what is this guy doing chained to my bed? Finally, he came in and removed the electrical tape from my eyes and said, 'Asaf Asaf,' meaning, 'I'm sorry, I'm sorry.' What else could he do? Another one of the bizarre things I remember is that while I was lying there waiting to die, waiting for someone to come in and cut my head off, the television set was showing English programming and it was a rerun of 'Hollywood 90210,' this stupid show with Luke Perry at like age 19. And I'm lying there thinking, this will be the last thing I'll ever see. Rich, spoiled kids in Hollywood trying to decide what to wear to the prom. Unbelievable."

Do the American military authorities in Iraq know exactly who kidnapped Taylor? "If, indeed, the Americans were interested to find out who put me in the car that night in Tal Afar, the timing is known to them," said Taylor. "I mean, it was just before 7 p.m. at the front gate at Tal Afar. The Americans can easily determine what police official was there if they are intent on following it up. Do I know his name? No, but could they have figured it out within a matter of hours? I would expect so."

At the conclusion of my interview with Taylor I asked him under what circumstances he would return to Iraq. After a long pause he answered, "Perhaps when it calms down, if that's at all possible. It's much too dangerous now, and once you become marked by the different groups, it's even worse. You know, you become a player as opposed to someone who's just going in to report. That does make you a target. I've got a wife and a kid. I've already done my bit."[97]

Chapter 4

Why Do They Hate Us?

The Nature of Modern War and Real-Time Reporting

After 9/11, the press joined political leaders in asking, "Why do they hate us?" The problem is in the pronouns. The popular wisdom after 9/11 was that Islamic fundamentalists were the killers and innocent Western civilians were the targets. For war correspondents in Afghanistan and Iraq, the truth is much more complex. For example, "Western" journalists are a minority among the war correspondents killed there in recent years, and American and Coalition troops are prominent among the killers.

What is so different about modern warfare that makes journalists appropriate military targets? Is it that the combatants themselves are more brutal, more indiscriminate in defining their targets? The frequent use of the term *terrorist* to characterize armed rebellion, insurgency, or resistance to foreign occupation suggests that local militias, unlike traditional armies, are likely to target civilians, including journalists. But the history of citizen-armies of resistance has a noble tradition, suggesting that we be cautious in depicting all who fight without a uniform as "terrorists." Adding to the confusion is the tendency of modern, well-trained armies to regard "unfriendly" journalists as spies or supporters of terrorism.

War correspondents themselves have complex explanations for the increasing hostility shown by all combatants toward journalists. Pulitzer Prize-winning reporter Philip Caputo, the first of the prominent journalists to be kidnapped in the Middle East, says,

The nature of war has changed somewhat, but the greater change has come about in the attitudes of combatants toward the press, toward the media. We used to talk about this when I was a correspondent, and we had begun to observe the change back in the 1970s. I remember my friend from *Newsweek*, Nick Profit, mentioning to me that there was a point in time when holding a press card, while not a guarantee of safety, was at least something of a flak jacket, and that was ceasing to be the case.

We were observing that change from the early to the late 1970s. Journalists were beginning to be seen as fair game for, you name it, murder, kidnapping, intimidation, things that had not occurred before. This was due not so much to a change in journalism as in the attitudes of combatants toward journalists. Combatants used to regard journalists as off limits, and would often seek to curry favor with them in the hope of gaining a favorable press. Certainly, by the time of the Lebanese civil war and some of the subsequent conflicts, it appeared that that attitude was vanishing, and now I believe it has vanished altogether.

I would agree that the change in the attitudes of combatants has been influenced by a change in the nature of war. Today's wars are seldom waged between traditional armies. The Pentagon uses one of their acronymic terms for it, 'ethnic religious civil conflicts' (ERCC). These are basically huge gang fights between ethnic or religious insurgent groups or terrorist groups. These are untrained gunmen, people who have no knowledge of the laws of war. It would be comparable to what would occur if the CRIPS or the BLOODS organized armies and went to war in Los Angeles and you found yourself caught between them. I think that's where the change in attitude came about.[1]

Jerry Levin, former CNN correspondent and kidnap victim in Lebanon, agrees that the violence directed at journalists may be unprecedented, but he believes the cause comes from outside the Middle East. "If the violence against western journalists is unprecedented, it is because of the unprecedented level of violent involvement in the Middle East by America and its fellow traveler governments," he says.

What happened to me and Terry Anderson and the others back in 1984 and '85 was pretty tough and pretty mean, but most of us emerged from that, not unscathed, but alive and with all ten fingers and ten toes. Remember, back then, this response by the terrorists, our adversaries, was seen as unprecedented and brutal. But as bad as that was, compare it to what's happening to journalists now and you find that the level of danger back then was infinitely less consequential than it is now. Why? In my opinion, it is because, back in the 1980s, the level of violent

American involvement was, relatively speaking, infinitesimal compared to what it is now. As this exponential increase of American violence in Iraq has occurred, there has been a logical and directly proportional exponential increase in the brutal response. I call Iraq "Gaza East." The general terrorist or guerrilla response, attacks on journalists, beheadings, kidnappings, what have you, is certainly, for these times, at an unprecedented level of brutality. But if one is honest, one has to see the connection with this horrendous increase of violence by the United States.[2]

Former AP correspondent Terry Anderson, America's longest held hostage, believes the nature of modern warfare is part of the reason for the increased vulnerability of war correspondents. "The wars we fight right now are wars without fixed lines," he told me. "They are chaotic. They involve a lot of what we used to call guerrilla action. Now we call them terrorists. It's very difficult to tell friend from foe, and that makes it very dangerous for journalists. I don't see that changing in the near future. We don't fight formal wars any more. The formal phase of this war [Iraq] was brief and overwhelmingly one-sided, and that's the way it's going to be. There was never any question that we were going to whip the crap out of the Iraqis. The problem came up after that was accomplished, because we had no idea what to do next. And that's the way it's going to be for the foreseeable future."[3]

Adi Ignatius of *Time* magazine is more specific in identifying what is new in the Iraq war. "To me, it's the kidnapping that makes this thing different," he said. "In that sense, journalists have become tools. There are the clearly politically motivated kidnappings meant to change a country's policies, and journalists are not viewed as exempt from this. We're frequently targeted. . . . And it's so lawless now that a lot of the kidnapers are just gangsters kidnapping for ransom. They might eventually trade you up to the Zarqawi level, [at which point] it becomes a political kidnapping. That, to me, is the fundamental difference in Iraq."[4]

Nik Gowing of BBC News says, "[A]lthough media reporting of war has been a dangerous business for a long time, it is now more dangerous than ever. . . . The new insidious development is that because of the impact of our real-time capability to bear witness immediately, we are being actively targeted by warriors, warlords and forces of even the most highly developed governments who do not want us to see what they are doing."[5]

Gowing says the journalists who have been murdered in Afghanistan, Iraq, and Palestine provide evidence of their vulnerability in "the new transparency of war." He describes the death of Italian photographer Raffaele Ciriello, who was shot dead in Ramallah, West Bank, in March 2002. An Israeli tank opened fire when Ciriello pulled out a small video camera. "For any journalist, the very act of pulling out a video camera now puts you at great risk if an army like the Israeli Defense Force (IDF) thinks you are threatening their operational security. . . . I am trying to highlight the real tension that exists now because of the new, light-weight, go-anywhere nature of our business. . . . This technology is now part of the new information dynamic of war that is making journalists far more intrusive, and therefore more vulnerable."[6]

Jerry Levin, former CNN correspondent in Lebanon, where he was kid-napped and held for a year, says, "Journalism is such that you want to be where the story is, and electronic journalism has given us far more opportunities. But there has been a grim trade-off. First, electronic journalism, which now includes the Internet, has created jobs for an exponentially larger universe of journalists being sent to dangerous places than ever before. And second, more journalists chasing after the same dangerous stories creates the potential for more journalists flirting with danger because of the excruciating pressures that electronic journalism has put on the entire business to meet the demands of news scoops and exclusive interviews."[7]

Reuters chief David Schlesinger notes that the new technology has made jour-nalism particularly dangerous for photographers. "There's a real difference in media," he says. "The two people who were killed for Reuters . . . were both camera-men. Cameramen have to be on the scene quickly. It's a very very dangerous job. We just had another incident at the end of last week. We don't have any problems get-ting volunteers for text [reporting], because for text you can always lock down in the house and rely on stringers and make phone calls and get information in other ways. But in the visual area, journalists think several times about whether they really want to be in a place where they have to go out and put themselves in danger."[8]

Canadian war correspondent and publisher Scott Taylor has observed first-hand how both the warlords and the occupation armies in Iraq are exploiting jour-nalists. "Reporters are targeted at the same time they're being used," says Taylor, who survived abduction and torture by mujahidin in Iraq. "Every side is now real-izing that they need to get their message out. . . . The rebels know that what they're actually giving you as interviews or showing you will be made public almost immediately, but what's made public can then be used as intelligence by the other side. So it's become like the bumblebee of the battlefield. Both sides need it, because they want to glean information, not covert information, but information to confirm or correct what they have observed."[9]

Cash Is a Dangerous Magnet

In his recent book on the media and terrorism, Stephen Hess spoke to a number of war correspondents concerning the dangers posed by the large amounts of money they carried with them on assignment. Hess quoted Michael Gettler, ombudsman for the *Washington Post*, who called reporters in Afghanistan "walking ATM machines" because of their practice of carrying so much cash, and asked the reporters how much cash they carried.

"Thousands," said Michael Gordon, author and London-based correspondent for the *New York Times*, "in hundred dollar bills."[10]

Tom Squitieri, a war correspondent for *USA Today*, said he carried a similar amount, but added, "I wrap all my hundreds and fifties in ones, the dirtiest ones and fives I could scrounge up, because that would immediately turn off people. They didn't want small bills."[11]

Carol Morello, a *Washington Post* reporter with wide experience in the Middle East, said, "Even [when I traveled with] the marines, I think I carried $5,000 in hundreds and fifties, the idea being that I didn't know what was going to happen, and I could easily find myself in a situation where I'd turn around and the marines would be gone and I'd have to figure how to get out myself. So I went to the ATM and American Express and got 5,000 bucks before I went in."[12]

New York Times photographer Vincent Laforet says reporters in Afghanistan were made more conspicuous by the money and equipment they carried. "[I]t's hard to be inconspicuous when one is not only Caucasian but also carrying $10,000 in cash, $30,000 in computer equipment and a $6,000 satellite phone among brown-skinned people whose per capita income is in the hundreds of dollars. . . . You were the lottery, walking right in there, unguarded."[13]

Apparently, most American reporters feel that carrying cash will buy them protection, not define them as targets. But not all war correspondents take that view. Scott Taylor, the Canadian reporter who was kidnapped and tortured in Iraq, runs a small organization that operates on a limited budget. Even so, that's not what determines the amount of money he carries when covering conflicts. He carries only what he needs to do his job. Anything more just makes him conspicuous and vulnerable.

"There are ways to deposit a little money in locations inside the country," says Taylor. "Let's say I could leave a little in Kirkuk with a friend or a family, knowing that if all went to hell I could get back there and still have $300 and make it to the border. You know, once you've got some experience in a country like Iraq you can begin to travel with less cash. You know exactly what your budget will be, because it becomes like going to work in the morning, right? I would carry about $300, a flexible amount, just in case something went wrong. You know, it costs as little as 25 to 50 dollars a day for a driver who also works as an interpreter. My budget doesn't include money for a guide plus a driver plus a car, requiring 400 U.S. dollars per day. That would require you to carry a lot of money. When you go into a country where you know there is no way to recharge your money, there's no credit card use, no banking, you need to have some contacts."

Why not just carry a lot of cash, as the big news organizations do?

"It's dangerous," Taylor said simply. "They become targeted because they've got cash. That much money would make you look like a spy. For me, a couple of thousand dollars is a lot of money. I've never taken that much. I don't have that kind of money. On the last trip, I had paid my driver on the way. Normally, it's about a fifty dollar drive into Iraq, and you work out how many days you need to stay. I stayed with a friend, and it's really cheap once you're in there."

Taylor rejects the notion of carrying "protection money," saying, "The minute you start doing that, they're going to say, 'Give me everything.' I had about 700 U.S. dollars when I was grabbed by the Ansar al Islam guys in Tal Afar. We were taken the first night, strip-searched and relieved of our cash. They said, 'You're not going to need money.' They know that whatever money you have, you have on your person. I mean, $700 is a lot of money in a country where 50 bucks is a good monthly wage, even for a doctor. From that point on it was like the Big House: free room and board. It wouldn't have mattered how much I carried. They would have taken whatever I had. So, in the end I gave it all up front, but I was going to spend it anyway."[14]

Loss of Objectivity

The perceived lack of objectivity in Western reporting on Middle Eastern conflicts has led local insurgents to regard journalists as mouthpieces for their governments. David Schlesinger, chief correspondent for Reuters wire service, has raised the question of the "we" factor in Western reporting. "I think that in journalism there's been a certain loss of objectivity," said Schlesinger.

> The use of "we" [in Iraq] to mean not "we" the organization or "we" the profession, but "we" representing the United States or the Coalition means that in many people's minds journalists are not objective observers of the situation. They are actually in play, and I think that is one of the things that makes it more dangerous today. They kidnap French journalists because they want to influence French policy. They target American journalists because they want to influence American policy. I think we the press have a responsibility to go back, in a sense, to a much purer objectivity to show that we are not part of the government. . . .
>
> I would like to make the point that it's always very dangerous when journalists become part of the story. I think the difficulty that journalists have had, the deaths of journalists, the injury of journalists, has to some extent made journalists part of this story. I think that's something that they and we as editors have to guard very much against.[15]

Chris Hedges, celebrated war correspondent turned critic, believes reporters will always be part of the story when they cover military conflicts. After the first Gulf War, he wrote, "The notion that the press was used in the war is incorrect. The press wanted to be used. It saw itself as part of the war effort. . . . For we not only believe the myth of war and feed recklessly off of the drug but also embrace the cause. We may do it with more skepticism. We certainly expose more lies and misconceptions. But we believe. We all believe. When you stop believing you stop going to war."[16]

Jerry Levin, former CNN correspondent and kidnap victim in Lebanon, agrees with Hedges. "Mainstream journalism has never been neutral," he says. "Do you really suppose that when the *New York Times* or the *Birmingham News* or the *Associated Press* covers a war in which the United States is involved that they are going to be pulling for the other side to win? They may be critical of the conduct of the war, but they acknowledge that there is an enemy. Having said that, be assured that there have been plenty of times throughout history when mainstream journalism has exceeded the boundaries of, if you will, appropriate one-sidedness."[17]

Susan Chira, foreign editor of the *New York Times*, does not fully agree with the claims of bias in the press, saying that as far the print media are concerned, "most news organizations that I see [in Iraq] have not really assumed the point of view or perspective of the Coalition authorities." She does, however, acknowledge that "in certain television organizations the flag-waving that has gone on has perhaps colored people's perceptions, . . . and I think there's been a bleed from TV into all journalism."[18]

John McWethy, chief national security correspondent for ABC News, described the change of atmosphere in his own organization as they covered Iraq. "[T]he worm began to turn as the issues turned: Are you an American? Or a journalist? These two issues immediately began to be debated within my news division. . . . The greatest criticism of the American press during this period is that international journalists saw us as being nothing more than cheerleaders for the administration."

Even the question of whether journalists should wear an American flag lapel pin when on the air became hotly contested. ABC eventually decided no. "It's like waving a flag," said McWethy. "When you are on television you are a symbol for your network. I would no more wave an American flag while trying to report in a non-biased way about conflict overseas than I would a Canadian flag or a British flag if I were a citizen of those countries. I'm a reporter."[19]

Marjorie Miller, foreign editor of the *Los Angeles Times*, says the appearance of partisanship among journalists in Iraq has placed them at increased risk. "You could always get killed by being in the wrong place at the wrong time," she says.

"Here, just by being a westerner, you're perceived, or fear you're perceived, as a partisan. Reporters don't want to be seen as partisan at a cost of their lives."[20]

I asked Canadian journalist and publisher Scott Taylor if he felt that war correspondents were being targeted because of their lack of objectivity in covering foreign conflicts. "I can understand that view with respect to American journalists and the British as well to some degree," he said. "They're involved in a war, and you can expect a lot of that patriotic jingoism—you know, play down the defeats, exaggerate the victories, we're all part of the war effort, keep up the morale on the home front. . . . The reality of the war is not being brought home to American readers and viewers, whereas we Canadians have a little more latitude. Our government stayed out of the war. On the other hand, I don't think the insurgents in Iraq distinguish much between American, Canadian, Danish, whatever, journalists. If you're from the west, they associate that with the CNN reports, which are incredibly one-sided."[21]

Journalists as Intelligence Agents

In February 1996, when the Council on Foreign Relations (CFR) recommended that the CIA "resume sending out spies posing as journalists," the Senate Intelligence Committee immediately called on CIA director John M. Deutsch to clarify current CIA practice on the use of journalists. Deutsch surprised the Senate committee by revealing that earlier restraints on the CIA had already been modified by "waivers" that allow CIA agents to pose as journalists or to enlist American journalists in clandestine operations. In summary, the current CIA policy authorizes unlimited recruitment of foreign journalists, unlimited use of "voluntary" press relationships, and secret criteria under which the Director of Central Intelligence may "waive" all agency regulations regarding the media.

Even the CFR's project director, Richard Haass, was unaware of the "waiver" policy. "Our assumption was the use [of journalists] was totally banned," he said.[22]

On April 24, 1996, Jane Kirtley, executive director of the Reporters Committee for Freedom of the Press, wrote to CIA Director Deutsch:

> I am writing to express our deep concern over CIA policies regarding the use of journalists and news organizations in intelligence activities. During your testimony before the Senate in February, you acknowledged that the use of journalists as "cover" or as intelligence agents is not precluded by current agency policy. . . . As you can surely understand, anything less than an unqualified rejection of these practices poses a palpable threat to the safety of countless American journalists working

abroad. It also undermines the independence of the press by compromising the First Amendment-mandated separation of the government and the news media.

We join our colleagues in urging you to rescind the policy that would permit the CIA to recruit journalists for intelligence work or to allow agents to impersonate journalists.[23]

Kirtley's concern that the continuing CIA policy of recruiting journalists would put foreign correspondents at risk is more appropriate today than ever. Every reporter kidnapped while covering American military action in the Middle East has been charged with being a spy for his or her government. The fact that the charges are probably specious does not change the fact that the CIA's policy provides motivation to the kidnappers and some legitimacy to their claims.

Terry Anderson, America's longest-held hostage, was abducted in Lebanon while serving as chief Middle East correspondent for the Associated Press. He, like virtually all kidnapped journalists, was charged with being a spy. In a recent interview, I asked him if journalists would be safer if the CIA renounced the use of reporters as agents. "Oh, absolutely," he said. "I protested against that policy and testified against it before a Senate committee. And you know what's particularly stupid about it? Just between you and me, the CIA can do any damn thing it wants to, but they don't have to announce to the world that this is their policy. They can lie. They're allowed to lie. By acknowledging that they do use journalistic cover and may in the future, they are simply confirming a suspicion that these mujahadin already hold. That's dangerous. They already assume that I'm a spy, or that any journalist is a spy, because in their own countries there is no tradition of journalistic independence. So they assume that's true everywhere. The only way the press can deal with this problem is to insist over and over again—and have the CIA confirm—that we don't do that. But the CIA is unwilling to play the game. They have done this for many years and they're just not willing to change."[24]

Philip Caputo, a former correspondent and hostage in Lebanon, sees limited benefit to a public renunciation of the CIA's policies with respect to recruitment of journalists. "When I was captured, they thought I was a spy, either for the Israelis or the CIA or both," he told me. "I can't count the number of times people over there said, 'Oh, you're a spy, you're in the CIA.' That's the standard excuse given for capturing journalists. A change in CIA policy would help only marginally, because the kidnappers come from cultures where there is no separation between the press and those in power. In their countries, the press is an arm of government, it is the arm of those in power, so for them it is a logical assumption that Western journalists are spies.

"I'm sure the insurgents looked at the recently abducted Italian journalist [Giuliana Sgrena] and said, the Italian government has sent soldiers over here and you're out asking questions, ergo, you're a spy for the enemy. I think that no matter how emphatically the CIA says, 'We do not do this, we will not do it,' it would not deter these people from capturing journalists and saying they are spies. It would possibly help in cases where governments, rather than insurgent groups, capture journalists, because then a case could be built against that government for a violation of international law, custom and practice. But against these unaffiliated groups, I don't think it would help whatever."[25]

Jerry Levin, former CNN correspondent and kidnap victim in Lebanon, recently told me that no CIA policy statement could help journalists at this point. "I don't think it would help because we've had too many instances in the past of journalists working on behalf of our government. There have been so many such examples that no matter what we say, our history speaks for itself. When we get into bitter conflict, there will always be that legitimate suspicion. The horse is out of the barn. I don't think anybody will ever know how many journalists were working for the CIA. I would make a wild guess that for every John Scali incident that became public, there probably were, and still are, many others doing the same. I can understand America's enemies being suspicious about that, because we're suspicious of any foreign journalist working here."[26]

Canadian war correspondent Scott Taylor was held hostage by mujahidin in Iraq, who accused him of being a spy. Taylor says a lot of journalists suspect each other of having intelligence links. "I always wonder who might be CIA, who isn't, who is an agent, who is not. It's one of those things where you don't necessarily have to be under contract. The agency will take reports from someone they know has been in an area that they can't get into. They'll glean information. I'll sure there are some that are being used deliberately, and that does endanger the rest of us. When I returned home after my ordeal, the Canadian government sent over an intelligence officer from the Foreign Affairs Ministry to interview me. I said, 'Look, I'll do the interview as a private citizen who has been held hostage, but not as a journalist per se. I made it very clear that anything I gave her was either going to be made public in my reports or was already public. I also stipulated that such information was for Canadian purposes only, and was not to be forwarded to the U.S. or the Brits. She was aghast that I would withhold such information."[27]

Death from Friendly Fire

The current hostility of the American and British military toward "unfriendly" media in Iraq derives directly from the aggressive NATO policy in the Balkans during the 1990s. Because of the censorship proclivities of the nineteen NATO countries who were officially involved in the war against Serbia, an increasing amount of American and European television footage, including disturbing images of civilian casualties from the American bombing of Belgrade, was coming from Serbian television studios. As a result, on April 8, 1999, NATO's military spokesperson, David Wilbey, announced, "Serb radio and TV is an instrument of propaganda and repression. It is therefore a legitimate target in this campaign. If [Yugoslav] President Milosevic would provide equal time for Western news broadcasts in its programmes without censorship three hours a day between noon and 1800 and three hours a day between 1800 and midnight, then his TV could become an acceptable instrument of public information."

The assembled journalists were dumbfounded. "Can we take it that that reply should be seen as either a threat or a promise that you will be bombing the television transmitters unless they allow three hours of Western television?" asked a BBC reporter.

"I think you can take it as a public statement, a public announcement," answered Wilbey.[28]

American planes immediately began intensive bombing of all media facilities in Serbia, destroying broadcast studios and killing numerous journalists in the process. The Serbian radio and television network, RTS, was hit particularly hard, and on April 23, 1999, an American attack on their studios in Belgrade killed at least eleven people.

Outraged news organizations around the world protested the bombing as a threat to all journalists, but NATO spokesperson Jamie Shea simply declared, "RTS is not media. It's full of government employees who are paid to produce propaganda and lies. . . . [T]herefore, we see that as a military target."[29]

Robert Leavitt, associate director of the Center for War, Peace, and the News Media, gave two reasons for opposing NATO's policy: "The first is that this is really a deliberate targeting of civilians, which is questionable in any circumstance. This is not a military target, no matter what NATO says. The second is that it really creates a dangerous precedent with respect to freedom of the press. Once we start defining journalists as legitimate targets, it becomes very hard for us to criticize any other attacks on media. . . . There are many governments around the world who are very happy now that NATO has said it's legitimate to target journalists. And they will be doing that in the future."[30]

Canadian journalist Scott Taylor, who had reported extensively on the Balkans before his ill-fated experience in Iraq, says events in Serbia and Kosovo were a prelude to the targeting of journalists in Iraq. "We saw this in Serbia when the U.S. bombing took the Serb media off the satellite in order to undermine popular support for the war effort. The decision to bomb the RTS studios in Belgrade and take them off the air is the point at which our media became a legitimate target. And that took us down a slippery slope."[31]

Indeed. As described earlier, insurgents in Iraq, Afghanistan, and elsewhere currently regard Western journalists as propagandists for their governments and therefore as legitimate targets. The irony, of course, is that Coalition armies in Iraq and Afghanistan regard many of these same journalists as propagandists for the insurgents. A double whammy!

Nik Gowing of BBC World TV has written extensively on the intrusive new technology available to war correspondents, and he concludes, "[T]he price is that we are seen potentially as spies by some at the military and government command levels."[32]

Tom Squitieri, foreign correspondent for *USA Today*, said that from a reporter's point of view one of the more chilling realities to emerge in Iraq recently was "the way the U.S. Special Forces and those guys in the field felt towards journalism. The attitude toward journalists . . . , letting the locals hold them at gunpoint, saying, 'Oh, don't worry, they won't kill you.' This sends a really bad signal to local militias. . . . The idea that journalists could be manhandled, . . . U.S. Special Forces doing this to reporters or other journalists—the local people see that, the local gunmen see that [and] they think it's OK."[33]

Scott Taylor, the Canadian journalist who was kidnapped and tortured in Iraq, told me, "Even as a western-looking reporter I've had more guns put to my head for trying to snap a picture of an American soldier than for filming insurgents. We've almost been killed as a result of their fear. If you're not embedded, they see you as potentially hostile. Anybody with a camera. We've had that problem on the main highway where you get stuck behind U.S. convoys because they block both lanes. They won't let anyone pass them because they are understandably afraid of car bombs. Well, one time we were just cooling our heels behind one of those convoys and I took the opportunity of snapping a photo of the guy in the Hummer who was aiming his weapon at us. Shortly thereafter the whole convoy ground to a halt and they came rushing at us. They had guns to my driver's temple and they were screaming at us to give them our camera, our press papers, etc. It was a very, very tense moment. I know that if anybody had sneezed at that moment, we would all have been killed, because they were so afraid they didn't know what was going on.

"These guys were all from a logistics unit that normally wouldn't be out doing convoys, and they didn't know what to do. You're an ex-soldier yourself Herb, you know what I'm talking about. Not everyone should be a front line soldier. They saw someone with a camera and they jumped on it, because they were afraid of being ambushed."[34]

Taylor said it was a different situation for the Reuters cameramen killed by U.S. forces. "They were local stringers who probably looked Arabic," he said, "and sometimes that's all it takes. If you're filming any aftermath of an attack, they get very antsy, very suspicious. Remember, you've got a lot of National Guardsmen over there who probably don't want to be there, and they're scared out of their minds. They're dealing with a culture they don't understand, and it becomes very polarizing, us against them."[35]

In November 2004, David Schlesinger of the Reuters news agency told a media conference that the United States was entirely "to blame" for the deaths of three of its employees in Iraq since the start of the war in March 2003. "All of them were killed by the American army," he declared.[36]

Two months earlier, Schlesinger had told a conference of overseas editors, "We've had two people killed by U.S. fire in Iraq. We've had three of our employees in Iraq arrested, detained and brutalized by U.S. soldiers. . . . We've had a number of deaths and a number of other unfortunate encounters with the U.S. military."[37]

When asked for details on the "brutalized" staff, Schlesinger explained:

In our case it was three Iraqi employees. I think one of the difficulties that I've had when I tried to engage the Pentagon on this issue is getting them to understand that for an organization like ours, nationality just doesn't matter. We have more than 100 nationalities among the 2,300 journalists in Reuters. So for me it doesn't matter whether the person is Iraqi or American or whatever. But for a U.S. troop or his commander, the fact that someone is not American or British somehow makes them suspicious, and I think this is a real issue for us. In this instance, three of our guys were in Fallujah when I think a helicopter went down. They were on the scene very, very quickly, which aroused suspicion. We like our people to get to places quickly. That's what journalists do. But the implication in the minds of the troops apparently was that because they were there quickly, they were somehow in the know, they were part of the bad guys. And they looked like bad guys, because they were Iraqis.

They were taken into detention, and, according to their statements, which were before any of the allegations of maltreatment in prisons [like Abu Ghraib] came out, some pretty bad things happened to them. They were forced to lick their shoes, forced to stick their fingers in their anus and then lick it, told they were to be raped, all sorts of really bad things. Now we've complained repeatedly, and basically we were turned away. We provided statements from our guys, but they were never re-interviewed by the military. The military said that the statements that we provided were not internally credible. Whether they are internally credible or not, I find it difficult to think that a proper investigation was done if they were not interviewed professionally. We have really not got much satisfaction on this, and in my mind, the fact that this happened before Abu Ghraib came out, the fact that our guys made their statements before any of this was in the press gives it at least enough credibility to be investigated thoroughly and independently.[38]

The abuse of the three Reuters employees—cameraman Salem Ureibi, freelance television journalist Ahmed Mohammad Hussein al-Badrani, and driver Sattar Jabbar al-Badrani—was described in a Reuters dispatch dated May 18, 2004. Two of the three Reuters employees said they had been forced to insert a finger into their anus and then lick it. They were also forced to put shoes in their mouths, something considered particularly humiliating in Arab culture. All three said they were forced to make demeaning gestures or assume demeaning positions as soldiers laughed, taunted them, and took photographs. The soldiers deprived them of sleep, placed bags over their heads, kicked and beat them, forced them to remain in stress positions for long periods, and threatened to send them to the U.S. detention center in Guantanamo, Cuba.

Cameraman Ureibi said the U.S. soldiers told him they were going to have sex with him, and he feared he would be raped. He drew a parallel between the abuse of the Reuters employees and that of the prisoners at Abu Ghraib. "When I saw the Abu Ghraib photographs, I wept," he said. "I saw they had suffered like we had."[39]

The victims told Reuters of their ordeal immediately after their release, but they decided to make it public only after two events: the insistence by the U.S. military that no abuse had occurred, and the shocking revelations of abuse of prisoners by the U.S. military at Abu Ghraib. The U.S. military, in a report issued before the Abu Ghraib abuses became public, claimed there was no evidence that the Reuters staff had been abused or tortured. A summary of an investigation dated January 28, 2004, said soldiers responsible for the detainees were interviewed under oath and "none admit or report knowledge of physical abuse or torture."[40]

Reuters was disappointed at the perfunctory nature of the military investigation, and on February 3, Schlesinger wrote to Lawrence Di Rita, special assistant to Defense Secretary Donald Rumsfeld, saying the investigation was "woefully inadequate" and should be reopened.

"The military's conclusion of its investigation without even interviewing the alleged victims, along with other inaccuracies and inconsistencies in the report, speaks volumes about the seriousness with which the U.S. government is taking this issue," he wrote.[41]

The Pentagon failed to respond to Schlesinger's request.

In June 2005, Aidan White, General Secretary for the International Federation of Journalists, expressed concern over the mounting casualties suffered by journalists in Iraq at the hands of both insurgents and Coalition forces. "Most of the 85 journalists and media staffers who have died have been killed by terrorists," he wrote. "But 14 have been killed by U.S. soldiers since the invasion in March 2003. None of these deaths has, to date, been satisfactorily explained by the U.S. military."[42]

White complained that the U.S. military often issues no explanatory report on such deaths, and when they do, the reports follow the same pattern: secrecy about the detail and nature of the report, selective examination of the evidence, insensitive "shrugs of regret," and exoneration of responsibility of U.S. personnel at all levels of command. "Perhaps most worrying," said White, "the absence of credible inquiry leads to speculation about the targeting of journalists by U.S. soldiers."

White dismissed the argument that the U.S. military targets journalists, but warned, "[U]nless U.S. authorities address concerns about the paltry response to media deaths, the anger and sense of injustice felt by many in journalism will remain."[43]

There have been numerous attacks on journalists by U.S. troops in Iraq, but official military accounts describe the casualties as unavoidable collateral damage, resulting from mistaken identities or journalists being caught in free fire zones. International press organizations find these explanations simplistic. The Moroccan National Press Union declared that U.S. troops had "knowingly targeted journalists" in order to "terrorize journalists." Reporters Without Borders demanded an investigation into the March 2003 killing of British ITV journalist Terry Lloyd by U.S. fire. Daniel Demoustier, a French cameraman injured in the same attack, accused U.S. troops of firing on their vehicles "to wipe out troublesome witnesses." He said American forces had continued to fire on the vehicles even after Lloyd had been killed."[44]

The American attack on the Italian journalist Giuliana Sgrena (see Chapter 2) after she had been released by her kidnappers in March 2005 became a particularly embarrassing international incident. Western news organizations continue to say they have no evidence that U.S. troops have targeted journalists, but they find the military accounts of the attacks to be perfunctory and contradictory. Jerry Levin, former CNN correspondent held hostage in Lebanon, says simply, "Forgive me if I don't rush to accept the official military versions in cases like the attack on the Italian journalist and so many others. Forgive me if I do not rush to acceptance. I was not born yesterday."[45]

Levin also points out the increasing number of mysterious deaths of what he calls "Iraqi fact-finders," people performing a journalist function outside of the traditional news organizations. "These very courageous fact-finders, working for international human rights organizations, are being bumped off in wholesale numbers," said Levin. "These guys are being assassinated too. And remember, their function is just as journalistic as those who are writing for news organizations, and their work is equally as dangerous, because they're trying to find the facts about the excesses of the occupation. So pay attention. In most cases, they're documenting the excesses of the occupation when they're being bumped off. By whom? Talk about unfriendly friendly fire."[46]

Terry Anderson, former AP correspondent and hostage in Lebanon, is concerned about the number of journalists killed by "friendly fire," but he places limited blame on the U.S. military for the killings of journalists. "I refuse to believe that American forces are deliberately shooting journalists," says Anderson, himself a former Marine. "I do believe that they are highly suspicious of any Arab media. I believe that they are told in their intelligence briefings that the insurgents are seeking information and that they will use local correspondents as spies. I also believe that when they go out into any sort of conflict or take direct fire, they go into full forward attack mode and they don't give a damn whom they kill. They simply open up. That's the way they react in Iraq. And that means that if there are any journalists out there with a camera trying to cover both sides, they're going to get shot. I do not believe that the U.S. military has a policy, or that the troops have a tendency, to shoot journalists.

"By the way, Israeli troops do often target Palestinian media quite deliberately. I don't know if it comes on orders from above, but they don't like 'em and they have on occasion quite deliberately shot journalists. I don't believe American troops have done that."[47]

I reminded Anderson that the Committee to Protect Journalists, on whose board he sits, has issued a report saying the killing of Arab journalists by U.S. forces was "avoidable but not deliberate."

Anderson responded, "Yes, it could have been avoided, but American troops are not going to take that into their calculations. It's a very dangerous place, and any time you go wandering into a live battlefield, you're putting your life on the line out there. Just because you're a journalist doesn't grant you immunity from the bullets and the shells."[48]

Military Attacks on Al-Jazeera

The pan-Arabic TV network al-Jazeera has been a thorn in the side of Coalition forces in both Afghanistan and Iraq. The fact that so many American attacks on Arab journalists have been shown on al-Jazeera while ignored on American television has caused journalists and the public at large to analyze the differences between the two kinds of coverage. In a speech in April 2005, Amy Goodman, author, journalist, and radio personality, shared an epigram commonly heard in the Middle East: "The U.S. media show where the American missiles take off. Al-Jazeera shows where the missiles land."[49]

The November 12, 2001, bombing of the Kabul, Afghanistan, offices of al-Jazeera by U.S. planes was widely interpreted as an expression of exasperation with the network's coverage of the American invasion of Afghanistan. In April 2002, Nik Gowing of BBC News presented his conclusions after months of investigation into the bombing. Gowing said the circumstances of the attack and the American motivation remained unresolved, with "outstanding ominous questions," such as, Why did the Americans bomb the bureau of a highly respected news organization? Why did the Americans hit the press building with two five-hundred-pound bombs?

Gowing notes the U.S. claim that there was "significant military activity" taking place inside the al-Jazeera building, but he questions how the activities of a news organization could reasonably be construed as significant military activity. "By that analysis," says Gowing, "our entire business of 'bearing witness' in conflict can be construed as 'significant military activity.' We record and transmit real-time information from a war zone that in many ways challenges and contradicts the official reported version of what is taking place. . . . [T]he Americans now say that they will hit any office or uplink facility that they consider to have some kind of potentially hostile military use. That could include a videophone from a front-line trench that is beaming up 'inconvenient' real-time details about fighting and targeting. . . . We could be hit in order to remove what warplane pilots have described to me as 'the threat of the media'. . . . Too many of the places from which our new technology can facilitate graphic reporting have become too dangerous, in particular due to the threat that our up-links will be bombed al-Jazeera-style because our reporting and electronic signatures can be construed as 'significant military activity.'"[50]

Just seventeen months later the U.S. Air Force showed al-Jazeera correspondents in Iraq that they were vulnerable as well. On April 2, 2003, al-Jazeera reporters in Basra had a close call when the Sheraton Hotel at which they stayed came under fire. Al-Jazeera TV reported that two shells landed in the hotel hallway, only one of which exploded. "Fortunately, however, our reporters were safe," said the TV announcer, who commented that the U.S. military had been advised that reporters were in the hotel. When al-Jazeera news director Ibrahim Hilal was asked if he suspected that the attacks were deliberate, he answered, "No, not so far, because if it is deliberate, it would be much worse."[51]

Then, on the morning of April 8, things became much worse for al-Jazeera—their Baghdad offices were bombed by U.S. planes. Al-Jazeera TV announced that its office, located near the Monsur Hotel not far from the Iraqi Information Ministry, "has been struck by American bombing, resulting in the martyrdom of Tarek Ayoub, al-Jazeera reporter in Baghdad."[52] Surviving al-Jazeera staff sought refuge in the nearby offices of rival satellite station Abu Dhabi TV, which then also came under U.S. attack. Abu Dhabi TV correspondent Shaker Hamed broadcast an emergency call for help, shouting into the microphone, "Twenty-five journalists and technicians belonging to Abu Dhabi television and . . . al-Jazeera are surrounded in the offices of Abu Dhabi TV in Baghdad." Hamed made an on-the-air appeal to the Red Cross, the International Organization of Journalists, Reporters Sans Frontieres, and the Arab Journalists Union "to intervene quickly to pull us out of this zone where missiles and shells are striking in an unbelievable way."[53]

Abu Dhabi television also announced that two more journalists were killed when a U.S. tank fired on the Palestine Hotel, headquarters for the international media in Baghdad. The U.S. military spokesperson in Baghdad extended condolences to the families of the dead journalists, adding, "We certainly know that we don't target journalists. That's just not something we do."[54]

Al-Jazeera correspondents were understandably skeptical. Indeed, the day before the attack, U.S. forces had fired on press vehicles for both Abu Dhabi TV and al-Jazeera. Concerned al-Jazeera correspondents immediately met with Michael Massing, media troubleshooter for the Committee to Protect Journalists, to express their concern that U.S. forces might attack their offices. Massing recalls, "On the night of April 7, I talked to them in my capacity [with CPJ]. . . , because they were worried about the security of their correspondents due to the number of incidents that had occurred, and sure enough, the next morning when I woke up, their office in Baghdad had been bombed and their correspondent there killed."[55]

Subsequently released details on the April 8 missile attacks do not unequivocally resolve the question of whether the attacks were deliberate. American planes, tanks, and ground troops were mopping up the scattered Iraqi resistance in Baghdad as journalists from around world watched and reported from their local offices or hotels. Prominent among the international press corps were correspondents from the three major Arab news networks: Abu Dhabi TV, al-Jazeera, and al-Arabiya. Abu Dhabi TV correspondent Amir al-Mounaiery joined several of his al-Jazeera colleagues on the roof of the building in which their offices were housed. From their rooftop perch, the military action could easily be observed and filmed.

When al-Mounaiery saw military activity about three hundred meters away he told his engineer and cameraman to switch to live broadcast. He recalls, "We saw aircraft coming in, buzzing. They were flying so close that if I wrote my name on my hand they could read it."[56]

When the American forces began firing at a nearby building, the Planning Ministry, the journalists on the hotel roof began to sense something was wrong. "Then I saw three aircraft maneuvering," recalls al-Mounaiery. "[W]e have a huge sign on the roof saying this is Abu Dhabi TV. They can see it from above." Al-Mounaiery saw one of the planes directly above him. He didn't realize that there was another one approaching from behind. "Suddenly, I heard the buzz of a rocket," he says. "I got down and then I saw the rocket hitting the wall in front of me. . . . If I hadn't gone down, the rocket would have hit me."[57]

The rocket exploded and sent shrapnel flying around. One piece hit Tareq Ayoub, an al-Jazeera cameraman. "It went straight to his heart," says al-Mounaiery. "He was an excellent man. I carried his body to the car below."[58]

Al-Mounaiery could not understand why the clearly marked building was hit. "There was noone [sic] with a weapon in our building," he said. "[T]he U.S. military snipers with their telescopes can see us clearly. We look like civilians."[59]

BBC reporter Rageh Omaar, who observed the bombing from a nearby hotel, said, "We were watching and filming the bombardment and it's quite clearly a direct strike on the al-Jazeera office. This was not just a stray round. It just seemed too specific." Al-Jazeera's Amman correspondent, Yasser Abu Hilalah, insisted that the attack was deliberate. "Al-Jazeera's office is located in a residential area and there's no way that the attack was a mistake," he said.[60]

For many Americans, the first real awareness of these new, devastating attacks on al-Jazeera came with the viewing of the award-winning documentary film, *Control Room*. In that film, Samir Khader, senior producer for al-Jazeera, recalled the bombing of their offices in Baghdad on April 8, 2003, and the death of correspondent Tarek Ayyoub. Khader said that shortly before 7 a.m. he was on the phone with one of his correspondents in Baghdad who described "a plane turning over us, and now it's coming towards us . . . , nose down, which means formation of attack, and the American plane came and launched the missiles against our office. And the explosion killed Tarek Ayyoub."

Even before the correspondent's death had been announced, Ayyoub's wife called al-Jazeera's office, saying "My heart tells me it's Tarek and something happened to him." Later, during an emotional impromptu press conference called by al-Jazeera, Ayyoub's wife addressed the assembled foreign journalists by speakerphone, telling them, "Please, my husband died trying to reveal the truth to the world. Please do not conceal it for any conditions. Not for the public opinion, not for the American policy, not for the British policy. Please be honest only for this time, for the sake of all those people who died. Innocent people, not military, not militia, not people in the army. Please tell the truth only this once. Thank you very much."[61]

In the film *Control Room*, Samir Khader is distraught over the death. "What can you say to her," he mumbles. "It was a hell of a morning. Everybody was crying. . . . You could see their tears flowing. . . . Except me. I managed to stay firm and not to cry, because it's too easy. For me, this was a crime that should be avenged, or at least investigated."[62]

A subsequent briefing by the U.S. military shed little light on the tragic incident. CNN's Tom Mintier recalled how two hundred correspondents awaited the military's explanation for the three shocking incidents: the missile strike against al-Jazeera's offices, followed by the strike against Abu Dhabi television, followed by the shelling of the Palestine Hotel. Mintier says that the many questions from reporters received basically the same answers from the military: that the battlefield is a dangerous place and that the only nearly safe position is with the embedded reporters with Coalition troops. Mintier recalled that when journalists asked how they could "surrender" to U.S. troops, perhaps by hanging white sheets out of their hotel windows, the military spokesman said basically that "you shouldn't be in this location."[63]

When the military press officer in Baghdad asked Mintier how the other journalists responded to the bombing of al-Jazeera, Mintier told him, "When you talk about killing three journalists in three separate strikes, journalists tend to stick together, just like soldiers stick together." Today, Mintier still wonders why Abu Dhabi TV and al-Jazeera were targeted. "Were they taking fire? I didn't get my question answered [by the U.S. military]." Shortly thereafter, the U.S. military did release a statement saying, "According to commanders on the ground, Coalition forces came under significant enemy fire from the building where al-Jazeera journalists were working, and consistent with the inherent right of self-defense, Coalition forces returned fire. Sadly, an al-Jazeera correspondent was killed in the exchange."[64]

Samir Khader found the American account unconvincing. "How come it got hit so direct," he wondered. "Everybody knows where we are. This is now twice [that] it happened to us, in Afghanistan and now in Baghdad, which makes me question it."[65]

Mohammed Jasem, general manager of al-Jazeera, was similarly perplexed. He said that after the American military had confirmed their knowledge of al-Jazeera's location, he advised all of his correspondents that the office was the safest place in Baghdad. "I was shocked when I heard the first bombs, after these confirmations from the American side," he said.[66] "We gave our locations in Mosul, Baghdad and Basra to the authorities in Washington and the Pentagon. We sent official letters to give our coordinates. They know the locations of our offices in Mosul, Baghdad and Basra."[67]

Nonetheless, Khader seemed resigned to al-Jazeera's vulnerability. "This objective of sending these missiles on the offices of al-Jazeera is to tell al-Jazeera, 'You're not siding 100 percent with us against Saddam Hussein, so we are going to punish you.' We are sending these missiles to kill people, OK? We have received the message. . . . We acknowledge the receipt of this message. . . . We cannot compete with the United States of America. We are a tiny channel in a tiny country. What can we do? We just shut up, and try to go on and do our job."[68]

Hassan Ibrahim, an al-Jazeera correspondent, concluded, "I think . . . they now want this war to be done without any witnesses. . . . If it [al-Jazeera] was intentionally targeted, it's a real disaster for journalism. It's a real disaster for al-Jazeera. We don't want to be more involved in this war. We just want to cover it."[69] In response to the continuing threat of U.S. attacks on its offices, al-Jazeera pulled its correspondents out of Iraq. Mohammed Burini, al-Jazeera's Mosul correspondent, later described the circumstances of his departure: "I was in Baghdad first, and then I went to Mosul. People were very nice [there], but after [the U.S.] hitting our office in Baghdad, everybody was scared and they just didn't want to receive us, because they said, 'You are targeted, so if you start your machines here, the American airplanes will target you.' This is shame! This is shame! We are media. We are not supposed to be targeted."[70]

Al-Jazeera would later reopen its offices in Baghdad, hoping that the end of formal hostilities in Iraq would make Coalition forces less trigger-happy. But the provisional Iraqi authorities promptly shut down al-Jazeera's offices, charging that its broadcasts incited violence. The interim prime minister, Ayad Alawi, defended the shut down, saying "Al-Jazeera is helping the terrorists."[71]

This characterization of al-Jazeera, though rejected by Arab public opinion, is frequently acted upon by the intelligence agencies of American allies in the Middle East. An example of such interagency cooperation was seen in the arrest and detention of al-Jazeera cameraman Sami Muhyideen al-Haj by Pakistani authorities along the Afghan border in December 2001. According to the al-Jazeera reporter who was on assignment with al-Haj at the border, al-Haj was arrested by order of Pakistani intelligence. He was then taken to a U.S. detention camp in Afghanistan, classified as an "enemy combatant," and subsequently transferred to Camp X-ray in Guantanamo Bay, Cuba, where he remains to this day.

Al-Haj's London-based lawyer, Clive Smith, says, "There is very little against him in terms of the official allegations. They are mostly trying to get Sami to become an informant against al-Jazeera."[72]

In September 2002, the Committee to Protect Journalists (CPJ) wrote to Secretary of Defense Donald Rumsfeld, calling on the Pentagon to reveal the basis for al-Haj's detention. CPJ received no response. In an October 2005 press release CPJ protested al-Haj's continued detention and "attempts by the U.S. military to recruit a detained journalist as a spy." CPJ said, "U.S. military interrogators allegedly told [al-Haj] that he would be released if he agreed to inform U.S. intelligence authorities about the satellite news network's activities."[73]

CPJ's Executive Director Ann Cooper said the most disturbing aspect of the case was "the U.S. military's long-term detention of Sami al-Haj without putting forward evidence that he has committed a crime. The implication here is that the military can detain a journalist in the field . . . and hold him for months or years without due process or establishing a legal basis for his incarceration. The United States should credibly explain the basis for Sami al-Haj's detention or release him immediately."[74]

Such questionable detention of an individual al-Jazeera employee is not evidence that U.S. forces have *targeted* al-Jazeera, but that charge gained a degree of credibility in November 2005, when a Top Secret British document suggesting American plans to bomb al-Jazeera's headquarters was leaked to the *London Daily Mirror.* The document, a five-page transcript of an April 2004 conversation between President Bush and British Prime Minister Tony Blair, reveals Bush advocating an attack on al-Jazeera's headquarters in Doha, Qatar, as Blair attempts to dissuade him.

An unnamed source told the *Mirror,* "The memo is explosive and hugely damaging to Bush. He made clear he wanted to bomb al-Jazeera in Qatar and elsewhere. Blair replied that would cause a big problem. There's no doubt what Bush wanted to do—and no doubt Blair didn't want him to do it."[75]

One government source claimed that President Bush's threat was "humorous, not serious," but another said, "Bush was deadly serious, as was Blair. That much is absolutely clear from the language used by both men."[76]

The *Mirror* story concluded that the leaked memo "casts fresh doubts on claims that other attacks on al-Jazeera were accidents."[77]

The leak of the Top Secret document occurred when civil servant David Keough gave the memo to a researcher in the office of British MP Tony Clarke. Accused of "a damaging disclosure," Keough was threatened with prosecution under Britain's Official Secrets Act. Blair's office would not comment on the memo itself, saying it never comments on leaked documents. The Bush White

House said it would not dignify the *Mirror* report with a response. Meanwhile, al-Jazeera issued a statement saying it was investigating the report which, if accurate, "would be both shocking and worrisome not only to al-Jazeera but to media organizations the world over" and would "cast serious doubts" on American explanations of earlier attacks on al-Jazeera.[78]

The British government's response to the *Mirror*'s revelations was not to explain or rebut them, but to suppress them. Attorney General Lord Goldsmith threatened to prosecute the *Mirror* if it published further details on the leaked memo, and the *Mirror* admitted, "We have essentially agreed to comply."[79] The *Mirror* and two other British newspapers—the *Times* and the *Guardian*—said the government's highest legal advisor had warned them that they would be prosecuted under the Official Secrets Act if they pursued the story. The *Guardian* described the threat as "a legal gag."

Peter Kilfoyle, a former defense minister in Blair's government, was among the first to demand that the secret document be released to the public. "If it was the case that President Bush wanted to bomb al-Jazeera in what is after all a friendly country, it speaks volumes and it raises questions about subsequent attacks that took place on the press that wasn't embedded with coalition forces."[80]

Kilfoyle said past U.S. attacks on press organizations lent credibility to the *Mirror* report. "There was an attack on the hotel in Baghdad used by al-Jazeera journalists, which caused great controversy," he said. "The U.S. also attacked a Serbian TV station [during the Kosovo War]. It is easy to dismiss this as a glib comment, but I don't find it very funny at all."[81]

It should be noted that, even if the leaked British document is eventually acknowledged by the Blair government, it would not confirm that American forces deliberately attacked al-Jazeera in 2002 and 2003. After all, the gist of the memo is that Blair *dissuaded* Bush from taking military action against the news network in 2004. Thus, the memo may suggest hostile American intentions toward al-Jazeera—a matter of common knowledge—but it is not evidence that those intentions were carried out.

I recently asked award-winning author and investigative reporter Seymour Hersh whether he thought the American military in Iraq was targeting unfriendly journalists. "Nobody wants journalists around," he answered. "They never do. . . . It's very hard to prove there's deliberate shooting of journalists, but there's always been antagonism toward journalists in a war zone. If the military does something terrible and there's a journalist around, that journalist has a problem. But it's not clear that they're targeted in a categorical way. Certainly the insurgents target journalists in Iraq, and there's a lot of reason to believe sometimes American forces will target journalists, but it's not proven. Remember, we destroyed the offices of al-Jazeera, and there's a lot of reason to think that it was deliberate. I find it hard to believe it wasn't, but there's no evidence."[82]

Hersh later told me, "We need a lot more reporting on the al-Jazeera story. I would just offer this thought: You don't have to use kinetic means, by which I mean a bomb, to destroy al-Jazeera. Our government has an enormous capability, classified capability, to keep the press from getting things done, from going on the air. I don't think we know everything there is to know about the hostility of the [Bush] administration toward al-Jazeera. . . . I would not want to be a journalist in Iraq, because the belief seems to be pretty widespread among the American military that if you're a journalist and you speak Arabic and you're a Muslim, then you're working with the insurgency. There's no question that Muslim and Arabic-speaking journalists, journalists for the Arab networks, are under tremendous duress."[83]

Attack on the Palestine Hotel

Just before noon on April 8, 2003, a U.S. tank fired a shell into Baghdad's Palestine Hotel, which housed over one hundred international journalists. The blast hit a fifteenth floor balcony of the hotel, killing Reuters cameraman Taras Protsyuk and Spanish cameraman Jose Couso of Telecinco, and wounding three other journalists. The attack, which came just a few hours after an American air attack destroyed al-Jazeera's Baghdad office, damaged the fourteenth to seventeenth floors of the hotel, including the Reuters and al-Arabiya offices. The tank shell knocked a hole in the hotel facade, blew out windows, and shook the entire building, sending reporters and media workers scurrying outside in fear. Journalists carried colleagues out on blood-stained sheets. Others were driven to hospitals.

American military spokesmen claimed that the tank was firing at snipers within the hotel. U.S. Brigadier General Vincent Brooks, spokesman for Central Command, initially said, "Reports indicate the coalition force operating near the hotel took fire from the lobby of the hotel and returned fire." When asked why the tank would have fired on the fifteenth floor of the hotel if the fire came from the lobby, Brooks replied, "I may have misspoken on exactly where the fire came from." He then declared, "This coalition does not target journalists so anything that has happened . . . would always be considered as an accident."[84]

The BBC's Paul Wood said, "We didn't hear or see any outgoing fire whatsoever. . . . We can't say for certain, but we're not aware of this hotel being used by the Iraqis to target the Americans."[85]

Swiss television correspondent Ulrich Tiger said in a report from the hotel, "In all the three weeks I have worked from this hotel I have not heard a single shot fired from here and I have not seen a single armed person enter the hotel."[86]

Sky News correspondent David Chater said he had seen the tank parked on a bridge with its barrel pointed directly at the press building. "They knew we were there . . . there was absolutely no mistake," said Chater. "I never heard a single shot coming from any of the area around here, certainly not from the hotel. That tank shell . . . was aimed directly at this hotel and directly at journalists."[87]

France 3 TV footage showed the U.S. tank slowly moving its turret toward the hotel and waiting two minutes before firing. Photojournalist Herve de Ploeg said he heard no shots directed toward the tank. "There was no shooting at all," he said. "Then I saw the turret turning in our direction. . . . It was not a case of instinctive firing."[88]

The video footage of the attack on the Palestine Hotel has been seen and analyzed by numerous journalists. In his award-winning documentary film *Weapons of Mass Deception,* Danny Schechter narrates the video: "Look at this! An American tank on the bridge across from the Palestine Hotel. . . . Listen carefully. There are no sounds. . . . No one firing at U.S. soldiers. Suddenly, without provocation . . ."[89]

Schechter, a former CNN and ABC News journalist, interviewed one of the victims of the Palestine Hotel attack, Reuters reporter Samia Nakhoul, who said she and the other Reuters staff moved to the Palestine Hotel on the advice of the Pentagon. Reuters and the other news organizations notified the Pentagon immediately upon completion of the move. "Why would they target us?" asked Nakhoul. "What have we done to them?"

When asked to describe her personal injuries, Nakhoul answered in matter-of-fact tones: "I was hit in the brain. I had a brain operation and it took me a long time to recover. . . . It was emotional damage and physical damage. Emotional also because I lost a colleague."[90]

Reuters Editor-in-Chief Geert Linnebank said, "The incident raises questions about the judgement of the advancing U.S. troops, who have known all along that this hotel is the main base for almost all foreign journalists in Baghdad."[91]

Michael Massing, award-winning author and media troubleshooter for the Committee to Protect Journalists (CPJ), said none of the journalists at the Palestine Hotel saw any evidence that U.S. troops had been fired on from the hotel, and he called for a full investigation of the incident. He said, "While it was a black eye for the military, certain sectors of the military probably don't care. . . . It's possible that if we keep at it long enough, they will adopt procedures to try to prevent something like this from happening again." Massing said that the CPJ would like to see the U.S. military agree that identifiable sites housing international journalists "be regarded as sensitive sites, similar to schools, hospitals, and religious sites, which the U.S. does regard as special cases that are to be avoided."[92]

Al-Jazeera correspondent Hassan Ibrahim was enraged as he watched TV reports of the attacks on the hotel. "The Palestine Hotel, where all the journalists are staying," he mumbled. "There were 300 reporters in that hotel. The International Union of Journalists is considering it a war crime."[93]

There have been several investigations into the Palestine Hotel killings. The first was a secret internal report prepared by the Coalition Forces Land Component Command just three days after the attack on the hotel. A revised version, also secret, was issued the following month. Both reports were eventually acquired through a Freedom of Information Act request by the press organization Reporters Without Borders, but the contents provided little more than a whitewash of the military action, concluding that no fault or negligence could be attributed to the U.S. Army and that the attack was a proportionate and justifiable response to what was believed to be an enemy firing platform and observation post.

The most extensive investigation of the Palestine Hotel attack was issued by the Committee to Protect Journalists on May 27, 2003. Relying on interviews with about a dozen reporters who were at the scene, including journalists embedded with the military, the CPJ report suggested that the attack on journalists at the hotel was avoidable, but not deliberate. Chris Tomlinson, an AP reporter embedded with a U.S. infantry division, told CPJ that the U.S. tank fired a heat round, an incendiary shell intended to kill people and not destroy buildings. He said that after the round was fired, the commanding officer, Lieutenant Colonel Philip DeCamp, began screaming over the radio, "Did you just f**king shoot the Palestinian [sic] Hotel? . . . . You're not supposed to fire on the hotel."[94]

Photographs commissioned by CPJ and taken at the bridge where the tank fired show that the seventeen-story Palestine Hotel was distinct against the Baghdad skyline, towering over the other buildings. A large sign in English reading "Palestine Hotel" was clearly discernible. Patrick Baz, an AP reporter who covered the battle from his balcony in the Palestine Hotel described the attack, "I was taking pictures the whole morning. We were watching everything, and they could see us. From the first day . . . they could see us the same way we could see them."[95]

The tank shell hit the fifteenth-floor balcony of the suite used by Reuters, killing Taras Protsyuk, a Ukrainian-born Reuters cameraman who had set up his camera on the balcony. Jerome DeLay, an AP photographer, told CPJ, "Taras was lying on the floor on his back, unconscious. . . . We forced open his jaws to get some air into him."[96] Protsyuk was taken to a Baghdad hospital but died on arrival. Paul Pasquale, a Reuters satellite dish technician, was injured, along with two other Reuters journalists. Debris from the explosion crashed through to the floor below, mortally wounding Spanish cameraman Jose Cuoso, who had been filming there.

In the CPJ report, journalists who were eyewitnesses to the incident flatly denied the Centcom claim that the tank was returning fire from the hotel. AFP reporter Sammy Ketz, who was on a fifteenth floor balcony during the attack, said, "I think that's quite impossible because on each floor and each room . . . even on the roof, there were journalists and photographers and they were looking at what was going on." Ann Garrels, an NPR correspondent and member of the CPJ board, said, "All of us were on our balconies watching the battle. We would have seen snipers in the building."[97]

In an April 8, 2003, letter to Secretary of State Donald H. Rumsfeld, CPJ said that "[w]hile sources in Baghdad have expressed deep skepticism about reports that U.S. forces were fired upon from the Palestine Hotel, even if that were the case, the evidence suggests that the response of U.S. forces was disproportionate and therefore violated international humanitarian law."[98]

Later, the army seemed to change its story. Captain Philip Wolford, commander of the tank unit that fired on the hotel, said that he had given the order to fire after one of his gunners noticed someone at the hotel observing his unit with binoculars. Dozens of reporters had been observing the battle with binoculars.

Based on the information obtained in its investigation, CPJ called upon the Pentagon to conduct a full and public investigation into the shelling of the Palestine Hotel, "not only to determine the causes of this incident, but to ensure that similar episodes do not occur in the future."[99]

Meanwhile, the family of slain Spanish cameraman Jose Couso has taken matters into their own hands, initiating legal action in Spanish courts. Under Spanish law, a crime committed against a Spaniard abroad can be prosecuted in Spain if it is not investigated in the country where it was committed. On this basis, a Spanish judge, Santiago Pedraz, issued arrest warrants on October 19, 2005, against the three U.S. military personnel directly involved in the attack on the Palestine Hotel: Lt. Col. Philip de Camp, Captain Philip Wolford, and Sgt. Shawn Gibson, all of whom were to be extradited to Spain. If the soldiers are brought to trial there, they face jail sentences of up to 20 years for murder and "crimes against the international community."[100]

After the judge issued the arrest warrants, Javier Couso, brother of the slain journalist, held a press conference at which he declared: "What we are going to urge the U.S. government to do is to begin the process for the extradition as soon as possible. This is a crime against the international community and a crime of war."[101]

Incidents, Investigations, and Recriminations

The investigations into the Palestine Hotel attack have had little effect on the tense relationship between the U.S. military and foreign correspondents in Iraq. Dangerous incidents have continued, with no end in sight. On March 18, 2004, al-Arabiya cameraman Ali Abdel Aziz and reporter Ali al-Khatib were shot by U.S. troops near a military checkpoint in Baghdad. The two journalists were covering the aftermath of a rocket attack on the Burj-al-Hayat Hotel and had parked about 150 yards away from the checkpoint. They approached the soldiers on foot, spoke to them for a while, and prepared to depart. As they drove away, they were struck by gunfire from the troops. Abdel Aziz died instantly of wounds to the head, and al-Khatib died in a hospital the next day, also from head wounds.

Like al-Jazeera, al-Arabiya had been publicly accused by occupation officials of encouraging—and even collaborating with—resistance to the occupation. As a result, Arab correspondents were generally cautious in dealing with the U.S. military. Prior to the al-Arabiya shootings, reporter Ali Khatib had spoken with U.S. troops for about ten minutes, requesting permission to film the hotel that had suffered the rocket attack. After permission was denied, the two journalists drove away. Their driver recalls hearing shooting after driving about fifty yards. "I don't believe they're attacking me until I find my friend's head on my shoulder." he said. Khatib, who was in the front passenger seat, slumped over with a bullet in his brain. He died the following morning. Abdel-Aziz, who was in the back seat with his camera, died immediately from a bullet in the back of the head.

"What happened yesterday, it's a homicide," said the driver. "It was not a random shooting."[102]

The day after the shootings, Iraqi journalists staged a high-profile protest when Secretary of State Colin Powell visited Baghdad to celebrate the first anniversary of the war. As Powell and occupation administrator Paul Bremer strode into the briefing room for a news conference, Iraqi journalists, joined by international reporters, stood and called for a moment of silence for the slain al-Arabiya journalists. After demanding greater security for journalists and "a full and open investigation into the murders," more than two dozen Arab journalists walked out of the conference.

Najem Rubaie, an editor at the Iraqi daily al-Distoor, read a statement signed by fifty Iraqi journalists saying that the United States had failed to create a secure environment in Iraq after a year of occupation. Rubaie said the Iraqi journalists demanded "an open investigation, before all the media, of the entity that committed this murder of journalists."[103]

Secretary of State Powell then told the remaining journalists that he regretted the deaths, but was "confident it wasn't deliberate."[104]

A subsequent military investigation concluded that the al-Arabiya car, a Kia, was between 55 and 164 yards behind a white Volvo—the actual target of the U.S. troops—when the firing began. "Due to the location of the Kia, and the range and orientation of the weapons used to stop the Volvo, it is likely that the Kia was unintentionally struck by four to six rounds aimed at the Volvo," said the military report.[105]

An al-Arabiya spokesperson expressed appreciation to the U.S. military for its investigation but said it contradicted the eye-witness accounts provided by journalists at the scene. Al-Arabiya's news director, Salah Negm, questioned how the U.S. fire could have been so far off the mark, given the distance—up to one and a half football fields—between the Kia and the Volvo. "This is a long distance, in fact, to miss a car."[106]

Fatalities of Arab journalists at the hands of U.S. troops in Iraq continued to mount. On March 26, 2004, Burhan Mohamed Mazhour, a freelance Iraqi cameraman working for the American television network ABC, was killed in the city of Fallujah. Agence France-Presse reported that Mazhour was standing among a group of working journalists when "U.S. troops fired in their direction."[107] On April 19, 2004, Asaad Kadhim, a correspondent for the U.S.-funded al-Iraqiya TV, and his driver, Hussein Saleh, were killed by U.S. forces near a checkpoint close to the Iraqi city of Samara. On November 1, 2004, Dhia Najim, an Iraqi freelance cameraman on assignment for Reuters, was shot and killed by U.S. troops in the city of Ramadi while covering a gun battle between the U.S. military and Iraqi insurgents. "Video shot from an upper floor of a building nearby shows Najim, at first half-hidden by a wall, move into the open," Reuters reported. "As soon as he emerges, a powerful gunshot cracks out and he falls to the ground, his arms outstretched. Civilians are seen gathering calmly at the scene immediately afterwards to look at his lifeless body."[108]

Because many of the journalists involved in these deadly incidents have been television correspondents, video footage of their deaths has often been available, though seldom seem in the United States. A typical example was the September 2004 attack on an al-Arabiya journalist, Mazin Tumaisi, who was filming a crowd of civilians near a burning U.S. Army vehicle in Baghdad. Tumaisi was working with his video crew in the center of Baghdad when they were attacked. The film footage that survived shows the young reporter speaking into the camera: "The Americans promised beautiful dreams, but the reality is different. The streets of Iraq have been transformed into a war zone." Tumaisi stops, motions to the cameraman and says, "Can we do this again?"[109]

Suddenly, U.S. helicopters swooped down and fired two missiles at the TV crew. The bouncing camera is still running, capturing Tumaisi being hit by fire and showing a blood-spattered lens. The camera catches Tumaisi's last words, "I'm dying, I'm dying."[110]

The U.S. military announced that two helicopters had been sent to the crowded area where the al-Arabiya crew was filming "to prevent looting and harm to the Iraqi people." But Reuters cameraman Seif Fuad, who was seriously injured in the attack, said the helicopters showed no interest in crowd control. They went right for the camera. "I looked at the sky and saw a helicopter at very low altitude," said Fuad. "Just moments later I saw a flash of light from the Apache. Then a strong explosion. Mazin's blood was on my camera and face."[111]

Fuwad, who works for Reuters, says, "We were colleagues and friends for a few years. Our friendship got deeper, and it's not simple to forget. . . . Every day when I wake up, I hope nothing bad will happen. But I also wish to work, and my work is to film bombings."[112]

Fuwad's boss, Jalid Romani, worries about sending his people out on dangerous assignments. "I don't want to feel guilty [that] one day I sent this cameraman to do this and to lose him," he says. "They know I'm saying to them, 'Please be careful' . . . I don't want . . . to lose him even for one picture or for a big exclusive."[113]

At the al-Arabiya offices in Baghdad, employees wept as they watched the video footage of their colleague being killed. A picture of Tumaisi was posted on the doors of the offices with an inscription, "Martyr Mazin Tumaisi, who was killed by the American forces on September 12th 2004." Laith Ahmed, operations manager at al-Arabiya, said Tumaisi had called the office to report that he was filming the destroyed U.S. Army vehicle. Five minutes later he called back and shouted, "Help me. Send someone right away. I am injured in my leg and head. Please help. Please help me quickly."[114]

Ahmed wept as he recalled, "I couldn't help him." He called the U.S. attack "a big scandal" and asked, "What excuse they have? The tank was destroyed, why should they hit it again?"[115]

Aside from the investigations of the Palestine Hotel incident, attacks by Coalition Forces against journalists have not been scrutinized by the military or by press organizations. Some have suggested that this is because the other attacks killed Arab journalists rather than "Western" correspondents, but regardless of the nationality of the victims, one would have expected press fatalities from friendly fire to be treated as a hot story in the mainstream media. Instead, there has been an uncomfortable silence in the press. Even the full-scale investigations of the Palestine Hotel attack received scant mention by the American media, leaving the issue dormant until a recent bureaucratic controversy at CNN opened the door to public debate. As we shall see, that door was closed before the light of day could be shed on the issue.

The one thing all journalists agree on is that American forces could do more to prevent the deaths of journalists from "friendly fire." Indeed, most journalists agree that lumping press casualties at the hands of U.S. forces under the category of "collateral damage" shows a misunderstanding of the new face of war and journalism. Collateral damage is a phrase used in past wars to characterize unavoidable casualties to noncombatants who happened to be near a military target. But war correspondents in Iraq and Afghanistan have not been protected, even when they prominently identify themselves and their locations to military commanders.

Correspondents, editors, and news executives are at once concerned and infuriated by this new vulnerability, but their CEOs in the media corporations seem more concerned with profits and politics. Few newspapers and none of the TV networks were acknowledging the growing complaints from journalists over the deaths of their colleagues at the hands of U.S. and Coalition troops. The sensitivity of this debate within the press corps was seen recently in the highly publicized forced resignation of CNN's chief news executive, Eason Jordan, who made an off-the-record comment at a conference in Switzerland about the targeting of journalists by U.S. troops. Although he immediately modified his original statement by insisting that he never meant to imply that U.S. troops were deliberately attacking journalists, Jordan's comments were soon paraphrased by Internet bloggers who, for the most part, pilloried him for his lack of respect for the U.S. military.

Jordan resigned on February 11, 2005. In a letter to colleagues posted on CNN's Web site, Jordan stated, "After 23 years at CNN, I have decided to resign in an effort to prevent CNN from being unfairly tarnished by the controversy over conflicting accounts of my recent remarks regarding the alarming number of journalists killed in Iraq. . . . While my CNN colleagues and my friends in the U.S. military know me well enough to know I have never stated, believed, or suspected that U.S. military forces intended to kill people they knew to be journalists, my comments on this subject . . . were not as clear as they should have been."[116]

The controversy became a front-page story in the mainstream media, causing blogger Jay Rosen to remark on the irony of a situation in which, for example, the *Los Angeles Times* was "reporting on Eason Jordan's resignation over a controversy that it had never told its readers about in the first place."[117] As the

Jordan controversy became big news, the question of U.S. targeting of journalists in Iraq remained somehow invisible.

David Gergen, Harvard professor and prominent journalist, was the moderator at the conference in Switzerland, where Eason Jordan made his controversial comments. He says that Jordan had just returned from his sixteenth visit to Iraq and "was very tightly wound because he was deeply concerned about the safety of CNN journalists in Baghdad. . . . CNN had lost three journalists over time there in Iraq. . . . So this is a man who cares—was under great stress and was very deeply concerned about safety of journalists on all sides."[118]

Congressman Barney Frank (D-MA), who was present at the conference, said "it sounded like he [Jordan] was saying it was official military policy to take out journalists." Frank told Jordan that the journalists' deaths had simply been collateral damage, and this clearly disturbed Jordan. Jordan said, "I was trying to make a distinction between 'collateral damage' and people who got killed in other ways."[119]

Gergen recalls, "He [Jordan] really just exploded, saying, 'Look, this is not all collateral damage there'. . . . And he left a very clear impression that journalists on both sides were being targeted, that Iraqi insurgents were targeting American journalists and in a limited number of cases . . . he left the impression that there had been targeting by American troops of journalists, perhaps al-Jazeera and others."[120]

Gergen says Jordan quickly realized that he had gone too far and immediately began to walk his conversation back. According to Gergen, Jordan said there was no official U.S. policy to target journalists, but he was concerned that troops may have been careless and that the Pentagon could push harder to protect journalists. In assessing the aftermath of Jordan's comments, Gergen said, "I think the punishment far exceeds the offense."[121]

BBC World Services Director, Richard Sambrook, another conference attendee, recalls that Jordan clarified his comments to say "he did not believe they were targeted as journalists. . . . They had been deliberately killed as individuals, perhaps because they had been mistaken for insurgents, we don't know. However, the distinction he was seeking to make is that being shot by a sniper, or fired at directly is very different from being, for example, accidentally killed by an explosion."[122] The media pilloried Jordan for the ambiguity of his off-the-record remarks but overlooked the brutally candid comments of Linda Foley, national president of the Newspaper Guild, at a conference just a few months later. On May 13, 2005, Foley told the National Conference on Media Reform that the U.S. military targets journalists, "not just U.S. journalists. . . . They target and kill journalists from other countries, at news services like al-Jazeera, for example. They actually target them and blow up their studios with impunity."123

In a column titled "Stories Not Told," in *U.S. News and World Report*, John Leo wrote: "Foley's comment was almost universally ignored by the news media. . . . [A] Nexis database search last week failed to turn up a straight news report on Foley's remark anywhere in America since Foley spoke on the panel."124

In the wake of the flak over Jordan's problems, the CPJ expressed dismay that the fundamental issue, safety for journalists, was being ignored: "Lost in all of the fulminating over Jordan's comments has been an honest look at the U.S. military's record on journalist safety in Iraq, something that should concern all journalists whether they are pundits, wire service reporters, or partisan bloggers. There is no evidence to conclude that the U.S. military has deliberately targeted the press in Iraq, but the record does show that U.S. forces do not take adequate precautions to ensure that journalists can work safely. And when journalists are killed, the military often seems indifferent and unwilling to launch an adequate investigation or take steps to mitigate risks."125

Chapter 5

Protecting Journalists at a Cost to Newsgathering

Caution Is the Watchword

Daniel Pearl, the *Wall Street Journal* correspondent who was kidnapped and murdered in Pakistan in 2002 (see Chapter 3), was a cautious man who carefully considered the risks of reporting in a "hot" zone. In 1999, Bill Spindle, news editor for the *Journal*, sent Pearl a memo suggesting that he apply for a visa for Afghanistan to cover the simmering civil war there. Pearl responded quickly: "I would refuse to go to Afghanistan, and I'd do so partly on the basis that I sent [John] Bussey [Deputy Managing Editor, *Wall Street Journal*] a detailed memo on reporter safety more than a year ago . . . and he hasn't responded. I'm not trained to be a war correspondent and I don't think it's responsible for a newspaper to send people without proper training into situations like that."[1]

Pearl's safety memo, ignored by the *Journal*, was titled, "Memo on Protection of Journalists," and it should have been heeded by Pearl's editors. Among the major safety issues addressed in the memo were the following:

CHECKING IN: Pearl described the danger that a reporter could be kidnapped and go missing for days without anyone realizing it. He said it should be part of editors' job descriptions to keep track of reporters who go into hazardous situations. Editors should have a system to remind them to check up on reporters and a list of numbers to call if a reporter is missing. The first contact, after the spouse, should be the translator/fixer, then other journalists in the country, then whatever government agency is responsible for visiting journalists, then the U.S. embassy. Other numbers to be called included the International Committee of the Red Cross and the Committee to Protect Journalists (CPJ).

GUIDANCE: Pearl said that one way to reduce risk for war correspondents is to discourage them from covering stories unless there is clear interest by their organization. Often, reporters in hot zones enter dangerous situations pursuing stories that their editors will not use. Pearl says expedited guidance from news organizations could prevent such unnecessary risk.

MONEY: Pearl noted the substantial amounts of cash that war correspondents must carry in order to operate, and he said that if reporters run low on money they may stick around dangerous places longer than necessary or may cut corners by dropping their regular drivers, going places without a fixer, and so on. He recommended maintaining a standing account of $5,000 or $6,000 for a trip.

TRAINING: Pearl recommended security training for all war correspondents. Such training would include basic first aid, armaments, human psychology, driving (e.g., how to maneuver out of hostile situations), what to wear to avoid becoming a target, how to stay safe during demonstrations, how to avoid mines, and similar training. He suggested two companies that offer such training: Centurion Risk Assessment Services (used by *New York Times* and BBC staff) and Andy Kain Enterprises (used by CNN and BBC).

Pearl's memo was never adopted, but even if it were issued to all reporters in Afghanistan and Iraq, it would probably be inadequate to protect them. Today's reporters and editors are forced to develop their own safety strategies on a hit-and-miss basis. As individual journalists and their news organizations become more sensitive to the growing dangers of war reporting, new policies and strategies for minimizing risks are necessary. Prudence and caution are the first line of defense, although some of the precautions may seem a little odd. For instance, John Pomfret of the *Washington Post* says, "Never wash your car. If somebody's going to put a bomb under your car, [you could spot their] fingerprints."[2]

In April, 2004, John Burns, the *New York Times*'s Baghdad bureau chief, and several colleagues were abducted by insurgents, blindfolded, and driven to a makeshift cell before being released after eight hours. Later, Burns said, "Did it change the way we operate? Yes it did. . . . [W]e feel now we have to be reasonably satisfied the hazards are acceptably low before we'll contemplate a trip. It's a very, very dangerous assignment. . . . And that's uppermost in the minds of all the reporters all the time."[3]

Bill Spindle, who oversees the *Wall Street Journal*'s reporters in the Middle East, Africa, and Asia, says, "Just coming out of your house . . . exposes you to various people who . . . have in many cases followed people and shot them. So simply leaving your compound puts you in danger. . . . The bedrock principle is to find level-headed, cautious people to go out and do these things. It's vastly preferable if they have lots of experience doing it before. . . . The people who do it the most often are the most cautious and the least likely to do anything silly. Then you sort of go from there. . . . My deal with them is they make their own calls on safety, but they need to talk through every decision with me in pretty great detail."4

Susan Chira of the *New York Times* says, "We try to send only people who have covered other hostile environments. It's volunteers only. Like most organizations, we have a full-time resident security consultant. Our drill is that he reviews with them [the reporters] the potential risks before they leave Baghdad. We essentially have a rule . . . that I need to be consulted for any major foray outside Baghdad. We never require anyone to go. We let them make the call."5

But Chira admitted that getting reporters to volunteer for assignments in Iraq is becoming difficult. When asked whether she can still get enough volunteers, Chira said, "It's been hard. We sustain four or five people in Baghdad, and it's not very easy. I'm struck by the fact that a lot of people don't want to go. A lot of our experienced people don't want to go, and they're not crazy, because the most experienced people understand the risk. But what I have to do a lot is hold back the young people. A lot of them want to go but . . . don't really have the experience to gauge the danger."6

David Schlesinger from Reuters says, "We send only volunteers, only experienced people who've gone through hostile environment training. We trust them, but . . . we talk through decisions. Should we have a complete lockdown? Should we allow people to go out, where should we go, how should we go, how should we get people in and out? A lot of consultation, but it's mostly trust of the people we know."7

Jeffrey Bartholet of *Newsweek* says, "We put somebody in charge of Baghdad who's one of our most experienced guys covering wars; level-headed. He's typed up a kind of booklet of rules for the Baghdad bureau, everything from what you must take in the car when you go out, to when you're allowed to travel to whether you're allowed to dine at night and under what circumstances and with whom, and so on."8

The editorial policy of assigning only volunteers to cover dangerous areas may have reached its limit in Iraq. Tim McNulty, assistant managing editor for the *Chicago Tribune*, admits, "The pool of people willing to go has steadily shrunk over the last two years. The number of people who have spent a good deal of time there have said they've done their time and are not eager to go back. . . . If they say no, I don't ask the reasons."9

Finding volunteers is simple for Canadian publisher and correspondent Scott Taylor. "I assign myself," he said.

We're a small company. We've got a lot of economic pressures on us. We're very "grass roots" and we don't have a deep reservoir of cash. So if I'm anywhere near a conflict area and we know we can make money from syndicated stories, then I will make it my endeavor to go in, if I know the area. I mean, I haven't just parachuted into Afghanistan or Chechnya. If I'm going into a conflict, it's going to be calculated in order to minimize the risk and maximize the number of contacts before I go. The more contacts you have, the more you know about the region, the less the risk. It helps if you know even a smattering of the language and know where the cultural divides are, where the friction lines are.

For instance, going into northern Iraq, I'm usually sponsored in by the Iraqi-Turkmen Front to cross the border from the Turkish side to the Kurdish side. Once I'm there, I'll take a Kurdish driver whom I know, who was recommended to me. He has good access right down to Kirkuk. From Kirkuk I'll use a Turkmen driver to get to Baghdad. In Baghdad I'll use an Arab driver that I've known for years. Pretty much anywhere in the Sunni Triangle I can do that, and he has excellent contacts with the Shiite community as well. So always traveling with someone from the group you're visiting and anticipating the difficulties you might have crossing the various police checkpoints is essential to the success and safety of reporting. You need to have all that arranged in advance.[10]

ABC TV News correspondent Brian Rooney told Public Television's Terrence Smith that the situation for reporters in Baghdad was "difficult but not impossible":

If you take security precautions you can go out in the city and get to certain locations to interview people. . . . The downside of it all is that you are just not well advised to go out into a market area of the city, if you have a face that looks like mine, and start asking people questions. It is dangerous. Just being in Baghdad is a dangerous thing. You have to be mindful that the car bombers are driving around in traffic with you. There are intermittent mortar rounds and rocket rounds landing. I had some near misses with that. You can report on this story, but you have to be very careful about it. You can't be casual about it by any means.

We would go in a short convoy, try to be low key and unrecognizable. We took security with us everywhere we went. We planned where we were going to go. We stayed there for as little time as possible, had an exit plan and got out as fast as we could. . . . You had to go in and do your business and go. And there were some places you just never did go. We tried to go to some car bombings, the aftermath. . . . We had some scouts ahead of us, some Arabic speaking people. It broke out in gunfire and we turned right around.

[W]e were pretty free to send an Arabic-speaking crew and people who looked Arabic to a lot of places, and they were fairly safe. But if you went there as a westerner, you never knew how the crowd was going to react, because there's a tendency to blame the United States for everything that happens, even if it was a car bombing. . . . So you just had to be careful going there. Your presence could incite a great deal of anger.[11]

Philip Caputo, former correspondent who was kidnapped in Lebanon, advises, "Journalists have got to exercise common sense, and they've got to make a thorough reconnaissance and thorough assessment of the situation they're in. They need to have indigenous people around them who can act both as their advisors and protectors. That would help reduce the risks somewhat, but beyond that, and beyond embedding themselves with a military unit, I don't think there's a lot to be done."[12]

Washington Post correspondent Carol Morello explained that even the cautious war correspondents are vulnerable. After four reporters were killed in one day in Afghanistan she said, "I think the killing of those four reporters spooked a lot of other reporters, because they seemed to have done everything right. When you heard about the three [reporters] . . . who were killed riding on top of an APC, you could say, well, that was sort of a dumb thing to do. But the four who were killed, they were part of a convoy. They didn't go in on the first day; they went in on the second day. They didn't go in the first car; they were in the second or third car. They had a local driver. . . . They did everything right. . . . You try to minimize the risk to a point where you feel, okay, it's safe enough. . . . They did everything 'right,' and they still ended up getting killed."[13]

Isolation in the Green Zone

When the streets of Iraq are prowled by kidnappers and murderers, prudence dictates that journalists spend their time at the hotel bar rather than venturing out into the hostile environment. In January 2005, the popular Doonesbury comic strip syndicated in newspapers around the country gave an indication of how isolated reporters in Iraq have become due to the pervasive danger there. Doonesbury shows a TV anchor saying,

"For more on the continuing chaos in Iraq, let's go live to Roland Hedley. Roland, can you give us the latest in Baghdad?"

"I'm afraid not, Lou," says the Baghdad correspondent.

"Um . . . why not?"

"I don't know anything. It's much too dangerous to leave the hotel."[14]

The next day, Doonesbury presented another image of press coverage in Iraq. Again, the TV anchor says, "For more on Iraq, we're joined by Roland Hedley in Baghdad."

Speaking into the camera, Hedley tells TV viewers, "Bowing to network pressure, I and my three bodyguards left my hotel in an armored car to cover the daily Coalition briefing. After two hours of creeping along unsecure streets, I am now at the briefing, where, I can assure you, no news will be committed. I'm Roland Hedley, alive."[15]

The Doonesbury satire of an intimidated and isolated press corps in Iraq is quite close to what the journalists themselves describe. Safety is, of course, the first concern of the news organizations remaining in Iraq, and two hotels reserved for journalists are the safest places, other than the fortified "Green Zone" for embeds.

Bill Spindle, the *Wall Street Journal's* Middle East editor, says his correspondents have been largely confined to Baghdad. "With the checkpoints and the kidnappings and the shootings that seem deliberately aimed at people working for Western organizations, moving around has been a dicey proposition."[16]

Fox News Senior Vice President John Moody says, "Some days our guys just don't get out of the building where we're located. Travel across the country is almost impossible now because the roads are too dangerous. It's constricted our ability to report stuff going on that's not just a comment from the CPA."[17]

A press corps that does not feel safe on Baghdad's streets is unable to investigate claims by either side in the conflict. "It enables Washington, London, and [Iraqi Prime Minister] Alawi to produce a picture of Iraq which is fantasy, but, ironically, we can't refute that because it's so dangerous," says Patrick Cockburn, a London-based correspondent for *The Independent*.[18]

Washington Post correspondent Rajiv Chandrasekaran described the "dramatic arc" of increased risk for reporters and the strategies for managing that risk. "As I was packing up about ten days ago in Baghdad I was looking at a map of Iraq, and all the major highways out of Baghdad were, in my mind, 'red,' meaning we don't send people there. Even within Baghdad you have to take care. There are certain neighborhoods where you can go and operate discretely, but there are other neighborhoods that are pretty much off limits. And when it comes to leaving the capitol and seeing the vast expanse of Iraq, it's almost impossible."[19]

Chandrasekaran said the problem extended beyond simply covering hot spots like Fallujah. "This problem extends to almost every other story that can be told across the country. I've long wanted to go down to the city of Hella, which is no more than about 40 miles south of Baghdad. . . . But the road from Baghdad to Hella is nicknamed The Road of Death. I went down there one day, and on the way back we saw shot-up cars. Seventeen people were killed just that one afternoon on that road. . . . one of whom, the Italian journalist, was later confirmed to have been killed on the road between Baghdad and Najaf."[20]

Brian Bennett of *Time* magazine described the relative ease with which he was able to move around Iraq shortly after the war, but he noted that now even print journalists were virtually confined to Baghdad. "During this last trip in August [2004] it was almost impossible to travel outside of Baghdad, because it was just so dangerous. The roads were so insecure and the kidnapping that was going on put us just too much at risk. . . . [Y]ou don't really get stories that take the temperature of the entire country. . . . I think that's a very important part of the story, to go to the more rural places, more out of the way places and talk to Iraqis. . . . That kind of scope and temperature-taking is almost impossible to do now."

Bennett admitted that there were stories he wanted to cover but couldn't reach because of security concerns. "I certainly wanted to go into Fallujah and get a sense of what it was like on the ground there for the average family, but that's just impossible. I tried to arrange it and get certain permissions from the mujahadin who control the city, but it was just too dangerous at the time. And I didn't even go and cover the siege of the shrine at Najaf. We sent Iraqi reporters that we had trained to go there and cover that simply because the road between Baghdad and Najaf was so dangerous."[21]

I asked Peter Spiegel, correspondent for the *Financial Times*, whether this kind of isolation was compromising reporting in Iraq. "Yes, absolutely," he said. "It's a frustration. That's one reason why I decided not to go back. The reason you go to a place like Iraq is to provide an eye-witness account of what's going on, and you just can't do that now. You're incredibly reliant on briefings from the military and, increasingly, from the Iraqi government. So there's no way it doesn't compromise the ability to get information."[22]

Drivers, Translators, Bodyguards, Fixers, Stringers, and Other Arab Surrogates

As described in Chapter 2, the increased vulnerability and isolation of Western journalists in Iraq and Afghanistan has forced news organizations to turn to local employees to perform on-the-scene reporting. This new reliance on local stringers and fixers has reduced the risk for Western journalists, but it has dramatically increased casualties among local news staff.

The term *stringer*, meaning a freelance journalist contracted by a news organization, has been a part of the lexicon of journalism for many years, but the term *fixer* is a product of the recent wars in Afghanistan and Iraq, where the dangers to Western journalists have forced them to rely on local staff. A fixer provides a variety of essential services to Western news organizations, including setting up interviews with local religious leaders and warlords and getting journalists to those interviews, often through dangerous areas. Sometimes fixers receive a monthly paycheck from the news organization, but in other cases they are hired on a per diem basis.

Joel Campagna, Middle East specialist for the CPJ, explained the increased role of local media in Iraq, including reporters, stringers, fixers, translators, and drivers:

> They have endured the lion's share of media casualties in 2004, and that's directly related to the increased role that Iraqi journalists now play in assisting western news organizations. During 2003, the year of the invasion, 13 journalists and just two media workers were killed. All but two of the journalists killed were from outside news organizations. In 2004, during the post-war phase of reporting, the numbers were reversed. Of the 23 journalists killed in 2004, 17 were Iraqis. In addition, all 16 of the media support workers killed were Iraqis. Again, it's indicative of the increasing role that Iraqi journalists and media workers are playing as front line personnel for international news gathering operations and as journalists for their own local media. We've seen journalists working for local news organizations threatened and killed. Today, Iraqi journalists and media support staff comprise the bulk of all media casualties in Iraq since 2003. They have become essential frontline personnel in the local newsgathering operations for the Iraqi press as well as for international news organizations. Their increasing role translates into increasing risk.[23]

In reality, the difference between a driver, a bodyguard, a translator, and a fixer is minimal. Often, a local person will perform all of these functions. I asked Peter Spiegel, defense analyst for the *Financial Times*, to describe how he goes about hiring a driver/translator in Afghanistan and Iraq:

> That was mostly coordinated by my bureau chief, both in Kabul and Baghdad. . . . You get a name passed on by someone else who knows a guy and that sort of thing. These people are absolutely essential to our operation. You could not function without them. They know the country. My guy in Afghanistan spoke English, but he was a little too young, didn't know the ways of the world. The guy in Iraq is my age, mid-thirties, a former army officer, actually a former member of the Baath Party. He's well-educated and speaks idiomatic English, though he has never left Iraq.

If, say, I wanted to go to the Oil Ministry, he would either call up or go to the Ministry the day before and see what he could do, that sort of thing. But he didn't have personal connections that would enable me have special access. So he wasn't a fixer in the pure sense of being a former official or something like that. These people are not only essential to getting around Iraq; he actually saved my life on a number of occasions.[24]

Spiegel's very broad description of a driver is similar to the description of a bodyguard provided by Michael Gordon, a London-based correspondent for the *New York Times*. "A bodyguard is not just a guy with a gun, because everybody has a gun," says Gordon. "It's a guy who's tied into the local power structure. They [the insurgents] recognize him; they say, 'Okay, you're with this guy. You must be alright.' They know a lot of the customs."[25]

The increasing reliance on such local assistance in Iraq has created virtual celebrity status for some of the fixers. One example is Hasan Aweida, also known as PJ, known in Kuwait and Iraq as "The Fixer"—the guy that reporters turn to if they want to get into Iraq and stay alive when they get there. He was born in Saudi Arabia, his mother is Lebanese, and his father is from Jerusalem. "Now I help the media people," he says. "Many of them were trying secretly to cross the border. I had to give them the clues how to get past the checkpoints. . . . When they got stuck, they would call me . . . by satphone, 'Please get us, PJ!'. . . . Wherever I would go, media people would ask me, 'PJ, what we have to do?'"[26]

Another mythic fixer is Mohammed Fahmy. Born in Egypt and educated in Canada, Fahmy moved to Kuwait, where he became a driver/translator for the *Los Angeles Times*. "To call him merely a translator and driver is terribly inadequate," says *Times* correspondent Tracy Wilkinson. "Mohammed was more like a colleague, helping us plan the next day's stories." Fahmy says, "I also did some editing for them, checked the Arabic names, checked the spelling. I made sure the feel of the story was right. . . . I felt that I was more than a driver and translator. We were a team."[27]

Rory McCarthy, correspondent for the British *Guardian* in Iraq, relies heavily on a stringer/driver/translator named Ossama. "More and more I'm asking Ossama . . . to go to the more tricky places and do some of the work for me," says McCarthy. Indeed, McCarthy has shared his byline with Ossama five times. Iraqi stringers are increasingly targeted because they work for Westerners, but Ossama has no complaints about the danger:

"I like working with tough people, and I think journalists are really tough," he says as he cautiously drives McCarthy around Baghdad. "It's a little bit dangerous. . . . A lot of people say it's really dangerous. . . . You just need to use your mind. Like now, I'm thinking of all situations. I'm looking in the mirror and I'm looking at all that and I'm talking to you. That's the way to do it. You just have to keep your eyes open. You're gonna die some day. Why don't we skip . . . thinking about getting killed. You won't make any money if you think like that . . . You *will* die if you just keep thinking about death, and death and death." He turns to McCarthy and asks, "So what do we have for tomorrow?"[28]

Susan Chira of the *New York Times* described a typical workday for a fixer with the *New York Times* in Baghdad. "You send so and so from the Baghdad bureau over to Fallujah," she says. "He has local connections, he knows people, he can get information. He goes in a car to Fallujah, sometimes with security people. You send him there with a list of questions. . . . You're trying, essentially, to train people to be your eyes and ears, but also to react in a journalistically effective manner. Some of the people have really grown and stretched, but then they come back and you debrief, and there are always things that someone didn't ask that you might have asked. So it's very frustrating for our guys. They come through trial and error to see which one of these Iraqi staff comes closest to the level that they would want."[29]

Lois Raimondo, photographer and reporter for the *Washington Post* in Afghanistan, was asked how she knew she had a good fixer with the Northern Alliance. "Because of the ways he gave me information," she answered. "I trusted him completely. . . . We'd go to the market, and he would tell me, this is what they said. . . . [H]e got me into conversations with commanders where they talked about globalization and things like that. I was led into safe houses when we took new towns. There were still snipers all about, and I was led into safe houses with the top commanders and we would be talking about these things. . . . I could listen and use it as background information. So he walked me into any number of situations that were incredibly rare."[30]

David Schlesinger, head of the Reuters news service, points out that for a wire service like his, developing a stringer network is nothing new. "We have 100 different nationalities among the full-time employees, and then among the stringers there are probably even more nationalities. One of the things you do is learn how to develop talent, spot talent, train talent, and inculcate the values of the agency, of the profession."[31]

Jeffrey Bartholet, foreign editor of *Newsweek*, says, "In the Pakistan/ Afghanistan area we're relying more on local journalists who work with us, stringers. We've got a really talented Afghan/Pakistani stringer who does a lot of the work in the tribal areas along the border zone where it's virtually impossible for someone like us to work now."[32]

But as the danger of covering the conflict forces Western journalists to rely on local help, these stringers and fixers are themselves targeted. Bill Spindle of the *Wall Street Journal* says, "Because they are locals, they are often the people that are left in the most vulnerable states when we leave. . . . We've had a large number of [violent] incidents with fixers. I've had to evacuate a number of fixers and translators from places like Iraq and Afghanistan."[33]

Time magazine's Adi Ignatius recounts, "One of our drivers/fixers was killed as he was driving into what was then the *Time* magazine compound in Baghdad. It's unclear exactly why he was killed, but it's very possible that he was killed because he worked for *Time*."

David Schlesinger, Reuters chief, believes that the increasing use of local stringers and fixers is what distinguishes the Iraq and Afghanistan wars from all previous conflicts. "It is no longer the white, Anglo-Saxon male [reporter] going off into battle as a reporter. It is local people, it is stringers, it is part-timers, it is the free-lancers trying to make their name. So it is a much different mix on the ground. I think that is different than in wars past."[34]

Susan Chira of the *New York Times* speaks very highly of the stringers and fixers employed by the Baghdad bureau of the *New York Times*, calling them "our eyes and ears" on whom "we increasingly rely." She noted, however, that they are increasingly targeted by the insurgents. In this regard, she said the *Times* had instituted a policy that some readers questioned. "We'd like to give them [Iraqi stringers and fixers] credit for their reporting, but we've allowed them to decide whether it's safe for us to publish their names, because people have been targeted."[35]

Despite her praise for the stringers and fixers, Chira says their increasing prominence raises serious journalistic questions. "You spend your whole life believing that what you see and you observe is the best litmus test," she says. "And yet you have to rely increasingly on people who were not trained as western journalists . . . and who haven't had the journalistic mentoring that we had."[36]

Brian Bennett of *Time* magazine was asked how the reporting by Iraqi staff differed from what he might have reported himself. "It's dramatically different," he said, "because you aren't there seeing things for yourself. You don't have an eye witness account of what's going on. They've been trained to ask good follow-up questions, to do good reporting and get as many facts as they can, but still, they're sort of reading it back to you over the phone, so you don't bring your own judgment to the observations that they're making. It really is like being once removed from the story."[37]

Washington Post correspondent Rajiv Chandrasekaran agreed. "Nothing beats looking somebody in the eye and talking to them. That's what foreign correspondence is all about. We're out there to try to find out the truth, to really find out what's going on. I've gone from a guy who sort of felt like I piloted my own airplane in the early days, and now I'm sitting in a shack piloting a predator drone. I'm sending out my Iraqis to go and ask questions. They report back, . . . but it's a very unsatisfactory way to cover the story, and ultimately our readers, our consumers of news lose out because it lacks a level of detail, it lacks immediacy and it lacks thoroughness."[38]

ABC correspondent Brian Rooney added, "There is a lot that is lost in the skill of this kind of reporting and a lot that is lost in translation. You have the military saying every night that they have conducted a precision attack on a certain location, and then civilians are saying you also killed non-combatants, women and children. The military is not verifying exactly who they killed, and we are not able to verify it. So places like Fallujah get lost in this kind of situation."[39]

Security Training for Journalists

The notion of survival skills and safety guidelines for journalists has been slow to catch on with media managers in the United States. Whereas in Europe, the BBC, ITN, and Reuters have long required security training for foreign correspondents, it took the 9/11 terrorist attacks to generate such policies within American news organizations. CNN, with three hundred correspondents assigned around the world at any time, has taken the lead in pushing for American safety standards. By 2002, 150 CNN correspondents had been sent through a week-long training with London's AKE Group that has also supplied security consultants to CNN crews in Afghanistan and the Middle East. The consultants manage, maintain, and transport the network's fleet of armored vehicles and design special protective gear, including flak jackets. Providing firearms to correspondents is a more sensitive issue. "They don't routinely carry weapons, but we don't really want to go into detail," said Eason Jordan, CNN's chief news executive. "There are extraordinary situations where that might be required."[40]

Chris Cramer, president of CNN's International Networks, calls it "criminal" and "a disgrace to the profession" when editors send correspondent's into harm's way without proper training, protective gear, or guidelines on how to pursue a dangerous story. "There are media organizations who refuse to confront the issue, refuse to spend the money on keeping their staff safe," says Cramer. "My message to them is quite simple: They should be ashamed of themselves."[41]

Christiane Amanpour, CNN's chief international correspondent says the most important safety issues are insurance, safety training, protective equipment, support, and counseling, none of which are receiving adequate support within press organizations. Brookings Institution scholar Stephen Hess believes it will take a cultural change in American newsrooms for safety standards to take root. "It's not part of the journalistic personality," he says. But in Europe, support for standards is widespread. Reuters has instituted a policy requiring any reporter going to a conflict zone to receive state-of-the-art training from military specialists. The two dominant companies offering such training are the British firms AKE Group Ltd. and Centurion Risk Assessment Services, which offers training in Woodstock, Virginia, as well as in Europe.

The Associated Press, BBC, CNN, ITN, and Reuters formed the News Security Group in late 2000 to set common guidelines to protect their foreign correspondents. Since then, CBS, ABC, and NBC News have joined. Rodney Pinder, the BBC's editor for video news, says, "News managers must guarantee the correspondent or cameraman the right to say no—to refuse to go into a dangerous situation or to withdraw from one on one's own initiative without consultation and with no fear of criticism or career damage. Our obligation is to provide the best available training, equipment, insurance and counseling to protect the exposed journalist from competitive pressure."[42]

American newspapers have been particularly slow in developing policies to protect journalists. As of late 2002, the *Los Angeles Times* had no written policy on safety in war zones, though it provides bullet-proof vests and armored vehicles for journalists who request them. Foreign editor Simon Li said only one *Times* correspondent had received hostile environment training. "The hurdles are money and time," he said.[43]

Until recently, the *Washington Post* had no formal guidelines, and foreign correspondent Douglas Farah said the paper was struggling with the moral, ethical, and financial implications of security training. "Do you train everyone on the foreign staff and people who are wanting to go overseas or go on short notice to hot spots like the Middle East or Afghanistan," he asked. "Who should be trained, when would you do it, and how much would it cost?"[44]

USA Today has adopted safety guidelines and offers some hostile-environment training to foreign correspondents. Editor Karen Jurgensen says, "At *USA Today*, it is a work in progress. We still are inventing our culture. . . . My position now is that everyone who goes should be trained."[45]

Washington Times foreign editor David Jones says the paper is in the process of creating safety guidelines. He says he is analyzing his travel budget "to make sure the next reporters we send into harm's way are better prepared to deal with whatever dangers they face."[46]

Loren Jenkins, National Public Radio's foreign editor, says NPR supplies safety equipment to correspondents "up to a point." She explains, "[W]e're still public radio. We can't afford what CNN does—bullet-proof Jeeps at $90,000 a whack. We provide what is necessary within reason."[47]

Robert Klamser, co-founder of Crisis Consulting International, says his company provides safety training to journalists using role-playing and demonstrations. He offers a grim assessment of the future for war correspondents:

"The risks will increase. Not only are you soft targets; you are attractive targets, because terrorism is about changing opinions. Using the leverage of a journalist as victim is one way to do it."[48]

After *USA Today* correspondent Mark Memmott received his hostile-environment training from Centurion, he sent a memo to his newsroom describing how much he had been helped by the training. World Editor Elisa Tinsley sighed in relief after reading the memo. "I personally take it so seriously," she said. "My anxiety level on a daily basis goes so high because I feel responsible for these people."[49]

Susan Chira, *New York Times* foreign editor, said of their correspondents in Iraq, "We require war training before they go. There are different operations that provide it. We contract with a group that is run by a bunch of ex-British army people. They have a five-day course they run them through. . . . They school them in different kinds of explosions, simulated kidnapping situations. They get advice about how to behave, and we don't let anyone go who hasn't had that."[50]

Small news organizations may not be able to provide expensive security training for their correspondents, but some reporters are military veterans who have had their own on-the-job training in hostile environments. Canadian war correspondent and publisher Scott Taylor says, "I started my magazine after serving as a commando in the army. That training was provided courtesy of the French army, if you will, as far as knowing how to handle weapons and handle myself in dangerous areas. Then, over the last 16 years I've just gained knowledge through experience, having been in hot spots like Croatia, Bosnia, Cambodia, Western Sahara, and, of course, Iraq."[51]

Guns and Military Equipment

Being hunted down like prey in Iraq and elsewhere has led some journalists to ask whether they should be prepared to defend themselves. Peter Spiegel, defense analyst for the *Financial Times*, says, "The U.S. military in Baghdad cannot protect journalists unless they're embedded. The other alternative is to totally armor up, wear a flak jacket and helmet, get a bullet-proof SUV with armed guards and that kind of thing. But I always felt that this was exactly the wrong thing to do because you just make yourself a target more than anything else. And frankly, if you're going to get kidnapped, your flak jacket and helmet aren't going to help you anyway. Instead, we would go out in my driver's beat-up sedan. I would put on a kafia and grow up my beard to the point where everyone said I looked like a Palestinian.

"As you may know, there's a big debate in news organizations about whether journalists should arm themselves or not. I have gone through several tense incidents where I felt if I had been armed and had a gun on me, it would have been very difficult to explain, 'I'm a journalist, not a combatant.' That happened two or three times where people accused me of being CIA and we had to explain who we were. For that reason, I'm very much among the group that thinks that carrying a weapon creates more danger than it solves."[52]

Joseph Caputo, kidnapped back in 1973 while covering the Lebanese civil war for the *Chicago Tribune*, says, "I was generally against the idea of carrying guns because that really brands the journalist as a combatant. Mind you, I was an ex-marine, very well trained in the use of fire arms. But let's assume I'm walking around with my own .45 automatic on my hip. About the best one could expect if captured by a group of insurgents is that you'll take a couple of them with you as they kill you. That's about it. The only time I had carried a weapon was in Afghanistan when I covered the conflict from the mujahadin as they fought the Soviet army. I had been with them for nearly a month and we had to make a night exfiltration through a gap in the Russian lines. The mujahadin gave me an old rifle and five rounds of ammunition, telling me that I would have to protect myself. I later told a friend that the best use I could have put that weapon to was to commit suicide. What am I going to do with this kind of Rudyard Kipling rifle, facing Russian tanks and helicopter gun ships? That night was the only time I carried a fire arm."[53]

Jerry Levin, former CNN correspondent and kidnap victim in Lebanon, agrees with Caputo. "Having journalists carry guns would be even more counterproductive than having the Red Cross carry weapons," he said recently. "Good heavens, journalists are already seen, quite appropriately in many ways, as being one-sided in their coverage. Carrying a gun would make it worse. It would be foolhardy, especially in my case. I would probably have shot myself in the foot."[54]

Joel Campagna, Middle East specialist for the CPJ, says carrying weapons would not make foreign correspondents safer. "Our position is that journalists should never carry firearms, because, in our opinion, it undermines their status as neutral observers and can potentially endanger other journalists in the future. There's a larger issue of debate in places like Iraq over whether news organizations should employ security escorts. Many organizations feel that they cannot cover conflicts like Iraq without such escorts. Our response is that those organizations have to be mindful that security guards and escorts can also potentially undermine the journalist's neutral status. One could make the case that for any journalist, especially broadcast journalists in Iraq, traveling overland is suicide. Nonetheless, we would remind them that traveling with a security escort brings its own risks. By giving the news crew the appearance of combatants, it makes them even more conspicuous targets while potentially undermining their neutral status."[55]

Terry Anderson, the Associated Press's chief Middle East correspondent when he was abducted and held for almost seven years in Lebanon, says carrying weapons would only increase the danger for reporters in war zones. "The only protection you have is the assumption that you're not part of the action," he said. "If you carry a gun, you're a fighter. I did not allow any guns to be carried by anyone in the Associated Press, local or correspondent. I think it's a very bad precedent to set. I'm not going to tell anyone you can't protect yourself, but I'll tell you what—What kind of gun are you going to carry that will get you out of trouble with a half dozen militiamen armed with AK-47s or M-16s? There are very few circumstances in which carrying a gun is going to help a journalist at all, and I can think of a lot of them where it's going to get him into serious trouble. So I think anyone who does that is being very unwise."[56]

Anderson felt that even traveling with bodyguards was unlikely to improve safety for journalists. "I would have had a very hard time justifying bodyguards in Lebanon," he said. "If it's that dangerous, don't go. A lot of journalists and news organizations got in trouble by using bodyguards. I'll tell you a little story. There was a TV news crew—two women, plus a cameraman and a soundman—in Beirut at one point, and their organization hired bodyguards, militiamen. I actually had to go down to their office and rescue them from their own militiamen who were holding them and wouldn't let them leave through the airport until they gave them more money. I had to go down there and tell these militiamen to back off, get out of the way, let these women go."[57]

Scott Taylor, the Canadian war correspondent who was abducted and tortured by the Ansar al-Islam group in Iraq in December 2004, said he has never carried a gun while on assignment. "I don't believe in it," he said. "As a soldier, I know that if I carry a gun I would be able to use it, but so what? When they've got ten guys with hand guns, how is it going to help me to have a gun? You're not going to shoot your way out of Iraq. It only endangers you, because it makes it that much more difficult to explain why or how you're a journalist. The absence of a weapon makes your claim of being a neutral observer that much stronger. To think that you're going to be able to access your weapon quickly enough to be able to shoot your way out of trouble like James Bond is absurd.

"You know, I was a commando. I know how to use guns. I was offered a weapon. Some guys I know in the Green Zone could always give me a temporary license, a permit to carry a Kalashnikov. But when am I going to start spraying, you know? If you drive up to a checkpoint with a gun hanging out the window, they're going to shoot you. And if you don't have the gun in your hands, then you wouldn't be able to get to it time in case of trouble. This is not the American Wild West. If you carry a gun in Iraq, it's only going to endanger you. To me, as long as you're talking and you are who you say you are, you should be able to get out of trouble. You shouldn't represent a threat to others. If you're armed, they're well within their rights to kill you."58

Rory McCarthy, correspondent for the British *Guardian*, was recently interviewed as he was driven through a dangerous section of Baghdad. He said he preferred to travel discreetly, rather than in large, bullet-proof vehicles. "I'm very reluctant to have guys with guns with us," he said. "We don't have any guns in this car. We don't have any guards with guns working for us. At the end of the day, we're journalists, and I don't think we should be armed. When you're dealing with a country that has front lines, you know where the danger begins, . . . and you can take steps to protect yourself. The problem here is that there are no front lines."59

Embedded Journalists

Journalists in Iraq feel safer when working under the formal protection of the U.S. military. This is accomplished by signing up as an "embed," which means living with the troops as you report on them. The most current official Pentagon memo on embedding, dated February 3, 2003, is titled, "Public Affairs Guidance (PAG) on Embedding Media. . . ." The memo states, "Media coverage of any future operation will, to a large extent, shape public perception of the national security environment now and in the years ahead. . . . Our people in the field need to tell our story. . . . To accomplish this, we will embed media with our units. These embedded media will live, work, and travel as part of the units with which they are embedded to facilitate maximum, in depth coverage of U.S. forces in combat and related operations."60

The memo defined a "media embed" as "a media representative remaining with a unit on an extended basis—perhaps a period of weeks or even months. Commanders will provide billeting, rations, and medical attention, if needed, commensurate with that provided to members of the unit, as well as access to military transportation and assistance with communications filing/transmitting media products, if required. Embedded media are not authorized use of their own vehicles while traveling in an embedded status."61

The prohibition on the use of private vehicles is significant, because it effectively precludes independent travel and reporting, leaving such activity to the "unilaterals."

Section 4.G. of the memo provides a lengthy list of "Categories of Information that Are Not Releasable." Among those are rules of engagement, information on intelligence collection activities, photos of enemy prisoners of war or detainees, and still or video images of custody operations or interviews with persons under custody.

The embedding policy began in Afghanistan where Nik Gowing of the BBC observed that journalists were relying on the military for "sparse and suspect" information, in addition to food, water, and sanitation. "This puts immense emotional and professional pressure on journalists who feel corralled by the military . . . ," said Gowing, "Such arrangements are a Faustian bargain. . . . They are the kind of controls that many in the military have wanted to re-impose for a long time and it has happened because of the danger of working in this transparent environment."[62]

Author and CNN contributor Robert Pelton says, "The idea of embedding is essentially the Stockholm syndrome. If you take an unarmed individual and put him amongst armed people, he becomes sympathetic to their cause. So the idea was, slap a helmet on these guys, stick them in a jeep or a Humvee . . . and let him do whatever the heck he wants and he will become sympathetic to our cause."[63]

In a hostile environment like Iraq it is safer for a reporter to embed, and it is easily accomplished. An e-mail to a lieutenant is usually all it takes. But safer doesn't mean safe, and Dexter Filkins of the *New York Times* can testify to that. He had been an embed for two weeks during the siege of Fallujah, during which he had to file stories from a latrine to avoid attracting gun fire. Filkins was with a company of 150 marines from the First Battalion, and a quarter of his company was killed during that offensive. "From the moment that we got out of the troop carriers and walked into the city . . . the RPGs were sailing out of the town and exploding right next to us. Everybody was on the ground trying to take cover, and I thought, 'My God, what have I signed up for?' We had continuous combat for 16 hours. . . . It was really intense. I mean, it made everything else I had covered look like a tea party. You know, I'm a writer, and words failed me, repeatedly."[64]

Philip Caputo, former marine and former *Chicago Tribune* correspondent who was kidnapped in Lebanon, says the safety of embedding comes with a price. He notes that even Dexter Filkins, who he says is the best correspondent currently working in Iraq, tends to identify unconsciously with the military in his reports from Iraq. "I noticed that even Filkins, when he was interviewed by phone on PBS, would sometimes say things like 'We moved up this street in Fallujah' or 'We came under fire.' That plural pronoun was revealing. It's like he's almost a member of the battalion, and in a sense he is. So the embedded reporter is seeing the war from the fighting man's point of view, the foxhole point of view. So obviously, when you're embedded, you see only one side of the story, and you're most likely to strongly identify with the soldiers you're with. They're your protectors."[65]

Canadian correspondent Scott Taylor, who functioned as a unilateral in Iraq, says he could never have reported on the damage done by American rocket attacks on Sadr City if he had been embedded. "On April 6, the morning of the night before the Americans launched major attacks to secure a big chunk of Sadr City, my driver and I were able to go in and film a lot of the damage, where rockets had taken out houses and hospitals, blown up vans. We were on one side in the morning, and then we crossed back to the American lines, and then we went back into Baghdad in the afternoon. . . . If you were an embedded journalist with that military unit, you couldn't do that. You'd have seen a lot of fighting, but you'd have no idea what it looked like from the other side. You wouldn't have seen the destroyed cribs and the beds in the hospitals and that sort of thing. It would look like a lot of puffs of smoke and tracer fire and that sort of thing, which is what we see on television."[66]

Washington Post correspondent Rajiv Chandrasekaran says, "These days, most western journalists, if they're gong out of Baghdad, they're going with the U.S. military, they're going as embedded reporters. . . . But what that means is you're only seeing one side of the story. You're having a very limited interaction with Iraqis."[67]

Former AP chief Middle East correspondent Terry Anderson has characterized the system of embedding journalists as "the most brilliant stroke of public relations that the U.S. military has ever thought up." But when I asked him if it was a good way to cover the war, he said, "For the military, yes. Journalists get great footage of American boys, well-trained, patriotic young heroes in battle. Such coverage became the entire story. Was there anything written that was not from the American point of view? Not by the American media. Embedding journalists with the military puts the news organizations in a position to get great footage from one side of the story, but it's very difficult to cover the other side."

But isn't embedding a safer way to cover a war?

"Yes, and that's a consideration," said Anderson. "You're obviously more relaxed when you're surrounded by heavily armed guys who like you. As my editor once told me, if you get your ass killed, you can't file the story, so there's no sense in going there to die."[68]

Anderson was not concerned over reports that the U.S. military had failed to assume responsibility for the safety of the unembedded journalists, the unilaterals. "The military should not have any responsibility for the unilaterals," he declared. "They should give them access, but they have no responsibility for their safety. I cannot tell you how many times I've been with American troops and they said, 'Oh, you can't do that, it's too dangerous, we can't protect you.' Well, if I wanted your protection, I wouldn't be in this business. I'm not looking for protection from the military. I'm trying to cover them.

"If I were covering Iraq today, what would be my best use? Should I be embedded with the U.S. military? No. My best use is to try to get out there and cover the war and its impact on civilians, which is always the most interesting story. In Iraq that's very dangerous. I can't promise you that I would be able to do it any better than the correspondents who are there, but I don't think the coverage of American troops should totally dominate the reporting. This war is not necessarily about American troops. It's mostly about Iraq and what happens to the people of Iraq. If a news organization can't cover the war in such a way as to tell the story of the Iraqis, then it hasn't done a very good job."[69]

Because proper coverage of the Iraq war requires going out on your own, some embeds are tempted to have the best of both worlds, bypassing restrictive military guidelines while accepting military protection. Correspondent Peter Arnett believes that the press restrictions imposed on both embeds and unilaterals force reporters to take greater risks to circumvent those restrictions. "It's not good for reporters to risk their lives in this way," he says. "[N]ot one journalist was killed in Vietnam because he had to go around [press restrictions] to get information. I don't think it should be up to the media to try to outwit our own side in these conflicts. It's too dangerous as it is."[70]

Christiane Amanpour also recognizes the quandary faced by embedded journalists. Embedding offers relative safety, but at the sacrifice of balanced reporting. "I preferred my own experience," she said, "which was sort of a hybrid between being embedded and going unilateral. . . . There's just one problem with the unilateral solution, and that is that it's very dangerous."[71]

Former hostage Jerry Levin says the practice of embedding in Iraq has reached the point of no return. "Whether journalists should or should not embed is no longer the question," he said. "The horse is out of the barn, and there are practical reasons associated with the increasing competition in journalism that force that choice on many journalists. I think the concept of embedding has, whether we like it or not, created more of a connection between mainstream journalism and the American government. It may not make journalists into combatants, but it at least gives them the appearance of jingoistic fellow travelers."[72]

Is the Story Worth the Risk?

The U.S. invasion of Afghanistan in 2001 was big news, and with the flood of journalists to the conflict came increased risks for war correspondents. But within a year or so the risks for reporters were considerably reduced. Afghanistan was still dangerous, but no longer as lethal for journalists. Why? Bill Spindel of the *Wall Street Journal* recently explained that the "toxic mix" for reporters comes when a regional story is both dangerous *and* important. "We're still covering Afghanistan," he said, "but we're not covering it anything like what we were doing before.

As time goes on, if the story [in Iraq] seems less important and is getting less play, yet remains very, very dangerous, we're going to have less ability to send people there; people aren't going to want to cover it . . . because the risks aren't worth it. And I think you could see that [in Iraq] if there's a dwindling interest in the story and it maintains a constant drumbeat of regular violence."

Speaking for *Time* magazine, Adi Ignatius said his organization relied on their reporters "to make the decision when a risk is worth it." He added, "We think hard about whether there's going to be a payoff, whether they go into a dangerous situation that's not going to lead to something major in the magazine."[73]

Philip Caputo, perhaps the first of the high-profile journalists to be kidnapped in the Middle East, says correspondents cannot allow themselves to be forced out of danger zones such as Iraq or Afghanistan. "Unfortunately, they have to cover them," he says. "To do otherwise would be total victory for, call it the forces of darkness. Press organizations cannot allow these forces to prevent journalists from covering these stories through terror and intimidation. Obviously, journalists have to be well prepared for such dangers. I wouldn't call it 'cautious' because of the connotation of timidity, but I would say that journalists have to be a lot smarter about the lay of the land than they have been in the past."[74]

Robert Klemser, co-founder of a security training company, urges news organizations to define trigger points, specific events, or circumstances that mean it's time for journalists to pull out of a war zone. He explained, "It is important for workers in hazardous situations to establish trigger points that mandate evacuation or withdrawal when dangerous events occur. . . . You don't wait for bullets to come through the window."[75]

Stuart Loory, editor of *IPI Global Journalist*, recently declared, "Despite all the publicity the safety problem gets, reporters continue to take chances, and their editors and producers apparently do not do enough to stop them. Part of the calculation that has to be made today in deciding whether or not to go after a story is solving the equation of whether or not the particular information sought is worth the life-threatening danger of going after it."[76]

Loory acknowledges that there are times when the risk of covering an important story could easily be considered necessary, but in such circumstances the reporter, after making the judgment, has to proceed with all due care to minimize the risks. "But there are other times," he cautions, "when the risk is not at all justified and at those times, the reporter cannot be criticized for turning away from the story. . . . Editors and producers must understand this. They must take steps to temper the zeal of journalists who might be described as overly committed to a story that is not worth the risk."[77]

Loory concludes, "The days when reporters were thought of as spectators sitting in a grandstand, watching the games people play and reporting on them are over. Reporters are now on the playing field, mixing it up with the players. They have to be certain they are getting deeply involved in the play only when necessary."[78]

Does the danger of covering a particular conflict ever reach the point where a news organization is justified in pulling out altogether? In 2004 a panel of foreign correspondents and editors was asked the hypothetical question, "When will events in Iraq dictate that it's time to bring the press corps home?" The answers were sober and pragmatic. Susan Chira of the *New York Times* said, "In Beirut, when people started getting kidnapped and held, as Terry Anderson was, . . . [correspondents] were ordered out of Beirut. We all are constantly asking ourselves, when does that point come? . . . I think it's the safety question that we have to ask ourselves over and over again. You weigh the risk versus the [story]. I think a significant American troop presence would mean that we would try to keep a significant foreign correspondent presence. Even if the troops are withdrawn, we would want to have some presence in Iraq to see what has been wrought."

Bill Spindle of the *Wall Street Journal* responded, "Those are questions we're already thinking a lot about, because of the cost issue. It's just staggeringly expensive, and our budget is teeny compared to what some of the folks on this panel spend. Just to hold two reporters in Baghdad we spend $23,000 a month simply on rent. So we're bumping up against those questions already. We're still committed, and as long as it remains a big story we'll remain committed, but budgetarily it's quite difficult."[79]

David Schlesinger, speaking for the Reuters wire service, declared, "We had a presence [in Iraq] before the war and we'll have a presence after the war. The question is size. When do you start to run it down? When do you make a decision that you will only have people with non-Coalition passports, for example? Safety is a part of it. Public interest is also part of it. There's no point in writing a lot or taking a lot of photographs if people aren't using them. So we have to judge what our clients want. We have to judge the status of our story, and we have to judge the safety aspect."

Adi Ignatius of *Time* magazine said it depended primarily on what the U.S. military did. He noted, "We have not walked away from the Afghanistan story, which was not as big a story for Americans as the Iraq story. We don't cover it as much as we did, but we have stayed with the story, and we will stay with the Iraq story. But a year from now, all bets are off."[80]

Notes

Foreword

1. News Dissector Danny Schechter blogs on these issues daily on media channel.org. For more on his new book, *When News Lies,* and the film, *WMD*, see www.wmdthefilm.com.

Introduction

1. "The Spanish American War," Small Planet Communications, c2000, 3. http://www.smplanet.com/imperialism/remember.html.

2. *War and the Media: Reporting Conflict 24/7*, Daya Thussu and Des Freedman, eds. London: Sage Publications, 2003, 4.

3. Michelle Ferrari, ed., *Reporting America at War: An Oral History,* New York: Hyperion, 2003, 99.

4. Author interview with Jeremy Levin, March 7, 2005.

Chapter 1

1. Patrick L. Cox, "From the Civil War to Iraq—Hostile Fire Front and Rear," *Digital Journalist*, March 2004, 3. http://www.digitaljournalist.org/issue0304/pcox.html.

2. Ibid., 4.

3. *Reporting America at War*, video, Insignia Films, Inc., narrated by Linda Hunt, 2003.

4. Mary Blume, "Martha Gellhorn: A Life of Wit and Rage," *International Herald Tribune*, February 19, 1998, 1–2. http://www.iht.com/IHT/MB/98/mb021998.html.

5. Ibid.

6. Martha Gellhorn, "High Explosives for Everyone," in *Her War Story: Twentieth Century Women Write About War*, edited by Sayre Sheldon. Carbondale: Southern Illinois University Press, 1999, 91.

7. Ibid.

8. Ibid., 94.

9. Michelle Ferrari, ed., *Reporting America at War: An Oral History.* New York: Hyperion, 2003, 47.

10. Caroline Moorehead, *Gellhorn: A Twentieth-Century Life.* New York: Holt, 2003, 232.

11. Moorehead, *Gellhorn,* 234.

12. Martha Gellhorn, "A New Kind of War," in *Her War Story: Twentieth Century Women Write About War,* edited by Sayre Sheldon. Carbondale: Southern Illinois University Press, 1999, 288.

13. Blume, "Martha Gellhorn," 1–2.

14. Ferrari, *Reporting America at War,* 48.

15. James Tobin, *Ernie Pyle's War: America's Eyewitness to World War II.* New York: The Free Press, 1997, 196.

16. Max Hastings, *Overlord.* New York: Simon & Schuster, 1984, 254.

17. Tobin, *Ernie Pyle's War,* 196.

18. Ibid.

19. Ibid.

20. Ferrari, *Reporting America at War,* 9.

21. Letter from Ernie Pyle to Geraldine Pyle, March 11, 1945. Pyle Letters, 1943–45, Lilly Library, Indiana University, Bloomington, Indiana.

22. *Reporting America at War,* video.

23. Letter from Ernie Pyle to Paige Cavanaugh, undated. Pyle Letters, 1943–45, Lilly Library, Indiana University, Bloomington, Indiana.

24. Tobin, *Ernie Pyle's War,* 239.

25. Tobin, *Ernie Pyle's War,* 2.

26. *Reporting America at War,* video.

27. Ferrari, *Reporting America at War,* 17.

28. Joseph E. Persico, *Edward R. Murrow: An American Original.* New York: McGraw Hill, 1988, 174.

29. *Reporting America at War,* video.

30. Bob Edwards, *Edward R. Murrow and the Birth of Broadcast Journalism.* New York: Wiley, 2004, 56.

31. Ibid., 76.

32. Persico, *Edward R. Murrow,* 220.

33. Ibid.

34. Walter Cronkite, *A Reporter's Life.* New York: Knopf, 1996, 99.

35. Ibid.

36. Ibid.

37. Ferrari, *Reporting America at War,* 19–20.

38. Ibid., 121.

39. Ferrari, *Reporting America at War,* 23.

40. Cronkite, *A Reporter's Life,* 122.

41. "The Writing 69th," from an article in *Look Magazine,* November 17, 1970. Online at: http://www.greenharbor.com/wr69/Biographies.html.

42. Andy Rooney, *My War.* New York: Times Books, 1995, 77.

43. Ibid., 116.

44. Ibid., 120–21.

45. Ibid., 121, 123.

46. *Reporting America at War*, video.

47. Rooney, *My War*, 126.

48. Ferrari, *Reporting America at War*, 55.

49. Ibid., 151–52.

50. Ibid., 165.

51. Ibid., 173.

52. Ibid., 175.

53. *Reporting America at War*, video.

54. Ward Just, *To What End: Report from Vietnam*. Boston: Houghton Mifflin, 1968, 181.

55. Ibid., 185.

56. Ibid., 186.

57. Ibid., 189.

58. Ibid., 190.

59. Ibid.

60. Peter Arnett, *Live from the Battlefield: From Vietnam to Baghdad, 35 Years in the World's War Zones*. New York: Simon & Schuster, 1994, 76.

61. Ibid., 150.

62. Ibid., 175.

63. Ibid., 178.

64. *Weapons of Mass Deception*, a film by Danny Schechter. Cinema Libre Distribution. Global Vision, 2005.

65. "A Thousand Day, a Hundred Battles," *Editor and Publisher*, November 13, 1965, 8–9.

66. Arnett, *Live from the Battlefield*, 232–33.

67. Ibid., 234.

68. Ibid., 240.

69. *Reporting America at War*, video.

70. Ibid.

71. Arnett, *Live from the Battlefield*, 355.

72. Ibid., 364.

Chapter 2

1. Philip Bennett, "Too Far from the Story?" *Washington Post*, June 6, 2004, B4.

2. Howard Kurtz, "Anchors Try to Get Close to the Story in Baghdad," *Washington Post*, January 27, 2005, C7.

3. "International Reporting," C-SPAN, aired on November 6, 2004. A panel discussion at the Overseas Press Club, New York City, September 14, 2004.

4. Ibid.

5. Howard Kurtz, "Scrambling for Cover—and Coverage," *Washington Post*, May 17, 2004, C4.

6. Ibid.

7. "Embattled Beat," Lehrer NewsHour, PBS TV, October 13, 2004.

8. Robin Wright, "In Baghdad, Capital Vistas Gradually Shrink with Insecurity," *Washington Post*, November 25, 2005, p. C7.

9. Ibid.

10. Ibid.

11. Ibid.

12. Author interview with Terry Anderson, January 8, 2005.

13. Scott Peterson, "In a Lawless Land, Hazards for Reporters Mount," *Christian Science Monitor*, November 29, 2001, 1.

14. Ibid.

15. Tim Weiner, "4 Foreign Journalists Are Shot and Possibly Killed in Ambush," *New York Times*, November 20, 2001, B1.

16. Ibid., B3.

17. "Press Release," Reporters sans Frontieres, November 19, 2001. http://www.rsf.org/uk/html/asie/cplp01.

18. *Embedded: The Media at War in Iraq; an Oral History*, edited by Bill Katovsky and Timothy Carlson. Guilford, CT: Lyons Press, 2003, 392.

19. Joseph Contreras, "No Sense of Safety," *Newsweek*, October 18, 2004, 6.

20. Ibid.

21. Seymour Hersh, "Declassified: Celebrating 20 Years of Keeping Government Honest," Conference sponsored by the National Security Archive, George Washington University, Washington, DC, December 9, 2005.

22. Bennett, "Too Far from the Story?" B4.

23. Jonathan Finer, "Assault on Hotel Kills 16 in Baghdad," *Washington Post*, October 25, 2005, p. A14.

24. Ibid.

25. "International Reporting," C-SPAN.

26. "WSJ Reporter Farnaz Fassihi Email From Baghdad," *Parapundit*, September 30, 2004, 1. http://www.parapundit.com/archives/002375.html.

27. Ibid.

28. Ibid., 2.

29. "Iraq: Reporting the War," *Frontline World*, PBS TV, January 11, 2005.

30. Ibid.

31. Ibid.

32. Ibid.

33. Author interview with Peter Spiegel, *Financial Times*, December 16, 2004.

34. Kurtz, "Anchors Try to Get Close to the Story in Baghdad," C7.

35. "Iraq: Reporting the War," *Frontline World*.

36. Ibid.

37. Author interview with Terry Anderson, January 8, 2005.

38. Author interview with Joel Campagna, Committee to Protect Journalists, January 13, 2005.

39. "International Reporting," C-SPAN.

40. Ibid.

41. Scott Johnson, "The Ping, Ping, Ping of Bullets Hitting My Car," in *Embedded: The Media at War in Iraq; an Oral History*, edited by Bill Katovsky and Timothy Carlson. Guilford, CT: Lyons Press, 2003, 392.

42. Ibid., 393.

43. Ibid., 396.

44. Ibid., 397.

45. Ibid., 398.

46. Ibid.

47. Ibid., 400.

48. "International Reporting," C-SPAN.

49. Author interview with Peter Spiegel, December 16, 2004. All Siegel quotes are from that interview.

50. Because Prime Minister Chirac of France had opposed American intervention in Iraq, French journalists in Iraq were usually treated with less suspicion than American journalists. However, the fact that two French journalists in Iraq were kidnapped in August 2004 and held for four months shows that being French is no guarantee of safety for journalists.

51. Roger Cohen, "A French Ex-Hostage Describes His Ordeal," *Hotel du Moulin,* January 10, 2005, 2. http://www.hotelmoulin.com/function_v2/read.php?id=today&no=455.

52. Ibid., 3.

53. Ibid.

54. "Hostages Freed," *Lehrer NewsHour,* PBS TV, December 22, 2004.

55. Cohen, "A French Ex-Hostage Describes His Ordeal," 3.

56. "French Journalists Released," *BBC World News,* PBS TV, December 22, 2004.

57. Ibid.

58. Dan Williams, "Reporting Under the Gun in an Ambush Zone," *Washington Post,* June 8, 2004, C1.

59. Ibid., C3.

60. Ibid.

61. Ibid.

62. Ibid.

63. Ibid.

64. Ibid.

65. John F. Burns, "Taken at Gunpoint, U.S. Journalist and Interpreter Are Missing in Iraq," *New York Times,* August 17, 2004, A10.

66. Dexter Filkins, "Reporter Freed as Rebel Cleric Brokers a Deal," *New York Times,* August 23, 2004, A1.

67. "Freed U.S. Reporter Hopes to Stay in Iraq," *UNAMI News and Events,* August 26, 2004, 1.

68. "Kidnapped Reporter Freed in Iraq," *BBC News, World Edition,* August 22, 2004, 1–2. http://news.bbc.co.uk/2/hi/middle_east/3589388.

69. "Horror at Treatment of Florence Aubenas," Reporters Sans Frontieres, March 1, 2005, 1. http://electroniciraq.net/news/1892.shtml.

70. Ibid.

71. "French Journalist Recalls Ordeal," *BBC News,* bbc.co.uk, June 14, 2005, 1. http://news.bbc.co.uk/1/hi/world/europe/4091838.stm.

72. Andy Mosher, "French Reporter, Iraqi Interpreter Freed," *Washington Post,* June 13, 2005, A12.

73. Ibid.

74. Anthony Shadid, "At Least 28 Killed in Iraq in Wave of New Attacks," *Washington Post*, February 8, 2005, A19.

75. Daniel Williams, "Italian Hostage in Iraq Pleads for Her Life," *Washington Post*, February 17, 2005, A12.

76. Ibid.

77. Ibid.

78. Giuliana Sgrena, "My Truth (La Mia Verita,)," translated by Eva Milan, *Il Manifesto*, March 6, 2005. Stop the War Coalition, http://www.stopwar.org.uk/GiulianaSgrena.html.

79. Daniel Williams, "Freed Hostage Wounded by U.S. Troops," *Washington Post*, March 5, 2005, A14.

80. Daniel Williams, "Italian Calls U.S. Gunfire Unjustified," *Washington Post*, March 6, 2005, A18.

81. Daniel Williams, "U.S., Italy Fail to Agree on Agent's Death in Iraq," *Washington Post*, April 30, 2005, A9.

82. Alan Cooperman, "Italian Leader Says U.S. Knew of Rescue Plan," *Washington Post*, March 10, 2005, A10.

83. Daniel Williams, "Italy Disputes U.S. Report on Agent's Death," *Washington Post*, May 3, 2005, A16.

84. Daniel Williams, "Italians Mourn Intelligence Agent Killed in Baghdad," *Washington Post*, March 7, 2005, A16.

85. Giuliana Sgrena, "My Truth (La Mia Verita)."

86. Scott Taylor, "Hostage Bungle: Chaos, Not Conspiracy," *ALJAZEERA.NET*, March 10, 2005, 2–3.

87. "Who Killed Steven Vincent," Reporters Without Borders, August 2, 2005, 1. http://www.rsf.org/article.php3?id_article=14599.

88. Jamie Glazov, "In the Red Zone," FrontPageMagazine.com, December 9, 2004, 1. http://www.frontpagemag.com/Articles/Printable.asp?ID=16214.

89. Ibid.

90. Jonathan Finer, "U.S. Writer Critical of Militias Is Found Shot Dead in Basra," *Washington Post*, August 4, 2005, A18.

Chapter 3

1. Author interview with Philip Caputo, February 28, 2005.

2. Philip Caputo, *Means of Escape: An Imagined Memoir*. New York: Harper Collins, 1991, 128.

3. Philip Caputo, "Prisoner of the Fedayeen," *Chicago Tribune*, May 20, 1973, 1.

4. Philip Caputo, "I Was Certain I'd Be Killed," *Chicago Tribune*, May 13, 1973, 8.

5. Caputo, *Means of Escape*, 130.

6. Ibid., 132.

7. Philip Caputo, "We'll All Be Killed in Here," *Chicago Tribune*, May 21, 1973, 4.

8. Caputo, *Means of Escape*, 141–42.

9. Caputo, "We'll All Be Killed in Here," 4.

10. Philip Caputo, "In a Prison Cell," *Chicago Tribune*, May 22, 1973, 4.

11. Caputo, "Prisoner of the Fedayeen," 1.

12. Caputo, *Means of Escape*, 160–61.

13. Caputo, "We'll All Be Killed in Here," 4.

14. Caputo, *Means of Escape*, 164.

15. Philip Caputo, "I Will Go Mad," *Chicago Tribune*, May 24, 1973, 2.

16. Caputo, *Means of Escape*, 165.

17. Caputo, "I Will Go Mad," 18.

18. Ibid.

19. Caputo, *Means of Escape*, 171.

20. Ibid.

21. Ibid., 172.

22. Ibid., 173.

23. Ibid., 174.

24. Ibid., 177.

25. Ibid., 8.

26. Author interview with Jeremy Levin, March 7, 2005.

27. Sis Levin, *Beirut Diary: A Husband Held Hostage and a Wife Determined to Set Him Free.* Downers Grove, IL: InterVarsity Press, 1989, 47.

28. Ibid., 54.

29. Ibid., 59.

30. Ibid., 67.

31. Ibid., 68.

32. Ibid., 91.

33. Ibid., 107.

34. Ibid., 120.

35. Ibid., 132.

36. Ibid., 131.

37. Ibid., 137.

38. Ibid., 147.

39. Ibid., 160.

40. Ibid., 163.

41. Nora Boustany, "Journalist in Lebanon Free After 11 Months' Captivity," *Washington Post*, February 15, 1985, A18.

42. George Boehmer, "Joyful TV Reporter Levin Reunited with Family," *Washington Post*, February 16, 1985, A15.

43. Ibid.

44. Ibid., A1.

45. Ibid., A15.

46. Kathy Sawyer, "Hostage's Wife Got 'Real Valentine's Day Present,'" *Washington Post*, February 15, 1985, A18.

47. Author interview with Jeremy Levin, March 7, 2005.

48. Ibid.

49. Author interview with Terry Anderson, January 8, 2005.

50. Ibid.

51. Ibid.

52. Terry Anderson. *Den of Lions: Memoirs of Seven Years.* New York: Crown Publishers, 1993, 7.

53. Ibid., 9.

54. Ibid.

55. Ibid., 13.

56. Ibid., 67.

57. Ibid., 109.

58. Ibid.

59. Ibid., 113.

60. Ibid., 146.

61. Ibid.

62. "Terry Anderson Begins Sixth Year of Captivity," *Congressional Record*, Senate, March 20, 1990, S2709.

63. Ibid., 261.

64. Ibid., 345.

65. Mark Dagostino, "Desperate Vigil," *Wall Street Journal*, February 18, 2002, 52.

66. Evan Thomas, "A Reporter Under the Gun," *Newsweek*, February 11, 2002, 18.

67. Steve LeVine, "A Murder's Aftermath," *Wall Street Journal*, January 23, 2003, A1.

68. Mariane Pearl, *A Mighty Heart*, New York: Scribner, 2003, 34.

69. Ibid., 82.

70. LeVine, "A Murder's Aftermath," A1.

71. Ibid., 105.

72. Ibid.

73. Ibid., 122–23.

74. Ibid., 119, 121.

75. Ibid., 129.

76. "A Conversation with Mariane Pearl," John F. Kennedy Library and Foundation Forum, Boston, Massachusetts, November 18, 2003, 7. http://www.jfklibrary.org/forum_ pearl.html.

77. Ibid., 184.

78. Ibid., 188.

79. Ibid., 198.

80. Kamran Khan, "Pearl Accomplice Tied to Attempt on Musharraf," *Washington Post*, May 28, 2994, A18.

81. Author interview with Scott Taylor, November 15, 2004.

82. Scott Taylor, "Hostage in Iraq: Five Days in Hell," September 15, 2004, espritdecorps @rogers.com.

83. Ibid.

84. Scott Taylor, *Among the 'Others': Encounters with the Forgotten Turkmen of Iraq*, Ottawa, Canada: Esprit de Corps Books, 2004, 194–95.

85. Ibid., 196.

86. Author interview with Scott Taylor, November 15, 2004.

87. Ibid.

88. Ibid.

89. Ibid.

90. Ibid.

91. Taylor, "Hostage in Iraq."

92. Author interview with Scott Taylor, November 15, 2004.

93. Taylor, *Among the 'Others'*, 207.

94. Ibid., 207–208.

95. Author interview with Scott Taylor, November 15, 2004.

96. Ibid.

97. Ibid.

Chapter 4

1. Author interview with Philip Caputo, February 28, 2005.

2. Author interview with Jeremy Levin, March 7, 2005.

3. Author interview with Terry Anderson, January 8, 2005.

4. "International Reporting," C-SPAN, aired on November 6, 2004. A panel discussion at the Overseas Press Club of America, New York City, September 14, 2004.

5. Nik Gowing, "Journalists and War: The Troubling New Tensions Post 9/11," 232, in *War and the Media: Reporting Conflict 24/7*, edited by Daya Kishan Thusu and Des Freedman. London: Sage Publications, 2003.

6. Ibid.

7. Author interview with Jeremy Levin, March 7, 2005.

8. "International Reporting," C-SPAN.

9. Author interview with Scott Taylor, Canadian journalist and publisher, November 15, 2004.

10. *The Media and the War on Terrorism,* Stephen Hess and Marvin Kalb, eds. Washington, DC: Brookings Institution, 2003, 180.

11. Ibid.

12. Ibid.

13. "Alum: Foreign Correspondents 'Alone,'" *Medill*, Northwestern University, May 2, 2002, 2. http://www.medill.northwestern.edu/medill/inside/news/alum_foreign_correspondents.

14. Author interview with Scott Taylor, November 15, 2004.

15. "International Reporting," C-SPAN.

16. Chris Hedges, *War Is a Force That Gives Us Meaning.* Public Affairs, 2002, 143.

17. Author interview with Jeremy Levin, March 7, 2005.

18. "International Reporting," C-SPAN.

19. *The Media and the War on Terrorism,* Stephen Hess and Marvin Kalb, eds.

20. Howard Kurtz, "Anchors Try to Get Close to the Story in Baghdad," *Washington Post,* January 27, 2005, C1.

21. Author interview with Scott Taylor, November 15, 2004.

22. Reva, Susan. "Deja Scoop: Journalists and the CIA," *American Journalism Review,* April 1996, 10.

23. Jane E. Kirtley, Executive Director, Reporters Committee for Freedom of the Press, letter to John M. Deutsch, Director of Central Intelligence, April 24, 1996. Press release by Reporters Committee for Freedom of the Press.

24. Author interview with Terry Anderson, January 8, 2005.

25. Author interview with Philip Caputo, February 28, 2005.

26. Author interview with Jeremy Levin, March 7, 2005.

27. Author interview with Scott Taylor, November 15, 2004.

28. NATO press conference, April 8, 1999, 6–7. http://www.nato.int/docu/speech/1999/s990408a.

29. "Off the Air," *Online NewsHour*, May 4, 1999, 2–3. http://www.pbs.org/newshour.

30. Ibid.

31. Author interview with Scott Taylor, November 15, 2004.

32. Gowing, "Journalists and War,", 234.

33. *The Media and the War on Terrorism,* Stephen Hess and Marvin Kalb, eds., 177.

34. Author interview with Scott Taylor, November 15, 2004.

35. Ibid.

36. "News Update from Citizens for Legitimate Government," November 18, 2004. http://www.legitgov.org.

37. "International Reporting," C-SPAN.

38. Ibid.

39. Andrew Marshall, "Reuters Staff Abused by Bush's Troops in Iraq," Reuters, May 18, 2004, 2. http://wireservice.wired.com/wiredstory..asp?section=Breaking&storyId=866188&tw=wn_wire_story.

40. Ibid.

41. Ibid.

42. Aidan White, "U.S. Must Address Journalists' Deaths," *Washington Post*, June 18, 2005, A18.

43. Ibid.

44. Henry Michaels, "U.S. Bombs Al-Jazeera Center in Baghdad," *World Socialist Web Site*, April 9, 2003, 5–6. http://www.wsws.org/articles/2003/apr2003/jaz-a09.

45. Author interview with Jeremy Levin, March 7, 2005.

46. Ibid.

47. Author interview with Terry Anderson, January 8, 2005.

48. Ibid.

49. Amy Goodman, speech at the Unity United Methodist Church, Baltimore, Maryland, April 15, 2005.

50. Gowing, "Journalists and War," 234, 238.

51. "Exclusive to al-Jazeera," Public Television series *Wide Angle*. Produced by Ben Anthony. July 10, 2003.

52. Ibid.

53. Michaels, "U.S. Bombs Al-Jazeera," 1.

54. "Exclusive to al-Jazeera," Public Television series.

55. Michael Massing, "Lending Assistance to a Dangerous Profession," in *Embedded: The Media at War in Iraq; an Oral History,* edited by Bill Katovsky and Timothy Carlson. Guilford, CT: Lyons Press, 2003, 377.

56. Amir Al-Mounaiery, "The Arab Perspective," in *Embedded: The Media at War in Iraq; an Oral History,* edited by Bill Katovsky and Timothy Carlson. Guilford, CT: Lyons Press, 2003, 284.

57. Ibid., 285.

58. Ibid.

59. Ibid.

60. Michaels, "U.S. Bombs Al-Jazeera," 2.

61. *Control Room*, video, Lions Gate Home Entertainment, Inc., Noujaim Films, 2004.

62. Ibid.

63. Ibid.

64. Ibid.

65. "Exclusive to al-Jazeera," Public Television series *Wide Angle*.

66. Ibid.

67. *Control Room*, video.

68. Ibid.

69. "Exclusive to al-Jazeera," Public Television series.

70. *Control Room*, video.

71. Rajiv Chandrasekaran, "Blast Kills 15 Policemen in Northern Iraq," *Washington Post*, September 5, 2004, A28.

72. "Detained Al-Jazeera Cameraman Allegedly Asked to Inform on Station," Committee to Protect Journalists, press release, October 26, 2005, p. 2. http://www.ifex.org.

73. Ibid., 1.

74. Ibid., 3.

75. "Bush Plotted to Bomb Al-Jazeera," *The Australian*, November 22, 2005, p. 1. www.theaustralian.news.com.su/common/story_page

76. Ibid., 2.

77. Ibid.

78. Robert Barr, "Report: Bush Talked of Bombing Al-Jazeera," *Yahoo! News*, November 22, 2005, p. 1. http://news.yahoo.com/s/ap/20051122.

79. "Britain Gags Report that Bush Targeted Arab TV," Canadian Broadcasting Corp, CBC News, November 23, 2005, p. 1. www.cbc.ca/story/world/national/20051123/blair-bush051123.

80. Robert Barr, "Report: Bush Talked of Bombing Al-Jazeera," *Yahoo! News*, November 22, 2005, p. 1. http://news.yahoo.com/s/ap/20051122.

81. "Al-Jazeera Urges Probe into Bush Bomb Plot Report," *Jordan Times*, November 24, 2005, p. 3. www.news.yahoo.com/s/afp/20051122/wl_mideast_ afp/qatarusbritainmedia.

82. Seymour Hersh, lecture at the Maryland Institute College of Art, Baltimore, Maryland, March 17, 2005. Sponsored by the Midtown Academy, Baltimore, Maryland.

83. Seymour Hersh, "Declassified: Celebrating 20 Years of Keeping Government Honest," Conference sponsored by the National Security Archive, George Washington University, Washington, DC, December 9, 2005.

84. "Reuters, Tele 5 Cameramen Die in Iraq Hotel Blast," Reuters, April 8, 2003, 2, in "The March for Justice". http://www.marchforjustice.com/id278_ m.html.

85. Michaels, "U.S. Bombs Al-Jazeera," 4.

86. "Reuters, Tele 5 Cameramen Die," Reuters, 2.

87. Ibid.

88. Ibid.

89. *Weapons of Mass Deception*, a film by Danny Schechter. Cinema Libre Distribution. Global Vision, 2005.

90. Ibid.

91. Ibid.

92. Massing, "Lending Assistance," 375.

93. *Control Room*, video.

94. Joel Campagna and Rhonda Roumani, "Permission to Fire: CPJ Investigates the Attack on the Palestine Hotel," Committee to Protect Journalists, May 27, 2003, 4. http://www.cpj.org/Briefings/2003/palestine_hotel.html.

95. Ibid., 5.

96. Ibid.

97. Ibid., 6–7.

98. Ibid., 6.

99. Ibid., 2.

100. "Killing the Witness," Democracy Now! October 20, 2005, p. 1. Retrieved December 21, 2005, from www.democracynow.org/print.pl?sid=05/10/20/1410259.

101. Ibid., 2.

102. Glenn Kessler, "Iraqi Journalists Disrupt Powell Briefing," *Washington Post*, March 20, 2004, A12.

103. Ibid., A16.

104. Ibid., A12.

105. Sewell Chan, "Army Says Troops Killed Two Iraqi Journalists," *Washington Post*, March 30, 2004, A13.

106. Ibid.

107. Ibid., 8.

108. Ibid., 11–12.

109. "Reporting the War," *Frontline World*, PBS TV, January 11, 2005.

110. Ibid.

111. "Over 100 Killed across Iraq," *ALJAZEERA.NET*, September 13, 2004, 1–2. http://english.aljazeera.net/NR/exeres/7946C494-E2FA-4B3A-87E8-7BA549324484.

112. Ibid.

113. Ibid.

114. Jackie Spinner, "At Least 80 Civilians Die in Iraqi Violence," *Washington Post*, September 13, 2004, A17.

115. Ibid.

116. "CNN Executive Resigns after Controversial Remarks," *CNN.com*, February 11, 2005, 1. http://www.cnn.com/2005/SHOWBIZ/TV/02/11/easonjordan.cnn.

117. "Bloggers and Journalists," *Online NewsHour*, February 14, 2005, 5. http://www.pbs.org/newshour/bb/media/jan-june05/blog_2-14.html.

118. Ibid., 5.

119. Howard Kurtz, "Eason Jordan, Quote, Unquote," *Washington Post*, February 8, 2005, C1, C3.

120. "Bloggers and Journalists," *Online NewsHour*, 4.

121. Ibid.

122. Kurtz, "Eason Jordan, Quote, Unquote," C1, C3.

123. John Leo, "Stories Not Told," *U.S. News and World Report,* June 13, 2005, 78.

124. Ibid.

125. Joel Campagna, "CNN's Jordan Is Gone, but Questions Remain over U.S. Security Record in Iraq," Committee to Protect Journalists, February 18, 2005, 1. http://cpj.org.

Chapter 5

1. Mariane Pearl, *A Mighty Heart*. New York: Scribner, 2003, 58–59.

2. *The Media and the War on Terrorism,* Stephen Hess and Marvin Kalb, eds. Washington, DC: Brookings Institution, 2003, 174.

3. Howard Kurtz, "Scrambling for Cover—and Coverage," *Washington Post*, May 17, 2004, C1.

4. "International Reporting," C-SPAN, aired on November 6, 2004. A panel discussion at the Overseas Press Club of America, New York City, September 14, 2004.

5. Ibid.

6. Ibid.

7. Ibid.

8. Ibid.

9. Howard Kurtz, "Anchors Try to Get Close to the Story in Baghdad," *Washington Post*, January 27, 2005, C7.

10. Author interview with Scott Taylor, November 15, 2004.

11. *Lehrer NewsHour*, "Embattled Beat," October 13, 2004, WETA Public Television.

12. Author interview with Philip Caputo, February 28, 2005.

13. *The Media and the War on Terrorism,* Stephen Hess and Marvin Kalb, eds. Washington, DC: Brookings Institution, 2003, 174.

14. Gary Trudeau, "Doonesbury Flashbacks," *Washington Post*, January 24, 2005, C4.

15. Gary Trudeau, "Doonesbury Flashbacks," *Washington Post*, January 25, 2005, C3.

16. Kurtz, "Scrambling for Cover—and Coverage," C4.

17. Ibid.

18. Joseph Contreras, "No Sense of Safety," *Newsweek*, October 18, 2004, 6.

19. *Lehrer NewsHour*, "Embattled Beat."

20. Ibid.

21. Ibid.

22. Author interview with Peter Spiegel, December 16, 2004.

23. Author interview with Joel Campagna, Committee to Protect Journalists, January 13, 2005.

24. Author interview with Peter Spiegel, December 16, 2004.

25. *The Media and the War on Terrorism,* Stephen Hess and Marvin Kalb, eds. Washington, DC: Brookings Institution, 2003, 173.

26. Hasan Aweidah, "The Fixer," in *Embedded: The Media at War in Iraq; an Oral History,* edited by Bill Katovsky and Timothy Carlson. Guilford, CT: Lyons Press, 2003, 56.

27. Mohammed Fahmy, "On the Road with Unilaterals," in *Embedded: The Media at War in Iraq; an Oral History,* edited by Bill Katovsky and Timothy Carlson. Guilford, CT: Lyons Press, 2003, 241–44.

28. "Reporting the War," *Frontline World*, PBS TV, January 11, 2005.

29. "International Reporting," C-SPAN.

30. *The Media and the War on Terrorism,* Stephen Hess and Marvin Kalb, eds., 171.

31. "International Reporting," C-SPAN.

32. Ibid.

33. Ibid.

34. Ibid.

35. Ibid.

36. Ibid.

37. *Lehrer NewsHour,* "Embattled Beat."

38. Ibid.

39. Ibid.

40. Sherry Ricchiardi, "Preparing for Battle," *American Journalism Review,* July/August 2002, 4. http://www.ajr.org/Article.asp?id=2556.

41. Ibid., 1.

42. Ibid., 3.

43. Ibid.

44. Ibid.

45. Ibid.

46. Ibid., 4.

47. Ibid., 5.

48. Ibid.

49. Ibid., 6.

50. Ibid.

51. Author interview with Scott Taylor, November 15, 2004.

52. Author interview with Peter Spiegel, December 16, 2004.

53. Author interview with Philip Caputo, February 28, 2005.

54. Author interview with Jeremy Levin, March 7, 2005.

55. Author interview with Joel Campagna, January 13, 2005.

56. Author interview with Terry Anderson, January 8, 2005.

57. Ibid.

58. Author interview with Scott Taylor, November 15, 2004.

59. "Reporting the War," *Frontline World.*

60. "Media Relations: the Military and the Media," Joint Air Force, Army, Navy, Marine Corps Public Affairs, February 28, 2003, 1–2. http://www.au.af.mil/au/awc/awcgate/dod/d20030228pag.pdf.

61. Ibid.

62. Gowing, "Journalists and War," 238.

63. *Weapons of Mass Deception,* a film by Danny Schechter.

64. Ibid.

65. Author interview with Philip Caputo, February 28, 2005.

66. Author interview with Scott Taylor, November 15, 2004.

67. *Lehrer NewsHour,* "Embattled Beat."

68. Author interview with Terry Anderson, January 8, 2005.

69. Ibid.

70. Michelle Ferrari, ed., *Reporting America at War: An Oral History.* New York: Hyperion, 2003, 156.

71. Ibid., 221.

72. Author interview with Jeremy Levin, March 7, 2005.

73. "International Reporting," C-SPAN.

74. Author interview with Philip Caputo, February 28, 2005.

75. Sherry Ricchiardi, "Preparing for Battle," 1. http://www.ajr.org/Article. asp?id=2556.

76. Stuart Loory, "When a Story Is Not Worth the Danger," *IPI Global Journalist*, 2003, Quarter Three, 1. http://www.globaljournalist.org/magazine/2003-3/final-word.html.

77. Ibid., 2.

78. Ibid.

79. "International Reporting," C-SPAN.

80. Ibid.

Selected Bibliography

Beeston, Richard. *Looking for Trouble: The Life and Times of a Foreign Correspondent.* London; Washington: Brasseys, 1997.

Behr, Edward. *Bearings: A Foreign Correspondent's Life Behind the Lines.* New York: Viking Press, 1978.

Bellamy, Christopher. *Expert Witness: A Defense Correspondent's Gulf War, 1990–91.* New York: MacMillan, 1993.

Bliss, Edward, Jr. *In Search of Light: The Broadcasts of Edward R. Murrow, 1938–1961.* New York: Knopf, 1967.

Bullard, F. Lauriston. *Famous War Correspondents.* New York: Beekman, 1974.

Davis, Richard Harding. *Notes of a War Correspondent.* New York: Scribner's Sons, 1910.

Foote, Joe S., ed. *Live from the Trenches: The Changing Role of the Television News Correspondent.* Carbondale: Southern Illinois University Press, 1998.

Geyer, Georgie Anne. *Buying the Night Flight: The Autobiography of a Woman Foreign Correspondent.* New York: Delacorte Press, 1983.

Gruber, Ruth. *Ahead of Time: My Early Years as a Foreign Correspondent.* New York: Wynwood Press, 1991.

Kendrick, Alexander. *Prime Time: The Life of Edward R. Murrow.* New York: Avon, 1970.

Kent, Arthur. *Risk and Redemption: A Foreign Correspondent's Journey.* Toronto: Penguin, 1997.

Knightley, Phillip. *The First Casualty: The War Correspondent as Hero and Myth-Maker from the Crimea to Iraq.* Baltimore: Johns Hopkins University Press, 2004.

Levine, Isaac Don. *Eyewitness to History: Memoirs and Reflections of a Foreign Correspondent for Half a Century.* New York: Hawthorne Books, 1973.

Mathews, Joseph J. *George W. Smalley: Forty Years a Foreign Correspondent.* Chapel Hill: University of North Carolina Press, 1973.

McLaughlin, Greg. *The War Correspondent.* London: Pluto Press, 2002.

Melzer, Richard. *Ernie Pyle in the American Southwest*. Santa Fe, NM: Sunstone Press, 1996.

Miller, Lee Graham. *The Story of Ernie Pyle*. Westport: Greenwood Press, 1970.

Mitgang, Herbert. *Newsmen in Khaki: Tales of a World War II Soldier Correspondent*. Lanham: Taylor Trade Pub., 2004.

Nichols, David, ed. *The Best of Ernie Pyle's World War II Dispatches*. New York: Random House, 1986.

Nicholson, Michael. *A Measure of Danger: Memoirs of a British War Correspondent*. London: Harper Collins, 1991.

Pollock, John Crothers. *The Politics of Crisis Reporting: Learning to Be a Foreign Correspondent*. New York: Praeger, 1981.

Redmont, Bernard S. *Risks Worth Taking: The Odyssey of a Foreign Correspondent*. Lanham: University Press of America, 1992.

Rollyson, Carl. *Nothing Ever Happens to the Brave: The Story of Martha Gellhorn*. New York: St. Martin's Press, 1990.

Shirer, William L. *Berlin Diary: The Journal of a Foreign Correspondent*. New York: Grosset & Dunlap, 1941.

Smith, R. Franklin. *Edward R. Murrow: The War Years*. Kalamazoo: New Issues Press, 1978.

Smith, Wilda M. *The Wars of Peggy Hull: The Life and Times of a War Correspondent*. El Paso: Texas Western Press, 1991.

Tuohy, William. *Dangerous Company: Inside the World's Hottest Trouble Spots with a Pulitzer-Prize-Winning War Correspondent*. New York: Morrow, 1987.

Index

About the Author

HERBERT N. FOERSTEL is the former Head of Branch Libraries at the University of Maryland, board member of the Freedom to Read Foundation, and editor of the Maryland Library Association's newspaper. He is the author of many books on free press issues, including *Refuge of a Scoundrel: The Patriot Act in Libraries* (Libraries Unlimited, 2004), *Banned in the U.S.A.: A Reference Guide to Book Censorship in Schools and Public Libraries* (Greenwood Press, 2002), *From Watergate to Monicagate: Ten Controversies in Modern Journalism and Media* (Greenwood Press, 2001), *Freedom of Information and the Right to Know* (Greenwood Press, 1999), *Banned in the Media: A Reference Guide to Censorship in the Press, Motion Pictures, Broadcasting, and the Internet* (Greenwood Press, 1998), *Free Expression and Censorship in America: An Encyclopedia* (Greenwood Press, 1997), and *Surveillance in the Stacks: The FBI's Library Awareness Program* (Greenwood Press, 1991).

08/06